ACC 304

INTERMEDIATE ACCOUNTING PROBLEM SOLVING SURVIVAL GUIDE

Chapters 8-16

2010 Custom Edition

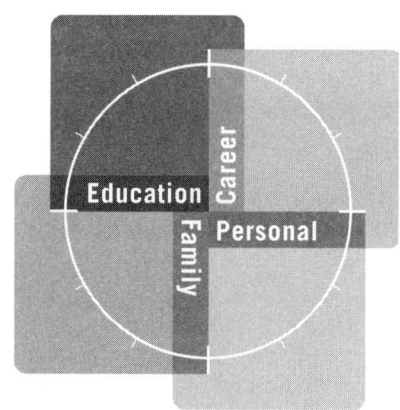

STRAYER. UNIVERSITY

WILEY *Custom*
LEARNING SOLUTIONS

ACC 304: INTERMEDIATE ACCOUNTING
PROBLEM SOLVING SURVIVAL GUIDE
2010 Custom Edition

To order books or for customer service, please call 1(800)-CALL-WILEY (225-5945).

Printed in the United States of America.

ISBN 978-0-470-57577-2
Printed and bound by Victor Graphics, Inc.

10 9 8 7 6 5 4 3 2 1

CONTENTS

Problem Solving Survival Guide
VOLUME I: CHAPTERS 1-14

INTERMEDIATE ACCOUNTING
Thirteenth Edition

Marilyn F. Hunt, M.A., C.P.A.

Donald E. Kieso, Ph.D., C.P.A.
KPMG Peat Marwick Emeritus Professor of Accounting
Northern Illinois University
DeKalb, Illinois

Jerry J. Weygandt, Ph.D., C.P.A.
Arthur Andersen Alumni Professor of Accounting
University of Wisconsin
Madison, Wisconsin

Terry D. Warfield, Ph.D.
Associate Professor
Director, Andersen Center for Financial Reporting and Control
University of Wisconsin
Madison, Wisconsin

WILEY
JOHN WILEY & SONS, INC.

COVER PHOTO: Jon Arnold Images/Superstock, Inc.

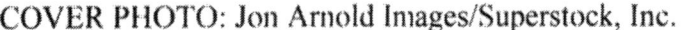

To order books or for customer service call 1-800-CALL-WILEY (225-5945).

ISBN-13 9780470380574
ISBN-10 0470380578

Printed in the United States of America

10 9 8 7 6 5 4 3 2 1

Printed and bound by Courier Kendallville, Inc.

CHAPTER 8

VALUATION OF INVENTORIES: A COST BASIS APPROACH

OVERVIEW

In accounting, the term inventory refers to a stock of goods held for sale in the ordinary course of business or goods that will be used or consumed in the production of goods to be sold. A number of questions regarding inventory are addressed in this chapter; these include: (1) How does a periodic inventory system differ from a perpetual system? (2) What goods should be included in inventory? (3) What costs are included in inventory? (4) How will the selection of a particular cost flow assumption affect the income statement and balance sheet? (5) How do you compute the various layers of inventory when the dollar-value LIFO method is used?

SUMMARY OF LEARNING OBJECTIVES

1. **Identify major classifications of inventory.** Only one inventory account, Merchandise Inventory, appears in the financial statements of a merchandising concern. A manufacturer normally has three inventory accounts: Raw Materials, Work in Process, and Finished Goods. Companies report the cost assigned to goods and materials on hand but not yet placed into production as raw materials inventory. They report the cost of the raw materials on which production has been started but not completed, plus the direct labor cost applied specifically to this material and a ratable share of manufacturing overhead costs, as work in process inventory. Finally, they report the costs identified with the completed but unsold units on hand at the end of the fiscal period are reported as finished goods inventory.

2. **Distinguish between the perpetual and periodic inventory systems.** A perpetual inventory system maintains a continuous record of changes in inventory in the Inventory account. That is, a company records all purchases and sales (issues) of goods directly in the Inventory account as they occur. Under a periodic inventory system, companies determine the quantity of inventory on hand only periodically. A company debits a Purchases account for purchases and the Inventory account remains unchanged during the period. A company determines cost of goods sold at the end of the period by subtracting ending inventory from cost of goods available for sale. A company ascertains ending inventory by physical count.

3. **Identify the effects of inventory errors on the financial statements.** *If a company misstates ending inventory:* (1) inventory and retained earnings will be misstated in the balance sheet, which leads to miscalculation of working capital and the current ratio, and (2) cost of goods sold and net income will be misstated in the income statement. *If a company misstates purchases (and related accounts payable) and ending inventory by the same amount:* (1) inventory and accounts payable will be misstated in the balance sheet, which leads to miscalculation of the current ratio. (2) cost of goods sold and net income will **not** be misstated in the income statement (even though purchases and ending inventory are both misstated in the income statement).

4. **Understand the items that should be included as inventory cost.** Product costs are the costs directly associated with the acquisition of goods and the conversion of such goods to a salable condition. Such charges would include purchases, freight charges on goods purchased, other

direct costs of acquisition, labor, and other production costs incurred in processing the goods up to the time of sale. Manufacturing overhead costs are also allocated to inventory. **Manufacturing overhead costs** include indirect material, indirect labor, and such items as depreciation, taxes, insurance, heat, and electricity incurred in the manufacturing process. Selling, administrative and interest costs are generally not included as inventory costs; they are period costs and thereby charged to expense in the period incurred.

5.   **Describe and compare the cost flow assumptions used in accounting for inventories.** (1) **Average cost** prices items in inventory on the basis of the average cost of all similar goods available during the period. (2) **First-in, first-out (FIFO)** assumes that costs are used in the order in which the related goods were purchased. The cost of inventory on hand at a balance sheet date must therefore represent the most recent purchase prices. (3) **Last-in, first-out (LIFO)** matches the cost of the last goods purchased against revenue.

6.   **Explain the significance and use of a LIFO reserve.** The difference between the inventory method used for internal reporting purposes and LIFO is referred to as the Allowance to Reduce Inventory to LIFO or the LIFO reserve. The change in the LIFO reserve is referred to as the LIFO Effect. Companies should disclose either the LIFO reserve or the replacement cost of the inventory in the financial statements.

7.   **Understand the effect of LIFO liquidations.** LIFO liquidations match costs from preceding periods against sales revenues reported in current dollars. This distorts net income and results in a substantial tax bill in the current period. LIFO liquidations can occur frequently when using a specific goods LIFO approach.

8.   **Explain the dollar-value LIFO method.** An important feature of the dollar-value LIFO method is that companies determine and measure increases and decreases in a pool in terms of total dollar value, not the physical quantity of specific goods in the inventory pool.

9.   **Identify the major advantages and disadvantages of LIFO.** The major advantages of LIFO are the following: (1) It matches recent costs against current revenues to provide a better measure of current earnings. (2) As long as the price level increases and inventory quantities do not decrease, a deferral of income tax occurs in LIFO. (3) Because of the deferral of income tax, cash flow improves. (4) A company's future reported earnings will not be affected substantially by future price declines (future earnings hedge). Major disadvantages are: (1) reduced earnings, (2) inventory is stated in terms of old costs which may be far below current costs, (3) the cost flow does **not** approximate the physical flow of the items except in unique situations, and (4) poor buying habits caused by involuntary liquidations.

10.   **Understand why companies select given inventory methods.** Companies ordinarily prefer LIFO in the following circumstances: (1) if selling prices and revenues have been increasing faster than costs; and (2) if a company has a fairly constant "base stock" (which is typical in companies dealing with refining, chemicals, and glass.) Conversely, LIFO would probably not be appropriate in the following circumstances: (1) if sales prices tend to lag behind changes in costs; (2) if specific identification is traditional such as in the sales of automobiles, farm equipment, art, and antique jewelry; and (3) when unit costs tend to decrease as production increases, thereby nullifying the tax benefit that LIFO might provide.

TIPS ON CHAPTER TOPICS

TIP: The term inventory (or merchandise inventory) is the label given to goods held by a merchandise firm (either wholesale or retail) when goods have been acquired for resale. The terms raw materials, work in process, and finished goods refer to inventories of a manufacturing entity.

TIP: The cost of an inventory item includes all costs necessary to acquire the item and bring it to the location and condition for its intended use. This cost would include the item's purchase price, transportation-in, and any special handling charges. However, transportation-out is **not** included in the cost of inventory; it is classified as a selling expense on the income statement for the period in which the expense was incurred.

TIP: The transportation terms designate the point at which title passes. F.o.b. shipping point (or seller) means the title passes to the buyer when it leaves the seller's dock. F.o.b. destination (or buyer) means the title passes to the buyer when it arrives at the buyer's dock. Assuming that Palmer Company in Bay Hill, Florida sells to Tiger Woods in Orlando, Florida, the following shows synonymous terms:

f.o.b. shipping point	**f.o.b. destination**
or f.o.b. seller	or f.o.b. buyer
or f.o.b. Bay Hill, Florida	or f.o.b. Orlando, Florida

TIP: FIFO (first-in, first-out) means the cost of the first items put into inventory are used to price the first items out to cost of goods sold. Thus, the earliest acquisition prices are used to price cost of goods sold for the period, and the latest (most current) acquisition prices are used to price items in the ending inventory. LIFO (last-in, first-out) uses the most recent costs to price the units sold during the period, and it uses the oldest prices to cost the items in the ending inventory. Thus, in a period of rising prices, the method that will yield the lowest net income on the income statement and the lowest ending inventory on the balance sheet is the LIFO method.

TIP: The cost of the ending inventory determined by using the weighted-average method is an amount between the cost of the ending inventory determined by using the LIFO method and the cost of the ending inventory determined by using the FIFO method.

TIP: When working a problem which requires the computation of either ending inventory or cost of goods sold, remember that the total of the ending inventory and the cost of goods sold should equal the total cost of goods available for sale during the period (beginning inventory plus the net cost of purchases).

TIP: Sales revenue represents the **selling prices** of goods sold, whereas cost of goods sold expense represents the **cost** of items sold.

TIP: The inventory pricing method selected by an entity does **not** have to correspond to the actual physical flow of goods. Thus, a company **can** use the LIFO method to determine the cost of ending inventory even though the first goods purchased are the first to be sold. (It is rare to find a company whose inventory has an actual physical flow of last-in; first-out. Examples would include piles of coal, sand, gravel, some feed bins, and the like.)

ILLUSTRATION 8-1
PERPETUAL VS. PERIODIC INVENTORY SYSTEMS (L.O.2)

Features of a Perpetual System

1. Purchases of merchandise for resale are debited to Inventory rather than to Purchases.
2. Freight-in, Purchase Returns and Allowances, and Purchase Discounts are recorded in the Inventory account rather than in separate accounts.
3. Cost of goods sold is recognized for each sale by debiting the Cost of Goods Sold account, and crediting the Inventory account
4. Inventory is a control account that is supported by a subsidiary ledger of individual inventory records. The subsidiary records show the quantity and cost of each type of inventory on hand. At any point during the accounting period (assuming all postings are up to date), the balance of the Inventory account reflects the cost of the items that should be on hand at that point in time.

Features of a Periodic System

1. Purchases of merchandise for resale are debited to a Purchases account.
2. The Freight-in, Purchase Returns and Allowances, and Purchase Discounts accounts are separate accounts which are used to record information about inventory acquisitions during the accounting period.
3. Cost of goods sold is recognized only at the end of the accounting period when the (1) ending inventory amount (determined by physical count, pricing, and extensions) is recorded in the Inventory account, (2) the Purchases, Freight-in, Purchase Returns and Allowances, and Purchase Discounts account balances are closed to the Income Summary account, and (3) the beginning inventory amount is transferred from the Inventory account to the Income Summary account.
4. There is no subsidiary ledger for inventory. All during the accounting period, the Inventory account reflects the cost of the inventory items on hand at the beginning of the period (beginning inventory). The Inventory account is **not** updated for acquisitions and withdrawals of inventory during the period; it is updated only at the end of the period to reflect the cost of the items on hand at the balance sheet date.

TIP: When a company uses a perpetual system, it must periodically do a physical count to verify the accuracy of the perpetual records. When a difference exists between the perpetual inventory balance and the physical inventory count, the company needs to record an adjusting entry. For example, assume the Inventory account reflects a balance of $58,000 when the physical count shows only $54,000 of goods on hand. The entry to record the difference is:

Inventory Over and Short	4,000	
Inventory		4,000

The over and short balance is normally included in cost of goods sold on the income statement, however, sometimes it is reported in the "Other expenses and losses" or "Other revenues and gains" section of the income statement.

ILLUSTRATION 8-1 (Continued)

EXAMPLE	
PERPETUAL SYSTEM	**PERIODIC SYSTEM**
1. There are 8 units in beginning inventory at a cost of $2,000 each.	
The Inventory account shows the inventory on hand at $16,000.	The Inventory account shows the inventory on hand at $16,000.
2. Purchase 12 items on account at $2,000 each.	

Inventory   24,000
    Accounts Payable   24,000
	Purchases 24,000
	    Accounts Payable 24,000

3. Return one defective item for $2,000 credit.	

Accounts Payable   2,000
    Inventory   2,000
	Accounts Payable 2,000
	    Purchase Returns
	      & Allowances 2,000

4. Sell 15 items on account for $3,000 each.	

Accounts Receivable   45,000
    Sales   45,000
 	
Cost of Goods Sold   30,000
    Inventory   30,000
	Accounts Receivable 45,000
	    Sales 45,000

5. End of period entries for inventory-related accounts (4 units on hand at $2,000 each).	

No entries are necessary:
The Inventory account shows the ending balance as $8,000 ($16,000 + $24,000 - $2,000 - $30,000)
	Inventory (ending, by
	  physical count) 8,000
	Purchase Returns &
	  Allowances 2,000
	Cost of Goods Sold 30,000
	    Purchases 24,000
	    Inventory
	      (beginning) 16,000

ILLUSTRATION 8-2
RECORDING PURCHASES DISCOUNTS—GROSS AND
NET METHODS (L.O.4)

A vendor may offer a discount for payment of items purchased within a specific time frame. The following illustrates the two methods of accounting for purchase discounts:

<u>Gross Method</u>			<u>Net Method</u>		
Purchase cost $40,000, terms 2/10, net 30:					
Purchases	40,000		Purchases	39,200	
Accounts Payable		40,000	Accounts Payable		39,200
Invoices of $16,000 are paid within discount period:					
Accounts Payable	16,000		Accounts Payable	15,680	
Purchase Discounts		320	Cash		15,680
Cash		15,680			
Invoices of $24,000 are paid after discount period:					
Accounts Payable	24,000		Accounts Payable	23,520	
Cash		24,000	Purchase Discounts Lost	480	
			Cash		24,000

TIP: If a company uses the net method, it considers purchase discounts lost as a financial expense and reports it in the "Other expenses and losses" section of the income statement. This treatment is considered better for two reasons: (1) It provides a correct reporting of the cost of the asset and related liability. (2) It can measure management inefficiency by holding management responsible for discounts not taken.

TIP: As you learned in an earlier chapter, if a company uses the gross method, it reports purchases discounts contra to purchases (i.e., as a reduction of inventory cost).

TIP: The net method is more in alignment with the cost principle in that the fair value of the item(s) received (cash equivalent price of the purchase) is the purchase price net of any discount allowed.

EXERCISE 8-1

Purpose: (L.O. 4) This exercise will give you practice in identifying the items that should be included as inventory cost.

Instructions
Indicate which of the items listed below would typically be reported as inventory in the financial statements by placing a "X" in the corresponding blank. If an item should **not** be included in the cost of inventory, indicate how it should be reported in the financial statements. The reporting period ends on December 31.

_____   1.   Raw materials on hand not yet placed into production by a manufacturing firm.

_____   2.   Raw materials on which a manufacturing firm has started production, but which are not completely processed.

_____   3.   Factory labor costs incurred on goods completed but still unsold by a manufacturer.

_____   4.   Factory supplies on hand.

_____   5.   Costs identified with units completed by a manufacturing firm, but not yet sold.

_____   6.   Goods out on consignment at another company's store.

_____   7.   Goods held on consignment from another company.

_____   8.   Goods purchased f.o.b. shipping point that are in transit at December 31.

_____   9.   Goods purchased f.o.b. destination that are in transit at December 31.

_____   10.   Goods sold f.o.b. shipping point that are in transit at December 31.

_____   11.   Goods sold f.o.b. destination that are in transit at December 31.

_____   12.   Goods sold on an installment basis.

_____   13.   Costs incurred to advertise goods held for resale.

_____   14.   Interest costs incurred to finance activities associated with making goods ready for sale; the goods are routinely manufactured items.

_____   15.   Interest costs on assets produced as discrete projects (such as ships or real estate) for sale.

_____   16.   Cost of sales brochures on hand.

_____   17.   Investments in stocks and bonds that will likely be sold within the next year.

_____ 18.   Office supplies on hand.

_____ 19.   Freight charges on goods purchased for resale.

_____ 20.   Supplies purchased for use in the delivery and sales functions of the enterprise.

Solution to Exercise 8-1

Items to be included in inventory: 1, 2, 3, 4, 5, 6, 8, 11, 15, and 19.

The following items would **not** be reported as inventory:

7.   Goods held on consignment from others are not reported in the financial statements because they are not owned by the reporting entity.

9.   Goods purchased f.o.b. destination that are in transit at December 31 are still the property of the vendor; title will not pass until they are received by the reporting entity.

10.   Goods sold f.o.b. shipping point that are in transit at December 31 are no longer the property of the seller; title passed at the date they were shipped which was before year-end. Thus, the sale should be recorded and cost of the items sold should be reported as cost of goods sold in the financial statements.

12.   Goods sold on an installment basis are accounted for as merchandise sold; therefore, the cost of those goods is reflected in cost of goods sold expense on the income statement.

13.   Costs incurred to advertise goods held for resale are classified as advertising expense on the income statement.

14.   Interest costs incurred for inventories that are routinely manufactured are expensed as incurred and are reflected as interest expense in the income statement. According to a FASB standard, these costs are **not** to be capitalized. (The word "capitalized" in this case means accounted for as a component of the cost of the asset, inventory). The FASB's standard on this subject states that companies should capitalize interest costs related to assets constructed for internal use or assets produced as discrete projects (such as ships or real estate projects) for sale or lease. (Such discrete projects should take considerable time to complete, entail substantial expenditures, and be likely to involve significant amounts of interest cost.)

16.   The cost of sales brochures on hand represents a cost of advertising. If this is considered to relate to sales of future periods, it will currently be an unexpired cost and reflected as a prepaid expense in the current asset section of the balance sheet. If there is doubt about these brochures being used in the future to generate sales, the cost should be reported as advertising expense on the income statement.

17.   Investments in stocks and bonds that will likely be sold within the next year are classified as short-term investments in the current asset section of the balance sheet.

18.   Office supplies on hand are reported as a prepaid expense in the current asset section of the balance sheet. When these supplies are later consumed, their cost will be reported as office expense in the general and administrative classification on the income statement.

20.   Supplies purchased for use in the delivery and sales functions of the enterprise should be reported as selling expense on the income statement.

Explanation: Inventory is the label given to assets that are to be sold in the normal course of business or to assets to be incorporated (directly or indirectly) into goods that are manufactured and then sold. The cost of inventory includes all costs necessary to acquire (or manufacture) goods and to bring them to the location and condition for sale to customers.

1.   Raw materials on hand are reported as Raw Materials Inventory. They will be reclassified as Work in Process Inventory when the materials are put into the manufacturing process and will become part of the cost of Finished Goods Inventory when the related goods have completed the manufacturing process. The cost of the finished goods will be charged to cost of goods sold expense in a later period when the goods are sold.

2.   Raw materials on which production has begun but has not been completed are called Work-in Process Inventory on the balance sheet.

3.   Factory labor costs are costs necessary for a manufacturer to manufacture an inventory item. For completed goods, the related factory labor costs are classified as Finished Goods Inventory on the balance sheet.

4.   Factory supplies are indirect materials, i.e., materials that are necessary in the production process but are not directly incorporated in the products; they simply facilitate production. Indirect materials on hand are reported as a part of a company's inventories since they ultimately will be consumed in the production process. Examples of factory supplies include oils and fuels for factory equipment, and cleaning supplies for factory equipment.

5.   Costs identified with goods completed but not yet sold by a manufacturer are reflected as Finished Goods Inventory on the balance sheet.

6.   Goods out on consignment at another company's store are merchandise owned by the entity but in the possession of others. The consignor retains title and includes the goods in inventory until the merchandise is sold by the consignee.

8.   Goods purchased f.o.b. shipping point that are in transit at the balance sheet date are to be included in the inventory of the buyer even though the buyer hasn't received them yet. When the terms of sale are f.o.b. shipping point, title passes to the buyer with the loading of goods at the point of shipment.

11.   Goods sold f.o.b. destination that are in transit at the balance sheet date are to be included in the inventory of the seller even though the seller no longer has possession of the merchandise. When terms of the sale are f.o.b. destination, legal title does not pass until the goods are received by the buyer. Therefore, the seller does not record

a sale and the related withdrawal of inventory until the buyer receives the merchandise.

15.   Interest costs related to assets produced as discrete projects for sale (such as ships or real estate) should be capitalized, that is, included as part of the cost of the asset.

19.   Freight charges on goods purchased for resale or to be included in the manufacturing of items for resale are to be included as the cost of inventory. They are part of the costs necessary to acquire goods and get them to the location of their intended use.

TIP: Costs incurred by a manufacturing company are often classified into two groups: product costs and period costs. **Product costs** such as material, labor, and manufacturing overhead attach to the product and are carried into future periods (as a balance in inventory) if the product remains unsold at the end of the current period, and, therefore, the revenue recognition is deferred to the period of sale. Product costs are thus expensed in the period the related product is sold. **Period costs** such as officers' salaries and other administrative expenses, advertising and other selling expenses, and interest expense (a financing cost) are charged to (expensed in) the period incurred.

TIP: Depreciation for the current period of the office building and any showroom facilities for a manufacturing company is charged to the current period. It is **not** a product cost. Depreciation on the office building relates to the general administration of the business (operating expense). Depreciation of showroom facilities relates to the sales function (operating expense) and thus is not a cost of manufacturing the product.

TIP: Depreciation of factory machinery is a component of manufacturing overhead; thus, it is an element of product cost. The amount of depreciation that pertains to the products produced during a period is first determined by use of the selected depreciation method. The amount of depreciation that ends up being reflected as an expense on the income statement for the same period depends on the number of products sold (not produced) during the period; it is included as part of cost of goods sold expense.

TIP: The amount of depreciation for the period of factory related items that pertains to the products that were produced during the current period but that remain unsold at the end of the period is reflected as part of Finished Goods Inventory at the end of the period. The amount of depreciation for the period that pertains to the goods that were partially processed during the current period and that remain in process at the end of the period is reflected as part of Work in Process Inventory at the end of the period.

EXERCISE 8-2

Purpose: (L.O. 3) This exercise will enable you to practice identifying the effects of inventory errors on the financial statements.

The net income per books of Wacky Wicks Company was determined without knowledge of the errors indicated.

Year	Net Income Per Books	Error in Ending Inventory	
2007	$ 150,000	Overstated	$ 9,000
2008	156,000	Overstated	21,000
2009	162,000	Understated	33,000
2010	168,000	No error	

Instructions
Compute the correct net income figure for each of the four years after taking into account the inventory errors⸴

Solution to Exercise 8-2

Year	Net Income Per Books	Add Over-statement Jan. 1	Deduct Under-statement Jan. 1	Deduct Over-statement Dec. 31	Add Under-statement Dec. 31	Corrected Net Income
2007	$ 150,000			$ 9,000		$ 141,000
2008	156,000	$ 9,000		21,000		144,000
2009	162,000	21,000			$ 33,000	216,000
2010	168,000		$ 33,000			135,000

Approach and Explanation: When more than one error affects a given year (such as in 2008), analyze each error separately then combine the effects of each analysis to get the net impact of the errors. The beginning inventory for 2008 (ending inventory for 2007) was overstated by $9,000. Therefore, cost of goods sold was overstated by $9,000, and net income for 2008 was understated by $9,000. The ending inventory for 2008 was overstated by $21,000. Therefore, cost of goods sold was understated, and net income for 2008 was overstated by $21,000. An understatement in net income of $9,000 and an overstatement of $21,000 in 2008 net to an overstatement of $12,000 for the net income figure reported for 2008. This overstatement of $12,000, combined with the $156,000 amount reported, yields a corrected net income figure of $144,000 for 2008.

Another way of analyzing the effects of an individual error is illustrated below for the $21,000 overstatement of inventory at the end of 2008.

		Effect on 2008		Effect on 2009	
	Beginning inventory			Overstated	$21,000
+	Cost of goods purchased				
=	Cost of goods available for sale			Overstated	21,000
-	Ending inventory	Overstated	$21,000		
=	Cost of goods sold	Understated	21,000	Overstated	21,000
	Sales				
-	Cost of goods sold	Understated	21,000	Overstated	21,000
=	Gross profit	Overstated	21,000	Understated	21,000
-	Operating expenses				
=	Net income	Overstated	21,000	Understated	21,000

Thus, the previously computed net income figure for 2008 must be reduced by $21,000 to correct for this error. Also, the net income figure for 2009 must be increased by $21,000 to correct for the same error.

> **TIP:** An understatement in ending inventory of year 1 will cause an understatement in net income for year 1 and an overstatement in net income for year 2. Thus, retained earnings and working capital at the end of year 1 are understated. However, assuming no more errors are committed at the end of year 2, retained earnings and working capital are **not** affected at the end of year 2.

EXERCISE 8-3

Purpose: (L.O. 5, 9) This exercise reviews the characteristics and the effects of using various pricing methods to determine inventory costs.

Instructions

Answer each of the following questions by inserting one of these abbreviations in the space provided:

SI	(specific identification)	FIFO	(first-in-first-out)
WA	(weighted-average)	LIFO	(last-in-first-out)

_____   1.   Which inventory cost method **best** matches current costs with current revenues on the income statement?

_____   2.   Which inventory cost method yields the most realistic amount for inventory, compared to replacement cost, on the balance sheet?

_____   3.   Which method results in the most exact ending inventory valuation when inventory items of the same type are **not** homogenous?

_____   4.   Which method is based on the assumption that inventory flow is "mixed" and therefore "mixes" all acquisition prices?

During a period of **rising prices**, which method yields the:

_____   5.   lowest net income figure?

_____   6.   lowest amount for inventory on the balance sheet?

_____   7.   lowest cost of goods sold figure?

_____   8.   lowest owners' equity figure?

_____   9.   lowest income tax bill for the current year?

During a period of **declining prices**, which method yields the:

_____   10.   lowest net income figure?

_____   11.   lowest amount for inventory on the balance sheet?

_____   12.   lowest cost of goods sold figure?

_____   13.   lowest owners' equity figure?

_____   14.   best cash flow?

Solution to Exercise 8-3

1.	LIFO	4.	WA	7.	FIFO	10.	FIFO	13.	FIFO
2.	FIFO	5.	LIFO	8.	LIFO	11.	FIFO	14.	FIFO
3.	SI	6.	LIFO	9.	LIFO	12.	LIFO		

Approach: Write down a description of the weighted-average, FIFO, and LIFO cost flow assumptions. Note the relative effects of these methods on the income statement and the balance sheet in a period of rising prices.

> **TIP:** **Inventory pricing method** is a synonymous term for **inventory costing method**.
>
> **TIP:** **FIFO (first-in, first-out)** means the cost of the first items put into inventory are used to price the first items out to cost of goods sold. Thus, the earliest acquisition prices are used to price cost of goods sold for the period, and the latest (most current) acquisition prices are used to price items in the ending inventory. **LIFO (last-in, first-out)** uses the most recent costs to price the units sold during the period, and it uses the oldest prices to cost the items in ending inventory. Thus, in a period of rising prices, the method that will yield the lowest net income on the income statement **and** the lowest ending inventory on the balance sheet is the LIFO method.

> **TIP:** Some corporations prefer to use the LIFO method for purposes of determining taxable income on the entity's tax return because, in periods of inflation, LIFO yields a lower taxable income figure than other inventory costing methods (and therefore the best cash flow situation). LIFO is said to defer holding gains; therefore, the payment of related income taxes is deferred also. For example, assume two inventory items are purchased for $50. One is sold for $75 and the other is held for a while. In the meantime, the supplier raises his price to $60. One more item is purchased to keep the inventory quantity at two. Then the old item is sold at a new selling price of $90. There is a $10 gain experienced because an item was purchased at $50 and held while prices (both acquisition and selling) increased. Using the FIFO method, that holding gain will be recognized in the current period as a part of the gross profit figure [sales of $165 ($75 + $90) minus cost of goods sold of $100 ($50 + $50) = gross profit of $65 ($25 + $40)]. Whereas if the LIFO method is used, that holding gain is deferred to a future period when the LIFO base is liquidated. Thus, the gross profit would only amount to $55 under LIFO [sales of $165 ($75 + $90) minus cost of goods sold of $110 ($50 + $60) = gross profit of $55 ($25 + $30)]. The difference between $65 gross profit under FIFO and $55 gross profit under LIFO is the $10 deferral of holding gain under LIFO.

EXERCISE 8-4

Purpose: (L.O. 2, 5) This exercise will allow you to practice performing calculations to determine inventory cost under each of three costing (pricing) methods, using both the periodic and the perpetual systems.

The Griggs Company is a multi-product firm. Presented below is information concerning one of their products, Infusion-39:

Date	Transaction	Quantity	Cost
1/1	Beginning inventory	1,000	$12
2/4	Purchase	2,000	18
2/20	Sale	2,500	
4/2	Purchase	3,000	22
11/4	Sale	2,000	

Instructions

Compute the cost of the ending inventory, assuming Griggs uses:
(a)   Periodic system, FIFO cost method.
(b)   Perpetual system, FIFO cost method.
(c)   Periodic system, LIFO cost method.
(d)   Perpetual system, LIFO cost method.
(e)   Periodic system, average cost method.
(f)   Perpetual system, moving-average cost method.

Solution to Exercise 8-4

(a)   **Periodic-FIFO:**

	Units	
Beginning inventory	1,000	
Purchases (2,000 + 3,000)	5,000	
Units available for sale	6,000	
Sold (2,500 + 2,000)	4,500	
Goods on hand (assumed)	1,500	1,500 units x $22 = $33,000

(b)   **Perpetual-FIFO:** Same as periodic: $33,000

TIP:	The use of FIFO with a perpetual system always yields the same results as the use of FIFO with a periodic system. The same does **not** hold true with the LIFO or average cost methods.

(c)   **Periodic-LIFO:**

1,000 units x $12	=	$12,000
500 units x $18	=	9,000
1,500 units	=	$21,000

(d)   **Perpetual-LIFO:**

Date	Purchased	Sold	Balance
1/1			1,000 x $12 = $12,000
2/4	2,000 x $18 = $36,000		(2,000 x $18) + (1,000 x $12) = $48,000
2/20		(2,000 x $18) + (500 x $12) = $42,000	500 x $12 = $ 6,000
4/2	3,000 x $22 = $66,000		(3,000 x $22) + (500 x $12) = $72,000
11/4		2,000 x $22 = $44,000	(1,000 x $22) + (500 x $12) = $28,000

(e)   **Periodic-average:**

1,000 x $12	=	$ 12,000	
2,000 x $18	=	36,000	
3,000 x $22	=	66,000	1,500 Units
6,000		$114,000 ÷ 6,000 = $19 each	x $19
			$28,500

(f)   **Perpetual-average:**

Date	Purchased	Sold	Balance
1/1			1,000 x $12 = $12,000
2/4	2,000 x $18 = $36,000		3,000 x $16[a] = $48,000
2/20		2,500 x $16 = $40,000	500 x $16 = $ 8,000
4/2	3,000 x $22 = $66,000		3,500 x $21.14[b] = $73,990
11/4		2,000 x $21.14 = $42,280	1,500 x $21.14 = $31,710

[a] 1,000 x $12 = $12,000
2,000 x $18 = 36,000
3,000 $48,000

$48,000   3,000 = $16.00

[b] 500 x $16 = $ 8,000
3,000 x $22 = 66,000
3,500 $74,000

$74,000   3,500 = $21.14

TIP: When using the average method and a perpetual system, a new average unit cost must be computed **only** after each new purchase; a sale will **not** affect the average unit cost. The average method applied to a perpetual system is often called the **moving-average** method.

TIP: Examine your solution to the exercise above and judge the reasonableness of your answers. What do you expect the relationship of the answers to be for the periodic system?
(1)   Because the trend of the acquisition costs was upward, the ending inventory computed under LIFO should be lower than the ending inventory figure computed under FIFO.
(2)   The cost of the ending inventory determined by using the average method should be between the amount of the ending inventory determined by using the LIFO method and the amount of the ending inventory determined by using the FIFO method.

EXERCISE 8-5

Purpose: (L.O. 4) This exercise will enable you to practice determining how to handle goods in transit and other items necessary for proper inventory valuation.

Jennifer Laudermilch Company, a supplier of artworks, provided the following information for the year ended December 31, 2010.

Inventory at December 31, 2010 (at cost, based on a physical count of goods in Laudermilch's warehouse on 12/31/10)	$ 820,000
Accounts payable at December 31, 2010	460,000
Net sales (sales less sales returns)	7,000,000

The Company has hired you to advise their bookkeeper on a list of items relating to goods in transit, consigned goods, and other issues. The list of items is as follows:

_____ 1. Laudermilch received goods costing $32,000 on January 2, 2011. The goods had been shipped f.o.b. shipping point on December 27, 2010, by Geoffrey Harrill Company.

_____ 2. Laudermilch received goods costing $41,000 on January 4, 2011. The goods had been shipped f.o.b. destination on December 28, 2010 by Nanula Company.

_____ 3. Laudermilch sold goods costing $18,000 to O'Toole Company on December 29, 2010. The goods were picked up by the common carrier on that same date and shipped f.o.b. shipping point. They were expected to arrive at the buyer's business as early as January 3, 2011. An invoice for $29,000 was recorded and mailed on December 29.

_____ 4. Laudermilch sold goods costing $30,000 to Matheson Company on December 31, 2010. The goods were picked up by the common carrier on that same date and shipped f.o.b. destination. They were expected to arrive at the buyer's store as early as January 2, 2011. These goods were billed to the customer for $45,000 on December 31 and were not included in the physical count at December 31, 2010.

_____ 5. Laudermilch is the consignor for a collection of prints. The prints are hanging in the showroom of The Dizzy Decorator. They cost Laudermilch $62,000 and are priced to sell at $95,000. They were not included in the physical count.

_____ 6. Laudermilch is the consignee for some goods from Asian Collectibles. They cost the consignor $50,000 and are priced to sell for $76,000 with Laudermilch to get a commission of 10%. They were included in the ending inventory at the selling price.

_____ 7. Included in the physical count were goods billed to a customer f.o.b. shipping point on December 31, 2010. These items had a cost of $24,000 and were billed at $38,000. The shipment was on Laudermilch's loading dock waiting to be picked up by the common carrier and was included in the physical count at December 31, 2010.

_____ 8. Goods received from a vendor on December 26, 2010 were included in the physical count. However, the related $44,000 vendor invoice was not included in accounts payable at December 31, 2010 because the accounts payable copy of the receiving report was lost. These goods are marked to sell for $65,000.

Instructions

(a)   Indicate which of the items listed above should be included as part of ending inventory cost in the December 31, 2010 balance sheet by placing an "x" in the corresponding blank before the item.

(b)   Using the format shown below, prepare a schedule of adjustments as of December 31, 2010 to the initial amounts per Laudermilch's accounting records. Show separately the effect, if any, of each of the eight transactions on the December 31, 2010 amounts. If the transactions would have no effect on the initial amount shown, state NONE.

Adjustments increase (or decrease)	Inventory	Accounts Payable	Net Sales
Initial Amounts	$ 820,000	$ 460,000	$ 7,000,000
1.			
2.			
3.			
4.			
5.			
6.			
7.			
8.			
Total Adjustments	$_____	$_____	$_____
Adjusted Amounts	$_____	$_____	$_____

Solution to Exercise 8-5

(a)   **Items to be included in inventory:** 1, 4, and 5.

(b)

Adjustments increase (or decrease)	Inventory	Accounts Payable	Net Sales
Initial Amounts	$ 820,000	$ 460,000	$ 7,000,000
1.	32,000	32,000	None
2.	None	None	None
3.	None	None	None
4.	30,000	None	(45,000)
5.	62,000	None	None
6.	(76,000)	None	None
7.	None	None	(38,000)
8.	None	44,000	None
Total Adjustments	48,000	76,000	(83,000)
Adjusted Amounts	$ 868,000	$ 536,000	$6,917,000

Explanation:

1.   When the terms of the purchase are f.o.b. shipping point, ownership of the goods passes to the buyer when the public carrier accepts the goods from the seller. Therefore, title passed to Laudermilch on December 27, 2010, but the goods were not physically present to be included in the physical count at December 31, 2010. The balance sheet at December 31, 2010, should reflect these goods as inventory and the related account payable.

2.   These goods would not have been included in the physical count at December 31, 2010, and are not to be included in the inventory at that date. Title did not pass to Laudermilch until the goods were received on January 4, 2011.

3.   With shipping terms of f.o.b. shipping point, title passed to the customer (O'Toole) when the goods were picked up by the common carrier on December 29, 2010. Therefore, the goods are properly excluded from the ending inventory, and the sale has been properly recorded in 2010.

4.   With shipping terms of f.o.b. destination, title did not pass to Matheson (the buyer) until the goods were received by the buyer, which had to be sometime in 2011. Therefore, the sale was improperly recorded in 2010. The goods were not on the premises late December 31, 2010, so were excluded from the physical count. However, their cost should be included in ending inventory to be reported on the balance sheet.

5.   Under a consignment arrangement, the holder of the goods (called the **consignee**) does not own the goods. Ownership remains with the shipper of the goods (called the **consignor**) until the goods are sold to a customer. Laudermilch, the consignor, should include merchandise held by the consignee as part of its inventory. The goods were not

in Laudermilch's warehouse when the physical count was taken; however, they should be included as part of the inventory balance at December 31, 2010.

6.   Laudermilch does not own the goods which it holds on consignment. Therefore, these goods should be excluded from its inventory; they should be included in the inventory of Asian Collectibles.

7   The $24,000 of goods on the loading dock were properly included in the physical count because they had not been released to the common carrier by the end of the day, December 31, 2010. However, the sale was improperly recorded; therefore, an adjustment is needed to reduce sales by the billing price of $38,000.

8.   The $44,000 of goods received on December 26, 2010 were properly included in the physical count of inventory; $44,000 must be added to accounts payable since the invoice was not included in the December 31, 2010 accounts payable balance.

> **TIP:**   Errors in accounting for goods in transit can affect the analysis of financial statements. For example, the failure to include inventory goods in transit that were shipped by the vendor f.o.b. shipping point will cause the current ratio to be misstated. Inventory and Accounts Payable will be understated by the same amount causing the current ratio to be overstated (assuming total current assets exceed total current liabilities). When this understatement of ending inventory and accounts payable is intentional, it is referred to as "window dressing" of the current ratio. You may be able to think of other ways a company might cause "window dressing" of the current ratio.

EXERCISE 8-6

Purpose: (L.O. 5) This exercise will illustrate the effect on net income when the LIFO cost method rather than the FIFO cost method is used in a period of rising prices. It also requires you to examine the effect of both the beginning inventory and the ending inventory on the net income computation.

Using the FIFO cost method, Rasulo Company had a beginning inventory of $24,000, ending inventory of $30,000, and net income of $80,000. If Rasulo had used the LIFO cost method, the beginning inventory would have been $20,000 and the ending inventory would have been $23,000.

Instructions
Compute what net income would have been if the LIFO cost method had been used.

Solution to Exercise 8-6

Using LIFO:
>   Beginning inventory would have been less by $4,000; therefore,
>>   Cost of goods sold would have been less by $4,000 and
>>   Net income would have been more by $4,000, and
>   Ending inventory would have been less by $7,000; therefore,
>>   Cost of goods sold would have been more by $7,000 and
>>   Net income would have been less by $7,000, therefore:

Net income using FIFO		$ 80,000
Decrease in beginning inventory using LIFO	4,000	
Decrease in ending inventory using LIFO		(7,000)
Net income using LIFO		$ 77,000

CASE 8-1

Purpose: (L.O. 6) This case will discuss the nature and use of a LIFO reserve. Many companies use LIFO for tax and external reporting purposes, but maintain a FIFO, average cost, or standard cost system for internal reporting purposes.

Instructions
(a) State a few reasons why a company may use LIFO for external reporting and FIFO for internal reporting purposes.
(b) Explain what a LIFO reserve is and how it works.

Solution to Case 8-1

(a) An entity may choose to use LIFO for tax purposes and for general purpose financial statements published for external users while using the FIFO inventory costing method for internal reports for several reasons such as:
 1. Companies often base their pricing decisions on a FIFO, average, or standard cost assumption, rather than a LIFO basis.
 2. Record keeping on some basis other than LIFO is easier because the LIFO assumption usually does not approximate the physical flow of the product.
 3. Profit-sharing and other bonus arrangements often depend on a non-LIFO inventory assumption.
 4. The use of a pure LIFO system is troublesome for interim periods, for which estimates must be made of year-end quantities and prices.

TIP: Many entities prefer to use the LIFO method for tax purposes because in periods of increasing prices, LIFO results in a lower taxable income figure for the current period thereby deferring the payment of income taxes.

TIP: A company can use one inventory cost method for financial reporting purposes and a different method for income tax reporting purposes. However, in the tax law, there is what we call the **LIFO conformity rule.** This rule requires that if a company uses LIFO for tax purposes, it must also use LIFO for reporting in the general purpose financial statements (although neither tax law nor GAAP requires a company to pool its inventories in the same manner for book and tax purposes). Even though this rule exists, a company often overcomes this disadvantage by providing supplemental disclosures in the notes to the financial statements. These supplemental disclosures often include non-LIFO income numbers as well as non-LIFO inventory numbers so that readers can more readily make meaningful interpretations of the statements and better comparisons with statements of other companies that do not use LIFO.

(b) A **LIFO reserve** is the difference between the ending inventory amount derived by the inventory method used for internal reporting purposes (FIFO, for example) and the ending inventory amount derived by the use of the LIFO method employed for external reporting purposes. This difference is often recorded in an account called Allowance to Reduce Inventory to LIFO. The change in the balance of this account from one period to the next is called the **LIFO effect**. For example, assume the Sullivan Company uses FIFO for internal reports and LIFO for external reports. At January 1, 2010, the Allowance to Reduce Inventory to LIFO account balance was $45,000. At the end of 2010, the inventory balance is $460,000 under FIFO and $400,000 under LIFO. The LIFO effect for 2010 is $15,000 and is recorded as follows:

Cost of Goods Sold...	15,000	
Allowance to Reduce Inventory to LIFO....		15,000

The Allowance to Reduce Inventory to LIFO balance of $60,000 would be deducted from the $460,000 Inventory account balance on the balance sheet to ensure that the inventory is stated on a LIFO basis at year-end. Either the amount of the LIFO reserve or the replacement cost of the inventory should be disclosed in the financial statements or the accompanying notes.

EXERCISE 8-7

Purpose: (L.O. 8) This exercise illustrates the use of the dollar-value LIFO method. It shows how a decrease in the ending inventory in terms of base prices from one year to the next affects the calculations and then what happens when an increase in the ending inventory at base prices occurs.

Presented below is information related to Tina Argentine Company.

Date	Ending Inventory (End of Year Prices)	Price Index (Percentage)
December 31, 2005	$ 160,000	100
December 31, 2006	231,000	105
December 31, 2007	216,000	120
December 31, 2008	247,000	130
December 31, 2009	308,000	140
December 31, 2010	348,000	145

Instructions
Compute the ending inventory for Tina Argentine Company for 2005 through 2010 using the dollar-value LIFO method.

Solution to Exercise 8-7

	Current $		Price Index (Percentage)		Base-Year $	Change
2005	$ 160,000	÷	100	=	$ 160,000	--
2006	231,000	÷	105	=	220,000	$+60,000
2007	216,000	÷	120	=	180,000	(40,000)
2008	247,000	÷	130	=	190,000	+10,000
2009	308,000	÷	140	=	220,000	+30,000
2010	348,000	÷	145	=	240,000	+20,000

Ending Inventory—Dollar Value LIFO:

2005 $ 160,000

2006	$160,000 @ 100 =	$160,000	
	60,000 @ 105 =	63,000	
		$223,000	
2007	$160,000 @ 100 =	$160,000	
	20,000 @ 105 =	21,000	
		$181,000	
2008	$160,000 @ 100 =	$160,000	
	20,000 @ 105 =	21,000	
	10,000 @ 130 =	13,000	
		$194,000	

2009	$160,000 @ 100 =	$160,000
	20,000 @ 105 =	21,000
	10,000 @ 130 =	13,000
	30,000 @ 140 =	42,000
		$236,000
2010	$160,000 @ 100 =	$160,000
	20,000 @ 105 =	21,000
	10,000 @ 130 =	13,000
	30,000 @ 140 =	42,000
	20,000 @ 145 =	29,000
		$265,000

Approach and Explanation: (1) The ending inventory must first be converted from current dollars to base-year dollars. This is done by dividing the ending inventory at current prices by the current price index. (2) Next, the ending inventory at base-year prices is apportioned into layers, according to individual years in which the inventory was acquired. (3) Each layer is then priced using the index of the year in which it was acquired in order to obtain the inventory at dollar-value LIFO cost.

TIP: When using the dollar-value LIFO method, you must determine the layers of inventory in terms of base prices. Then each of those layers must be priced in terms of the price level of the period in which each particular layer was added.

TIP: When performing the computations for the dollar-value LIFO method, watch that the results are what you would expect them to be. For instance, most companies experience a trend of increasing prices. Therefore, in converting the ending inventory at current cost to base prices, you would expect the ending inventory at base prices to be an amount that is less than the ending inventory at current cost.

TIP: Whenever a layer, or a portion thereof, is eliminated (such as is the case in 2007 above), it is gone forever and cannot be restored. Notice how in 2008, when there is again an increase in inventory, the newly added layer for 2008 is priced at the index of the year in which that layer was added (2008) and **not** at the index of the portion of the 2006 layer that was eliminated in 2007. This process is consistent with the last costs into inventory being the first costs out (LIFO); thus, inventory is valued at the earliest purchase prices.

TIP: When using the dollar-value LIFO method, a current price index may be given, or you may have to solve for it. For instance, if prices increased over the current year by 8%, the current price index would be 108. Using another example, if ending inventory is given as $128,800 at current cost and $115,000 at base prices, the current price index is 112 ($128,800 ÷ $115,000 = 1.12, which is 112 percent). This approach is generally referred to as the **double-extension method** because the value of the units in inventory is extended at both base year prices and current year prices.

ANALYSIS OF MULTIPLE-CHOICE TYPE QUESTIONS

QUESTION

1.   (L.O. 4) At December 31, 2010, a physical count of merchandise inventory belonging to Rhoda Corp. showed $1,000,000 to be on hand. The $1,000,000 was calculated before any potential necessary adjustments related to the following:

>   Excluded from the $1,000,000 was $80,000 of goods shipped f.o.b. shipping point by a vendor to Rhoda on December 30, 2010 and received on January 3, 2011.
>   Excluded from the $1,000,000 was $72,000 of goods shipped f.o.b. destination to Rhoda on December 30, 2010 and received on January 3, 2011.
>   Excluded from the $1,000,000 was $95,000 of goods shipped f.o.b. destination by Rhoda to a customer on December 28, 2010. The customer received the goods on January 4, 2011.

The correct amount to report for inventory on Rhoda's balance sheet at December 31, 2010 is:

a. $1,072,000.
b. $1,095,000.
c. $1,175,000.
d. $1,247,000.

Explanation:

(1)   The $80,000 should be added to the $1,000,000 because f.o.b. shipping point means the title transferred to Rhoda when the goods left the seller's dock on December 30, 2010.
(2)   The $72,000 is properly excluded from the ending inventory because title did not pass to Rhoda until Rhoda received the goods on January 3, 2011.
(3)   The $95,000 should be added to the $1,000,000 because the goods belong to Rhoda until they are received by the customer (in 2011).

$1,000,000
+ 80,000
+ 95,000
$1,175,000   Amount to report for ending inventory at December 31, 2010.

(Solution = c.)

QUESTION

2.   (L.O. 2) The following amounts relate to the current year for the Dan Harrier Company:

Beginning inventory	$ 40,000
Ending inventory	56,000
Purchases	332,000
Purchase returns	9,600
Freight-out	12,000

The amount of cost of goods sold for the period is:

a. $338,400.
b. $325,600.
c. $306,400.
d. $294,400.

Approach and Explanation: Write down the computation model for cost of goods sold. Enter the amounts given and solve for the unknown.

$ 40,000		Beginning Inventory
332,000	+	Purchases
9,600	-	Purchase Returns and Allowances
0	-	Purchase Discounts
0	+	Freight-in
362,400	=	Cost of Goods Available for Sale
56,000	-	Ending Inventory
$306,400	=	Cost of Goods Sold (Solution = c.)

TIP: Freight-out is classified as a selling expense, not a component of cost of goods sold. Freight-out is not a cost necessary to get the inventory item to the place and condition for sale; it is a cost incurred in the selling function.

QUESTION

3. (L.O. 2) The accountant for the Orion Sales Company is preparing the income statement for 2010 and the balance sheet at December 31, 2010. Orion uses the periodic inventory system. The January 1, 2010 merchandise inventory balance will appear:
   a. only as an asset on the balance sheet.
   b. only in the cost of goods sold section of the income statement.
   c. as a deduction in the cost of goods sold section of the income statement and as a current asset on the balance sheet.
   d. as an addition in the cost of goods sold section of the income statement and as a current asset on the balance sheet.

Explanation: The January 1, 2010 inventory amount is the beginning inventory figure. Beginning inventory is a component of the cost of goods available for sale for the period which is a component of cost of goods sold. (Solution = b.)

TIP: If the question asked about the December 31, 2010 merchandise inventory balance (ending inventory) rather than the beginning inventory balance, the correct answer would have been "c" (as a deduction in computing cost of sales and as a current asset).

QUESTION

4. (L.O. 3) If the beginning inventory for 2009 is overstated, the effects of this error on cost of goods sold for 2009, net income for 2009, and assets at December 31, 2010, respectively are:
   a. overstatement, understatement, overstatement.
   b. overstatement, understatement, no effect.
   c. understatement, overstatement, overstatement.
   d. understatement, overstatement, no effect.

Approach and Explanation: For questions dealing with inventory errors, assume a periodic system unless otherwise indicated. Write down the components of the cost of goods sold computation and analyze the resulting effects on net income.

		2009	**2010**
	Beginning inventory	Overstated	No effect
+	Cost of goods purchased		
=	Cost of goods available for sale	Overstated	
-	Ending inventory		
=	Cost of goods sold	Overstated	
	Net income	Understated	

The inventory at the end of 2009 and the inventory at the end of 2010 are both apparently free of error because the inventory at a balance sheet date is determined by a physical count and pricing process. Assume there are no errors in this process unless otherwise indicated. (Solution = b.)

> **TIP:** The fact that the inventory at the beginning of 2009 was in error indicates that the inventory at the end of 2008 was in error because the ending inventory of one period is the beginning inventory of the next period.
>
> **TIP:** When analyzing a question like this one, it is often helpful to create an example with numbers.

QUESTION

5. (L.O.3) If beginning inventory is understated by $7,000, and ending inventory is overstated by $3,000, net income for the period will be:
   a. overstated by $10,000.
   b. overstated by $4,000.
   c. understated by $4,000.
   d. understated by $10,000.

Approach and Explanation: Each error's effect on net income should be determined separately. The effect on net income is dependent on the effect on the computation of cost of goods sold (which is an expense affecting net income). The effects are then combined to compute the **total** effect on net income for the period. (Solution = a.)

	First Error	**Second Error**	**Total Effect**
Beg. Inventory	Understated $7,000		Understated $7,000
+ Purchases			
= Goods Available	Understated $7,000		Understated $7,000
- Ending Inventory		Overstated $3,000	Overstated $3,000
= Cost of Goods Sold	Understated $7,000	Understated $3,000	Understated $10,000
Net Income	Overstated $7,000	Overstated $3,000	Overstated $10,000

QUESTION

6. (L.O. 5, 9) Which inventory costing method most closely approximates current cost for each of the following:

	Ending Inventory	Cost of Goods Sold
a.	FIFO	FIFO
b.	FIFO	LIFO
c.	LIFO	FIFO
d.	LIFO	LIFO

Approach and Explanation: Write down which inventory method (LIFO or FIFO) reports current cost for ending inventory and which uses current cost to price cost of goods sold and then look for your answer combination. FIFO uses the first cost in as the first cost out, so the last (most current) costs are used to price the ending inventory. Therefore, FIFO is the answer for the first column. In contrast, LIFO uses the last cost in (current cost) as the first cost out (to cost of goods sold), so LIFO reflects the most current costs experienced in cost of goods sold. Therefore, LIFO is the answer for the second column. Answer "b" is the determined combination. (Solution = b.)

QUESTION

7. (L.O.4) Dr. Dong Company purchased goods with a list price of $50,000, subject to trade discounts of 20% and 10%, with a 2% cash discount allowed if payment is made within 10 days of receipt. Dr. Dong uses the gross method of recording purchases. Dr. Dong should record the cost of this merchandise as:
    a. $34,000.
    b. $35,000.
    c. $36,000.
    d. $50,000.
    e. None of the above.

Explanation: Trade discounts are not recorded in the accounts; they are means of computing a sales (purchase) price. Using the gross method of recording purchases, the cash discount allowed does not affect the amount recorded in the Purchases account; the cash discount allowed will be recorded if it is taken and will be recorded as a credit to Purchase Discounts. (Solution = c.)

Computations:

List price	$ 50,000
First trade discount ($50,000 x 20%)	(10,000)
Subtotal	40,000
Second trade discount ($40,000 x 10%)	(4,000)
Purchase price	$ 36,000

> **TIP:** A chain discount occurs when a list price is subject to several trade discounts. When a chain discount is offered, the amount of each trade discount is determined by multiplying (1) the list price of the merchandise **less** the amount of prior trade discounts by (2) the trade discount percentage.

QUESTION

8. (L.O. 4) Grennan Retail Company incurred the following costs in 2010:
    Freight-in on purchases
    Interest on loan to acquire inventory
    Selling costs

    Should the above items be included or excluded in determining Grennan's inventory valuation for its balance sheet?

	Freight-in	Interest	Selling Costs
a.	Include	Include	Include
b.	Include	Include	Exclude
c.	Include	Exclude	Exclude
d.	Exclude	Exclude	Exclude

Explanation: Freight-in is a product cost. The cost of inventory should include all costs necessary to get the inventory in the place and condition for its intended purpose (resale). Freight-in is necessary to get the merchandise to the location for resale. Interest costs should not be capitalized for inventories that are acquired by a merchandiser (because the goods do not require a period of time to ready them for sale) or inventories that are routinely manufactured or otherwise produced in large quantities on a repetitive basis. Therefore, the interest on this inventory is a period cost. Selling expenses are treated as a period cost. (Solution = c.)

QUESTION

9. (L.O. 5) For 2010, Selma Co. had beginning inventory of $75,000, ending inventory of $90,000 and net income of $120,000, using the LIFO inventory method. If the FIFO method had been used, beginning inventory would have been $85,000, ending inventory would have been $105,000 and net income would have been:
   a. $125,000.
   b. $115,000.
   c. $145,000.
   d. $95,000.

Approach and Explanation: Develop the answer by analyzing the effects on the cost of goods sold computation and resulting effects on net income. (Solution = a.)

	LIFO	FIFO	Effect on Cost of Goods Sold		Effect on Net Income	
Beginning Inventory	$ 75,000	$ 85,000	Increase	$10,000	Decrease	$10,000
+ Purchases						
= Goods Available						
- Ending Inventory	90,000	105,000	Decrease	15,000	Increase	15,000
= Cost of Goods Sold						
Net Income	120,000	?	Decrease	5,000	Increase	5,000

Net income using LIFO	$ 120,000
Increase in net income	5,000
Net income using FIFO	$ 125,000

QUESTION

10. (L.O. 2, 5) The following facts pertain to the cost of one product carried in the merchandise inventory of the Herara Store:

Inventory on hand, January 1	200 units @ $20 =	$ 4,000
Purchase, March 18	600 units @ $24 =	14,400
Purchase, July 20	800 units @ $26 =	20,800
Purchase, October 31	400 units @ $30 =	12,000

A physical count of the inventory on December 31 reveals that 500 units are on hand. If the FIFO cost method is used with a periodic inventory system, the inventory should be reported on the balance sheet at:
   a. $40,000.
   b. $36,600.
   c. $14,600.
   d. $11,200.
   e. None of the above.

Approach and Explanation: Think about what FIFO stands for: the first cost is in the first out to cost of goods sold. Therefore, ending inventory is comprised of the latest costs experienced. (Solution = c.)

400 units @ $30 =	$ 12,000
100 units @ $26 =	2,600
Ending inventory at FIFO	$ 14,600

QUESTION
11. (L.O. 2, 5) Refer to the data in question 10 above. If the average costing method is used, the cost of goods sold for the year amounts to:
a. $38,400.
b. $37,500.
c. $12,800.
d. $12,500.

Approach and Explanation: Read the question carefully. Notice it asks for the cost of goods sold and not for the ending inventory as you might expect.

Total cost of all units available for sale:

Beginning inventory	$ 4,000
Purchases ($14,400 + $20,800 + $12,000)	47,200
Cost of goods available for sale	$ 51,200

$51,200		Cost of goods available for sale
÷ 2,000[1]		Units available for sale
= $25.60		Average unit cost

$25.60 Average unit cost x 500 units = $12,800 Ending inventory
$25.60 Average unit cost x 1,500[2] units = $38,400 Cost of goods sold

[1]200 + 600 + 800 + 400 = 2,000 units available for sale.
[2]2,000 units available - 500 units in ending inventory = 1,500 units sold.
(Solution = a.)

QUESTION
12. (L.O. 5) Refer to the data in question 10 above. If the LIFO costing method is used, the cost of goods sold for the year amounts to:
a. $40,000.
b. $36,600.
c. $14,600.
d. $11,200.

Approach and Explanation: Notice the question asks for the cost of goods sold rather than the cost of the ending inventory. You may approach the solution one of two ways: You may cost the items sold or compute the cost of the ending inventory and deduct that cost from the cost of goods available for sale. Using the first of these two approaches, think of what LIFO stands for: the last cost in is the first cost out to cost of goods sold. (Solution = a.)

Units available	2,000
Units on hand at end of period	(500)
Units sold	1,500

400 units @ $30 =	12,000
800 units @ $26 =	20,800
300 units @ $24 =	7,200
1,500 units =	40,000 Cost of goods sold

TIP:	The cost of the ending inventory using LIFO would be:		
	200 units @ $20	=	$ 4,000
	300 units @ $24	=	7,200
	500 units	=	$ 11,200 Ending inventory

QUESTION

13. (L.O. 5) In a period of rising prices, which inventory flow assumption will result in the lowest amount of income tax expense?
    a. FIFO
    b. LIFO
    c. Average cost
    d. Income tax expense will be the same under all cost flow assumptions.

Explanation: Income taxes are determined by applying a tax rate to the amount of taxable income for the period. The inventory cost flow assumption yielding the highest cost of goods sold expense will yield the lowest income before tax figure. On a tax return, the cost of goods sold figure is a deduction in arriving at taxable income. The lower the taxable income, the lower the taxes due (thus, the lower the income tax expense) and the less cash required to pay taxes. In a period of rising prices, LIFO charges the highest costs experienced to cost of goods sold expense, yielding the lowest taxable income figure. (Solution = b.)

QUESTION

14. (L.O. 5) In a period of rising prices, which of the following inventory cost flow methods will yield the largest reported amount for cost of goods sold?
    a. Specific identification.
    b. FIFO.
    c. LIFO.
    d. Average.

Explanation: In a period of rising prices, the most recent purchase prices are the highest ones experienced by the entity. Using LIFO, the latest costs (the highest ones, in this instance) are used to price cost of goods sold and the earliest ones are used to price ending inventory. FIFO would give the lowest cost of goods sold in a period of rising prices. The results of the average method would fall between the results of the LIFO and FIFO methods. The specific identification method would likely yield a cost of goods sold figure similar to FIFO (but not more than LIFO) because specific identification would use the cost of the specific items sold to price the cost of the goods sold, and the specific items sold usually follow a first-in, first-out physical flow. (Solution = c.)

QUESTION

15. (L.O. 8) McGraty Corp. uses dollar-value LIFO. Its inventory was $500,000 in terms of base-year prices at December 31, 2010. At December 31, 2011, McGraty's inventory was $600,000 at base-year prices and $660,000 at current cost. McGraty's inventory at December 31, 2011, using dollar-value LIFO, is:
    a. $660,000.
    b. $610,000.
    c. $600,000.
    d. $550,000.

Approach and Explanation: Set up the problem as you normally would a dollar-value LIFO problem, even though the data given is not what you might expect.

Date	Ending Inventory @ Current Costs	Price Index (Percentage)	=	Ending Inventory @ Base Prices	Dollar-Value LIFO Cost
12/31/10				$500,000	$500,000
12/31/11	$660,000			600,000	?

Normally you are told the index and are then able to divide the inventory at current cost by the index to get the inventory at base-year prices. Here, you need to solve for the index by dividing $660,000 by $600,000 which gives you 1.10; so the index, in percentage terms, is 110. The ending inventory at dollar-value LIFO therefore is: (Solution = b.)

Base-Year $	%		Dollar-Value LIFO Cost
$500,000 x 100		=	$ 500,000
$100,000 x 110		=	110,000
			$ 610,000

CHAPTER 9

INVENTORIES:
ADDITIONAL VALUATION ISSUES

OVERVIEW

Sometimes a business is faced with the situation where impairments in the value of its inventory are so great relative to selling prices that items cannot be sold at a normal profit. In compliance with conservatism, any impairments in value should be recognized in the current period and the inventory should be reported at the lower-of-cost-or-market (LCM) on the balance sheet. By following the LCM rule, the impairment is recognized in the period in which it occurs, rather than in the later period of disposal of the inventory. Accounting for declines in inventory value is discussed in this chapter.

Sometimes a business may need to estimate the cost of inventory on hand at a certain date. Two estimation techniques—the gross profit and the retail method of inventory estimation—are discussed in this chapter. Although the conventional retail method yields results which are to approximate a lower-of-average-cost-or-market valuation for the inventory, the retail method also can be used to approximate FIFO cost, lower of FIFO cost or market, weighted-average cost, LIFO cost, etc. The conventional retail method and the LIFO retail method are discussed in this chapter.

SUMMARY OF LEARNING OBJECTIVES

1. **Describe and apply the lower of cost or market rule.** If inventory declines in value below its original cost for whatever reason, a company should write down the inventory to reflect this loss. The general rule is to abandon the historical cost principle when the future utility (revenue-producing ability) of the asset drops below its original cost. The conservatism principle (or constraint) is the justification for this departure from the historical cost principle.

2. **Explain when companies value inventories at net realizable value.** Companies value inventory at net realizable value when (1) there is a controlled market with a quoted price applicable to all quantities, (2) no significant costs of disposal are involved, and (3) the cost figures are too difficult to obtain.

3. **Explain when companies use the relative sales value method to value inventories.** When a company purchases a group of varying units at a single lump-sum price—a so-called basket purchase—the company may allocate the total purchase price to the individual items on the basis of relative sales value.

4. **Discuss accounting issues related to purchase commitments.** Accounting for purchase commitments is controversial. Some argue that a company should report purchase commitment contracts as assets and liabilities at the time the contract is signed. Others believe that the present recognition at the delivery date is most appropriate. The FASB neither excludes nor recommends the recording of assets and liabilities for purchase commitments, but it notes that if companies recorded such contracts at the time of commitment, the nature of the loss and the valuation account should be reported when the price falls.

5. **Determine ending inventory by applying the gross profit method.** Companies follow these steps to determine ending inventory by applying the gross profit method: (1) Compute the gross profit percentage on selling price. (2) Compute gross profit by multiplying net sales by the gross profit percentage. (3) Compute cost of goods sold by subtracting gross profit from net sales. (4) Compute ending inventory by subtracting cost of goods sold from total goods available for sale.

6. **Determine ending inventory by applying the retail method.** Companies follow these steps to determine ending inventory by the conventional retail method: (1) To estimate inventory at retail, deduct the sales for the period from the retail value of the goods available for sale. (2) To find the ratio of cost to retail for all goods passing through a department or firm, divide the total goods available for sale at cost by the total goods available for sale at retail. (3) To convert the inventory valued at retail to approximate a lower of cost or market figure, apply the cost-to-retail ratio.

7. **Explain how to report and analyze inventory.** Accounting standards require financial statement disclosure of: (1) the composition of the inventory (in the balance sheet or in a separate schedule in the notes), (2) significant or unusual inventory financing arrangements, and (3) inventory costing methods employed (which may differ for different elements of inventory). Accounting standards also require the consistent application of costing methods from one period to another. Common ratios used in the management and evaluation of inventory levels are inventory turnover and average days to sell the inventory.

*8. **Determine ending inventory by applying the LIFO retail methods.** The application of LIFO retail is made under two assumptions: stable prices and fluctuating prices. **Procedures under stable prices:** (a) Because the LIFO method is a cost method, both the markups and the markdowns must be considered in obtaining the proper cost-to-retail percentage. (b) Since the LIFO method is concerned primarily with the additional layer (or the amount that should be subtracted from the previous layer), the beginning inventory is excluded from the cost-to-retail percentage used to price a newly added layer. (c) The markups and markdowns apply only to the goods purchased during the current period and not to the beginning inventory. **Procedures under fluctuating prices:** The steps are the same as for stable prices except that in computing the LIFO inventory under a dollar-value LIFO approach, the dollar increase in inventory is found and deflated to beginning-of-the-year prices to determine whether actual increases or decreases in quantity have occurred. If quantities increase, this increase is priced at the new index to compute the new layer. If quantities decrease, the decrease is subtracted from the most recent layers to the extent necessary.

      *This material is discussed in Appendix 9A of the text.

TIPS ON CHAPTER TOPICS

TIP: As used in the phrase "lower of cost or market," the term **market** refers to the market in which the entity buys (not the market in which it sells). Thus, market means current replacement cost (by purchase or by reproduction) except that: (1) market should not exceed the net realizable value (ceiling) and (2) market should not be less than the net realizable value reduced by an allowance for an approximately normal profit margin (floor).

TIP: The **net realizable value of inventory** is the net amount of cash expected to ultimately be received from the sale of the inventory. Thus, the net realizable value of inventory is the estimated selling price in the ordinary course of business less reasonably predictable costs of completion and disposal.

TIP: If the utility of an inventory item declines prior to the period of sale (disposal), that loss of utility should be recognized in the period of decline rather than the period of disposal. Thus, if an inventory item has become obsolete, the amount of write down determined by the LCM rule should be recognized as a loss in the period of the decline in utility. This is in alignment with the concept of **conservatism.** That is, when doubt exists about the value of an asset, a company should choose the lower amount.

TIP: The **conventional retail method** is used to approximate a lower-of-average-cost-or-market figure for inventory valuation. There are other versions of the retail method. In each application, an amount of inventory expressed in terms of retail prices is converted to a cost or to a lower-of-cost-or-market amount by multiplying the retail figure by a ratio. The components of the ratio vary depending on which version of the retail method is desired.

EXERCISE 9-1

Purpose: (L.O. 1) This exercise reviews the steps involved in the determination of the lower-of-cost-or-market (LCM) valuation for inventory.

The Richard G. Long Company handles ten different inventory items. The normal profit on each item is 25% of the selling price.

Instructions

From the information below, complete the blanks to calculate the value to be used for the inventory figure for financial statements if the LCM rule is applied to individual items.

Item	No. of Units on Hand	Cost	Replacement Cost	Expected Selling Price	Expected Cost to Sell	Ceiling	Floor	Market	LCM	Item Total
				Per Unit						
1	100	$7.00	$ 7.50	$ 10.00	$ 1.00					
2	10	7.00	6.25	10.00	1.00					
3	50	7.00	9.25	10.00	1.00					
4	10	9.50	9.25	10.00	1.00					
5	20	5.00	6.25	10.00	1.00					
6	100	8.00	7.25	10.00	1.00					
7	30	12.00	11.50	16.00	1.00					
8	10	16.00	15.50	16.00	1.00					
9	20	14.00	11.00	20.00	2.00					
10	10	17.00	16.00	20.00	2.00					
					Grand Total					

Solution to Exercise 9-1

Item	Ceiling	Floor	Market	LCM	# of Units	Item Total
	Per Unit					
1	$ 9.00	$ 6.50	$ 7.50	$ 7.00	100	$ 700.00
2	9.00	6.50	6.50	6.50	10	65.00
3	9.00	6.50	9.00	7.00	50	350.00
4	9.00	6.50	9.00	9.00	10	90.00
5	9.00	6.50	6.50	5.00	20	100.00
6	9.00	6.50	7.25	7.25	100	725.00
7	15.00	11.00	11.50	11.50	30	345.00
8	15.00	11.00	15.00	15.00	10	150.00
9	18.00	13.00	13.00	13.00	20	260.00
10	18.00	13.00	16.00	16.00	10	160.00
				Grand	Total	$ 2,945.00

Approach and Explanation: Write down the two steps involved in determining the lower of cost or market and perform the steps in order for each of the items:

Step 1: Find market. Market is the middle value of replacement cost, ceiling, and floor. For example:

	Item 1	Item 2	Item 3	Item 4
Estimated selling price	$10.00	$10.00	$10.00	$10.00
- Cost to complete and dispose	1.00	1.00	1.00	1.00
= Net realizable value (ceiling)	9.00	9.00	9.00	9.00
- Normal profit margin	2.50*	2.50	2.50	2.50
= Floor	$ 6.50	$ 6.50	$ 6.50	$ 6.50

*$10.00 x 25% = $2.50.

Ceiling	$ 9.00	$ 9.00	$ 9.00	$ 9.00
Floor	6.50	6.50	6.50	6.50
Replacement cost	7.50	6.25	9.25	9.25
Middle of these three values	7.50	6.50	9.00	9.00

Step 2: Compare cost with market and choose the lower.

Cost	$ 7.00	$ 7.00	$ 7.00	$ 9.50
Market (from Step 1)	7.50	6.50	9.00	9.00
Lower of cost or market	7.00	6.50	7.00	9.00

TIP: There are two simple steps to follow in order to apply the **lower of cost or market rule** to an inventory item. Be sure to follow them in order:
Step 1: Find market: List the replacement cost, net realizable value (ceiling), and the net realizable value less a normal profit margin (floor) and choose the **middle** value of these three amounts. Thus:
(a) market is replacement cost if the replacement cost is in the range between the "ceiling" value and the "floor" value.
(b) market is the "ceiling" value if the replacement cost is equal to or above the ceiling.
(c) market is the "floor" value if the replacement cost is equal to or below the floor.
Step 2: Compare market (as determined in Step 1) **with cost and chose the lower** of the two. This choice is the amount at which the inventory is to be reported on the balance sheet.

EXERCISE 9-2

Purpose: (L.O. 1) This exercise will illustrate the effects of the failure to properly apply the LCM rule.

Bava uses the lower-of-cost-or-market rule to value its inventory. At December 31, 2010, the following facts pertain to Product X-17.

Original cost		$420
Replacement cost		365
Expected selling price	400	
Estimated selling expenses		50
Normal profit		25% of selling price
Quantity in ending inventory		100 units

The accountant for Bava used the replacement cost value ($365) to value Product X-17 at December 31, 2010.

Instructions

Answer the following questions:

1.   Is $365 the correct unit value for Product X-17 for balance sheet reporting at December 31, 2010? Explain.
2.   If $365 is not the correct value, explain the effect of the misstatement on the following: (a) income statement for the year ending December 31, 2010, (b) balance sheet at December 31, 2010, (c) income statement for the year ending December 31, 2011, and (d) balance sheet at December 31, 2011. Assume that all of Product X-17 on hand at December 31, 2010 was sold during 2011.

Solution to Exercise 9-2

1. $365 is **not** the correct value for Product X-17 at December 31, 2010.

    Explanation: The ceiling value of $350 should have been used for the market figure (replacement cost of $365 exceeds the ceiling value of $350) and the ceiling is lower than original cost ($420); hence, $350 is the correct unit value for ending inventory at December 31, 2010.

Computations:	
Expected selling price	$ 400
Estimated selling expenses	(50)
Ceiling	350
Normal profit ($400 x 25%)	(100)
Floor	$ 250
Ceiling	$ 350
Floor	250
Replacement cost	365
Middle of these three values	$ 350
Cost	$ 420
Market	350
Lower of cost or market	$ 350

2. (a)   Net income for 2010 is overstated by $1,500.
    (b)   Assets are overstated by $1,500 and owners' equity is overstated by $1,500 at December 31, 2010.
    (c)   Net income for 2011 is understated by $1,500.
    (d)   No effect on the balance sheet at December 31, 2011.

    Explanation:
    (a) $365 - $350 = $15.
          $15 x 100 = $1,500.
          The error will cause an overstatement of ending inventory which results in an understatement of cost of goods sold expense which causes an overstatement in net income for 2010 in the amount of $1,500.

    (b)   Ending inventory is overstated by $1,500, so assets at December 31, 2010 are overstated by $1,500. Owners' equity at December 31, 2010 is also overstated by $1,500 because net income for 2010 (which is overstated by $1,500) is closed into owners' equity at the end of the accounting period.

    > **TIP:**   Visualize the basic accounting equation. This error will maintain balance in the basic accounting equation. If assets are overstated, then something else in the equation must be effected to keep the equation in balance. In this case, it is an overstatement of owners' equity because the error affects income (and that effect flows into owners' equity).

(c) The inventory is all sold in 2011. Bava's accountant is using $365 as the carrying value for each of the 100 units when the correct unit value should be $350. This will cause net income for the year ending December 31, 2011 to be understated by $1,500 because cost of goods sold will be overstated by $1,500.

(d) The inventory in question is no longer on hand at December 31, 2011, so there is no effect on assets at that date. The $1,500 understatement in income for 2011 is closed into owners' equity which has a balance that is overstated by $1,500 at the beginning of 2011; thus, the owners' equity balance at December 31, 2011 is correct.

> **TIP:** The application of the lower-of-cost-or market rule incorporates only losses in value that occur in the normal course of business from such causes as style changes, shift in demand, or regular shop wear. A company should reduce damaged or deteriorated goods to net realizable value.

CASE 9-1

Purpose: (L.O. 1, 6) This case addresses three inventory topics: (1) inventoriable costs, (2) the LCM rule, and (3) the retail method.

Toastie Corporation, a retailer of small kitchen appliances, purchases its inventories from various suppliers.

Instructions

(a) 1. Explain what costs will be inventoriable for Toastie.
   2. Explain why Toastie's administrative costs would or would not be inventoriable.
(b) 1. Toastie uses the lower of cost or market rule for its inventory. What is the theoretical justification for this rule?
   2. The original cost of the inventory is above the replacement cost which is above the net realizable value of the inventory. Explain what amount should be used to value the inventory and why.
   3. Explain and illustrate the journal entry that should be made to record an excess of cost over market when the LCM method is used along with a perpetual inventory system.
(c) Toastie currently uses the average cost method to determine the cost of its inventory. To simplify the procedures involved in counting and pricing its ending inventory, Toastie Corporation is considering the use of the conventional retail method. How should Toastie treat the beginning inventory and net markups in calculating the cost ratio to use to determine the ending inventory? Explain why.

Solution to Case 9-1

(a) 1. Toastie's inventoriable costs should include all costs incurred to get the appliances ready for sale to the customer. It includes not only the purchase price of the goods but also the other associated costs incurred for the appliances up to the time they are ready for sale to the customer, for example, transportation-in.

2. Administrative costs are assumed to expire with the passage of time and not to attach to the product. Furthermore, administrative costs do not relate directly to inventories, but are incurred for the benefit of all functions of the business. Thus, administrative costs should be treated as period costs, not as product costs; that is, they are not inventoriable.

(b) 1. The lower of cost or market rule is used for valuing inventories because of the conservatism principle (constraint) and because the decline in the utility of the inventories below their cost should be recognized as a loss in (and matched with) the period in which the decline took place.

2. The net realizable value should be used to value the inventory because market is less than cost. In this instance, "market" is the ceiling (net realizable value) because replacement cost > ceiling > floor and "market" is the middle value. This indicates that there has been a decline in the utility of the inventory. The inventory should be written down and a loss recorded. The inventory should never be valued at more than net realizable value. Apparently, not only will Toastie Corporation fail to realize a profit when it sells the inventory, it will not even recover its original cost.

> **TIP:** The ceiling and floor values exist so as to reject the use of replacement cost as a market figure in the use of the lower-of-cost-or market rule where the replacement is not an appropriate figure for the valuation of an item in ending inventory. If the replacement cost of an item exceeds its net realizable value, a company should not report inventory at replacement cost; the company can receive only the estimated selling price less cost of disposal. Thus, anything more than the net realizable value figure will overstate the inventory item. The floor establishes a value below which a company should not price inventory, regardless of replacement cost. It makes no sense to value inventory below its net realizable value less a normal profit margin. This minimum amount (floor) measures what the company can receive for the inventory and still earn a normal profit. To value the inventory below the floor amount will understate the inventory.

3. There are two methods of recording the write down of the inventory from cost to market with a perpetual system. The **direct method** buries the loss in cost of goods sold. The indirect method is preferable because it clearly discloses the loss resulting from the market decline of inventory prices.

Direct Method	**Indirect Method**
Cost of Goods Sold	Loss Due to Market Decline of Inventory
Inventory	Allowance to Reduce Inventory to Market

> **TIP:** The Allowance account is reported on the balance sheet as a contra Inventory item.

(c)   Toastie's beginning inventory at cost and at retail would be included in the calculation of the cost-to-retail ratio because the conventional retail method approximates a lower of **average** cost or market valuation. An average cost method reflects all costs experienced (both from the beginning inventory and from purchases) in the ending inventory calculation. Net markups would be included in the calculation of the cost ratio. This procedure reduces the cost ratio because there is a larger denominator for the cost ratio calculation. Thus, the concept of balance sheet conservatism is being followed and a lower of cost or market valuation is approximated.

EXERCISE 9-3

Purpose: (L.O. 3) This exercise will demonstrate the use of the relative sales value method to value inventories.

Rhile Jones Corporation purchased a tract of unimproved land on Lake Sybelia for $1,000,000. Costs of subdividing and readying the land for residential lots amounted to $140,000. The lots are of two sizes and some are lakefront, so they vary in market prices as follows:

Type	No. of Lots	Sales Price per Lot
1	10	$ 60,000
2	15	80,000
3	6	100,000

Lots remaining unsold at December 31, 2010 were as follows:

Type	No. of Lots
1	4
2	9
3	2

Instructions
Compute the value to be reported for the inventory of lots on hand on the December 31, 2010 balance sheet.

Solution to Exercise 9-3

Type	# of Lots	Sales Price per Lot	Total Sales Price	Relative Sales Price	Total Cost	Cost Allocated to Lots	Cost per Lot
1	10	$ 60,000	$ 600,000	6/24	$1,140,000	$ 285,000	$ 28,500
2	15	80,000	1,200,000	12/24	1,140,000	570,000	38,000
3	6	100,000	600,000	6/24	1,140,000	285,000	47,500
			$2,400,000			$1,140,000	

Ending Inventory:

Type	Lots Left	Cost per Lot	Total
1	4	$ 28,500	$114,000
2	9	38,000	342,000
3	2	47,500	95,000
			$551,000

Explanation: When a group of varying units is purchased (acquired) at a single lump sum price (often called a basket purchase), the total cost is allocated to the various items based on their relative sales (market) values. (The petroleum industry widely uses the relative sales value method to value (at cost) the many products and by-products from a barrel of crude oil.)

EXERCISE 9-4

Purpose: (L.O. 5) This exercise will illustrate the use of the gross profit method of inventory estimation when: (1) gross profit is expressed as a percentage of cost, and (2) gross profit is expressed as a percentage of selling price.

Tim McInnes requires an estimate of the cost of goods lost by fire on April 2. Merchandise on hand on January 1 was $38,000. Purchases since January 1 were $72,000; freight-in, $3,400; and purchase returns and allowances, $2,400. Sales totaled $100,000 to April 2. Goods costing $7,700 were left undamaged by the fire; all other goods were destroyed.

Instructions
(a)   Compute the cost of goods destroyed, assuming that the gross profit is 25% of cost.
(b)   Compute the cost of goods destroyed, assuming that the gross profit is 25% of sales.

Solution to Exercise 9-4

(a)   (1)   Gross profit is 25% of cost.
Gross profit = 25%   (100% + 25%) = 20% of sales.
Gross profit = 20% of sales.

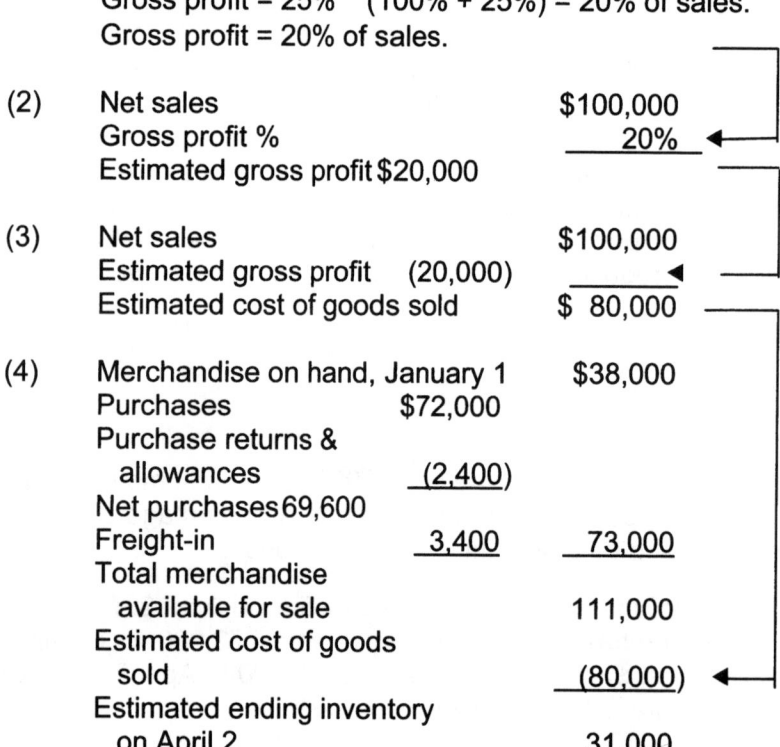

       (2)

Net sales	$100,000
Gross profit %	20%
Estimated gross profit	$20,000

       (3)

Net sales	$100,000
Estimated gross profit	(20,000)
Estimated cost of goods sold	$ 80,000

       (4)

Merchandise on hand, January 1		$38,000
Purchases	$72,000	
Purchase returns & allowances	(2,400)	
Net purchases	69,600	
Freight-in	3,400	73,000
Total merchandise available for sale		111,000
Estimated cost of goods sold		(80,000)
Estimated ending inventory on April 2		31,000
Undamaged goods		(7,700)
Estimated fire loss		$23,300

(b)   (1)   Gross profit is 25% of sales.

     (2)

Net sales	$100,000	
Gross profit %	25%	
Estimated gross profit	$25,000	

     (3)

Net sales	$100,000	
Estimated gross profit	(25,000)	◄
Estimated cost of goods sold	$ 75,000	

     (4)

Total merchandise available for sale [see part (a) (4) above]	$111,000
Estimated cost of goods sold	(75,000)
Estimated ending inventory on April 12	36,000
Undamaged goods	(7,700)
Estimated fire loss	$28,300

> **TIP:** It is important to understand that inventory is accounted for in terms of the **cost** of goods acquired, and the Sales account reflects the **selling prices** of goods that have been sold during the period. Therefore, the profit element must be removed from the sales amount to arrive at the estimated cost of the goods sold amount.

Approach: Use these steps to perform the calculations:

(1)   **Compute the gross profit percentage on selling price.**
In part (a), this must be computed; in part (b), it is a given piece of information.

(2)   **Compute estimated gross profit** by multiplying net sales by the gross profit percentage. **Caution:** *The gross margin percentage used here must be stated* in terms of *selling price.*

(3)   **Compute estimated cost of goods sold** by subtracting gross profit from net sales.

(4)   **Compute estimated ending inventory** on hand at the end of the period by subtracting cost of goods sold from total goods available for sale.

(5)   **Determine the estimated loss** from fire by deducting the cost of the undamaged goods from the estimated cost of inventory on hand at April 2, (Step 4).

> **TIP:** **Gross profit** is synonymous with **gross margin.**
>
> **TIP:** The gross profit percentage (expressed as a percentage of selling price) and the cost of goods sold percentage (also expressed as a percentage of selling price) are complements; that is, they sum to 100%. When the gross profit method of inventory estimation is used and the gross margin is expressed in terms of cost, the gross margin must first be expressed in terms of selling price before you can proceed with the computations. One method of conversion is to memorize and use the following formula:
>
> $$\frac{\text{Gross margin on}}{\text{Selling price}} = \frac{\text{Percentage markup on cost}}{100\% + \text{Percentage markup on cost}}$$
>
> Another approach to deriving this formula is shown below. It uses the familiar formula:

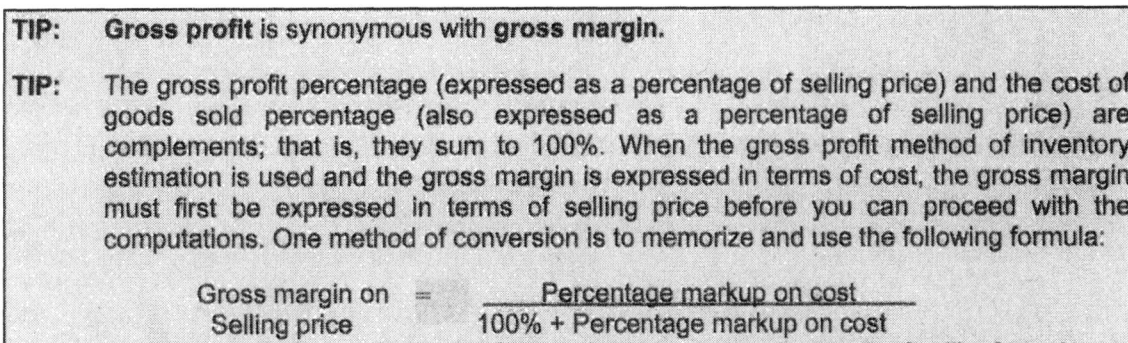

Sales (S) – Cost of Goods Sold (CGS) = Gross Profit (GP).

Example: If GP = 25% of cost, then cost of goods sold is 100%.
Putting this much information into our formula above: S – 100% = 25%.
Therefore S = 125%
Expressing GP as a percentage of S we get: 25% + 125% = 20%.
Thus, gross profit = 20% of sales

TIP: Gross profit on selling price will always be less than gross profit expressed as a percentage of cost.

TIP: The terms **gross margin percentage**, **gross profit percentage**, **rate of gross profit**, and **percentage markup** are thought of to be synonymous, although companies more commonly use the term **markup** in referring to a relationship to cost and then use the term **gross profit** in referring to a relationship to sales.

TIP: The gross profit (gross margin) method only provides an **estimate** of inventory cost. This method is deficient in that it uses past percentages in determining the markup and the markup is usually not uniform for all items in inventory. The method is normally unacceptable for financial reporting purposes (except for interim reports). The method is useful in estimating inventory when the inventory has been destroyed and for verifying the reasonableness of inventory amounts determined by other methods.

ILLUSTRATION 9-1
WHAT IS INCLUDED IN A CONVENTIONAL RETAIL INVENTORY COMPUTATION? (L.O. 6)

	Cost	Retail
Beginning inventory	$ 500	$ 1,000
Purchases	18,000	34,000
Purchase returns	(1,800)	(3,000)
Purchase discounts	(440)	
Purchase allowances	(460)	
Freight-in	2,000	
Goods available for sale	17,800	32,000
Markups		2,100
Markup cancellations		(700)
Subtotals	17,800	33,400
Markdowns		(1,110)
Markdown cancellations		300
Subtotals	17,800	32,590
Sales (gross)		(28,000)
Employee discounts		(1,070)
Sales returns		520
Estimated normal shrinkage		(840)
Ending inventory at retail		$ 3,200

Cost-to-retail ratio $= \dfrac{\$17,800}{33,400} = 53.3\%$

Ending inventory at lower of average cost or market = 53.3% X $3,200 = $1,706

TIP: Notice there is an amount in both the cost column and retail column for purchase returns because when an item is returned to a vendor by an enterprise, the item is physically removed from the shelves (inventory); thus, both the item's cost and retail price are no longer relevant to the computation. However, for purchase discounts and purchase allowances, an amount appears only in the cost column because the vendor reduces the cost of an inventory item, but the inventory item remains in inventory to be sold.

Payment of freight on purchases increases the cost of acquiring an inventory item but no new retail price is added to inventory; the original retail price of the inventory item was chosen to recover the purchase price plus freight plus a profit. Markups, related markup cancellations, markdowns, and related markdown cancellations all pertain to retail prices, not to cost. A merchandiser may increase or decrease the selling (retail) prices while holding merchandise, but that has no impact on the price paid to the wholesale vendor (cost) for the item.

Sales reduce the amount of retail goods on hand; hence sales are deducted in the retail column. Sales returns cause a return of merchandise to the shelves; hence, they are reflected as an addition in the retail column. When sales are recorded gross, companies do **not** use the sales discounts amount in the retail inventory calculations. The gross sales amount is the true reduction in retail prices from the shelves. Normal shrinkage is deducted from the amount of goods available at retail before applying a cost-to-retail ratio to compute ending inventory at

ILLUSTRATION 9-1 (cont.)

cost; therefore, the cost of ending inventory is effectively reduced because of estimated shrinkage. Typically employees are allowed an employee discount and the sales price is recorded net of it. Thus, employee discounts are deducted from the retail column in the same way as sales because they reduce the amount recorded for sales but they eliminate retail prices available for sale.

TIP: The following concepts apply to the **retail inventory method:**

Markup or markon: The difference between cost and original retail (sales price). Such as an item is purchased for $25 and is priced to sell for $45: the markup is $20.

Additional markup: The amount by which a selling price is marked above the original retail price. For example, the retail price is raised to $48 while it is being held for sale: the additional markup is $3. (It is confusing, but many retailers refer to the "additional markup" simply as "markup". Usually by context you can tell if an amount of "markup" is truly the (original) "markup" or "additional markup." Homework assignments or examinations may use either term.

Markup cancellation: The amount by which an additional markup is reduced or cancelled. For example, the item above is marked from a retail price of $48 to $46 while it is still held for sale: the (additional) markup cancellation is $2.

Markdown: The excess of the original retail price over a new lowered retail price. For example, if the item above is now marked from $46 to $40, there has been a(n) (additional) markup cancellation of $1 and a markdown of $5.

Markdown cancellation: A reduction in a markdown. For example, the item above is now marked from $40 to $44 while still being held for sale: there is a markdown cancellation of $4.

Net additional markup: Additional markups less additional markup cancellations.

New markdowns: Markdowns less markdown cancellations.

TIP: The conventional retail method **includes** net markups (often called net additional markups) but **excludes** net markdowns from the **ratio computation**. The reason for this is that a lower-of-cost-or-market valuation is desired when the conventional retail method is used. (Net markdowns would also be included in the ratio if a straight average cost value rather than a lower-of-average-cost-or-market valuation were desired.) The omission of the net markdowns from the ratio computation results in a higher denominator and therefore a lower resulting ratio than what would be derived if the net markdowns were to be included in the ratio computation. When there have been markdowns, any related writedowns in inventory should be reflected in the current income statement (from a conservative point of view). This is accomplished by reporting the inventory at a lower value which means more of the cost of goods available for sale goes to the income statement as cost of goods sold expense.

TIP: In using the conventional retail method, the net markdowns are **omitted** from the ratio computation, but they must be **included** in determining the estimated ending inventory at retail.

TIP: The retail inventory method can be used only if sufficient information is accumulated and maintained. Purchases are recorded in the accounts at cost. Although not recorded in the accounts, the retail value of purchases and the changes in that value (markups, markup cancellations, markdowns, and markdown cancellations) must be recorded in supplemental records for use in inventory calculations utilizing the retail inventory method.

ILLUSTRATION 9-2
HOW TO COMPUTE AND APPLY THE COST/RETAIL RATIO
FOR THE RETAIL METHOD (L.O. 6, 8)

Method (Basis)	Cost/Retail Ratio	How to Compute Ending Inventory
1. Conventional (Lower of Average Cost or Market).	(Beginning inventory at cost + net cost of purchases) ÷ (beginning inventory at retail + net purchases at retail + net markups).	Ending inventory at retail x ratio.
2. Average Cost	(Beginning inventory at cost + net cost of purchases) (beginning inventory at retail + net purchases at retail + net markups – net markdowns)	Ending inventory at retail x ratio
*3. LIFO Cost (ignoring change in price level). a. If ending inventory at retail is higher than beginning inventory at retail (added layer).	(Net cost of purchases) (net purchases at retail + net markups - net markdowns).	(Beginning inventory at cost) + (added layer at retail x ratio).
b. If ending inventory at retail is less than beginning inventory at retail.	Beginning inventory at cost beginning inventory at retail.	Ending inventory at retail x ratio.

*This material is covered in Appendix 8A in the text.

EXERCISE 9-5

Purpose: (L.O. 6, 8) This exercise illustrates two variations of the retail inventory method. It will provide an opportunity to compare and contrast these two approaches.

The records of Nancy Klintworth's Baubles report the following data for the month of May.

Sales	$ 79,000
Sales returns	1,000
Markups	10,000
Markup cancellations	1,500
Markdowns	9,300
Markdown cancellations	2,800
Freight on purchases	2,400
Purchases (at cost)	48,000
Purchases (at sales price)	88,000
Purchase returns (at cost)	2,000
Purchase returns (at sales price)	3,000
Beginning inventory (at cost)	30,000
Beginning inventory (at sales price)	46,500

Instructions
(a)   Compute the ending inventory by the conventional retail inventory method.
*(b)   Compute the ending inventory using the retail method to approximate a LIFO cost figure (assuming stable prices).

   *This material is covered in Appendix 8A in the text.

Solution to Exercise 9-5

	Cost		**Retail**
Beginning inventory	$ 30,000		$ 46,500
Purchases	48,000		88,000
Purchase returns	(2,000)		(3,000)
Freight on purchase	2,400		
Goods available for sale	78,400		131,500
Net markups:			
Markups		$ 10,000	
Markup cancellations		(1,500)	8,500
	78,400		140,000
Net markdowns:			
Markdowns		9,300	
Markdown cancellations		(2,800)	(6,500)
	$ 78,400		133,500
Net sales ($79,000 - $1,000)			(78,000)
Ending inventory, at retail			$ 55,500

(a)   Cost-to-retail ratio = $78,400 ÷ $140,000 = 56%
Ending inventory at lower of average cost or market = 56% x $55,500 = $31,080

(b)   Cost-to-retail ratio = $48,400^a ÷ 87,000^b = 55.63%

	Retail	**Ratio**	**LIFO Cost**
Beginning inventory layer	$ 46,500		$ 30,000
Layer added in May	9,000^c	55.63%	5,007
Ending inventory	$ 55,500		$ 35,007

^{a}$78,400 - $30,000 = $48,400   Net cost of purchases.
^{b}$133,500 - $46,500 = $87,000   Retail value of purchases plus net markups less net markdowns.

^{c}$55,500 - $46,500 = $9,000   Excess of ending inventory at retail over beginning inventory at retail.

Approach and Explanation:
(a)   Step 1:   **Compute the ending inventory at retail.** This is done by determining the retail value of goods available for sale, adjusting that figure for net markups and net markdowns, and deducting the retail value of goods no longer on hand (sales, estimated theft, etc.).

Step 2:   **Compute the cost-to-retail ratio.** The conventional retail method approximates an average cost amount so both beginning inventory and net purchases information is used in the ratio. The conventional retail method is to approximate a lower-of-cost-or-market value so the net markups are included but the net markdowns are excluded from the ratio computation.

Step 3:   **Determine the ending inventory at an approximate lower-of-average-cost-or-market value.** Apply the appropriate cost-to-retail ratio (Step 2) to the total ending inventory at retail (Step 1).

(b)   Step 1:   **Compute the ending inventory at retail.** This is done the same way as Step 1 in Part (a) above.

Step 2:   **Compute the cost-to-retail ratio.** When the LIFO method is used, ending inventory is priced in layers. If the ending inventory at retail is higher than the beginning inventory at retail, a new inventory layer was added during the period [Part (b) assumes stable prices] and the beginning inventory is intact. Therefore, the ending inventory is composed of the beginning inventory layer(s) and a new layer. A cost-to-retail ratio is needed to cost the new layer. Because the layer added came from purchases of the current period, beginning inventory information is **not** included in this ratio. Because LIFO cost rather than a lower-of-cost-or-market valuation is desired, both the net markups and net markdowns are reflected in the ratio computation.

Step 3:   **Determine the ending inventory at an approximate LIFO cost (assuming stable prices).** Determine the cost of each layer in the ending inventory. Because a new layer was added in May, the beginning inventory layer is still intact at the end of the period ($46,500 at retail and

$30,000 at LIFO cost). The ratio for the added layer (55.63% as determined in Step 2) is used to convert the $9,000 increase in inventory during the period at retail prices to a LIFO cost amount.

TIP:	If the ending inventory at retail had been equal to or less than the beginning inventory at retail figure ($46,500), then a different ratio would be needed. That ratio would be one which expresses the relationship of the cost of the beginning inventory ($30,000) to the retail value of the beginning inventory ($46,500). The ending inventory at retail would have been multiplied by that ratio (64.516%) to determine the LIFO cost of the ending inventory. Assuming an ending inventory at retail of $40,000, the ending inventory at LIFO cost would be $25,806.
TIP:	If prices had not been stable, additional procedures would have been required to eliminate the effects of price-level changes in order to measure the real increases in inventory, not the dollar increase.
TIP:	Compare the steps for each variation of the retail method utilized in this exercise. Notice that **Step 1** is the **same** for each of the two scenarios and, therefore, yields the same results ($55,500 ending inventory at retail). Notice that Step 3 always applies a ratio to this $55,500 (or a portion thereof). The differences between these two scenarios then stem from the appropriate ratio (Step 2) to be applied in each case and the layers that may exist in a LIFO situation. Look at each scenario and think through the logic of the ratio calculation as explained in this solution. This process should make it easier to recall how to handle similar situations as you encounter them. **Illustration 9-2** will help to summarize and compare these variations on the use of the retail method.

*EXERCISE 9-6

Purpose: (L.O. 8) This exercise will illustrate the use of the dollar-value LIFO retail method when there is: (a) a decrease in inventory and (b) an increase in inventory.

You assemble the following information for Henrietta's Department Store, which computes its inventory under the dollar-value LIFO retail method.

	Cost	Retail
Inventory on January 1, 2010	$ 227,200	$ 320,000
Purchases	340,400	460,000
Increase in price level for year		8%

Instructions

(a)   Compute the cost of the inventory on December 31, 2010, assuming that the ending inventory at retail is $286,200.

(b)   Compute the cost of the inventory on December 31, 2010, assuming that the ending inventory at retail is $351,000.

Solution to Exercise 9-6

(a)   Ending inventory at current retail prices $\qquad$ $ 286,200

   Ending inventory at base retail prices ($286,200 ÷ 1.08) $\qquad$ 265,000

   This calculation reveals that the inventory quantity has declined below the beginning level (compare $265,000 with $320,000); the ending inventory is merely a portion of the beginning inventory. Therefore, the cost-to-retail ratio reflected in the beginning inventory layer is used to price the ending inventory.

   $227,200 ÷ $320,000 = 71% Cost-to-retail ratio for beginning inventory

   $265,000 x 71% = $ 188,150

Approach and Explanation:

Step 1:   **Deflate the $286,200 ending inventory at current retail prices to base retail prices of $265,000.** The ending inventory at current retail prices is reduced to base retail prices by dividing the $286,200 by the ending price level index (108%). The price level increased 8% during the year so assigning an index of 100 (base) to the beginning of the year would mean the index at the end of the year would be 108% (8% higher than 100).

Step 2:   **Determine whether a real increase or a decrease has occurred in inventory.** This is done by comparing the ending inventory at base retail prices ($265,000) with the beginning inventory at base retail prices ($320,000).

Step 3: **Determine the ending inventory at dollar-value LIFO.** The ending inventory is merely a portion of the beginning inventory layer. The ending inventory at base retail prices is then converted to a cost figure by using the appropriate cost-to-retail ratio which is the ratio reflected in the beginning inventory.

(b) Ending inventory at current retail prices $ 351,000

Ending inventory at base retail prices ($351,000 ÷ 1.08)   325,000
Beginning inventory at base retail prices   320,000
Layer added—at base prices   5,000

Ending Inventory:	Retail at Base Price	Dollar-Value LIFO
Beginning inventory	$ 320,000	$ 227,200
Additional layer	5,000	3,996*
Ending inventory	$ 325,000	$ 231,196

*The $5,000 layer at base prices must be restored to the price level of the period in which it was added: $5,000 x 1.08 = $5,400 and then the cost-to-retail ratio for items purchased during the current year must be applied to that $5,400: $5,400 x 74%** = $3,996.

**The cost-to-retail ratio for items purchased during 2010 is computed as follows: $340,400 ÷ $460,000 = 74%.

Approach and Explanation:
Step 1: **Deflate the $351,000 ending inventory at current retail prices to base retail prices of $325,000.** This is done by dividing the $351,000 by 108%.
Step 2: **Determine whether a real increase or a decrease has occurred in inventory.** This is done by comparing the ending inventory at base retail prices ($325,000) with the beginning inventory at base retail prices ($320,000). A real increase of $5,000 in terms of base retail prices has occurred.
Step 3: **Determine the ending inventory at dollar-value LIFO.** The ending inventory is composed of two layers—the beginning inventory layer and a layer added during 2010. The cost of the beginning inventory layer is carried over from last period. The added layer must first be priced in terms of current retail prices (multiply $5,000 x 1.08) because the layer was added in 2010 and then that result ($5,400) is converted to a cost figure by multiplying it by the appropriate cost-to-retail ratio (74%). The appropriate cost-to-retail ratio is the relationship of cost to retail of the purchases made in 2010.

ANALYSIS OF MULTIPLE-CHOICE TYPE QUESTIONS

QUESTION

1. (L.O. 1) Crosby Co. is just beginning its first year of operations. Crosby intends to use either the perpetual moving average method or the periodic weighted average method, and to apply the lower of cost or market rule either to individual items or to the total inventory. Prices of most inventory items are expected to increase throughout 2010, although the prices of a few items are expected to decrease. What inventory system should Crosby Co. select if it wants to minimize the inventory carrying amount at the end of the first year?

	Inventory Method	Cost or Market Application
a.	Perpetual	Individual items
b.	Perpetual	Total inventory
c.	Periodic	Individual items
d.	Periodic	Total inventory

Approach and Explanation: Think about the results of using the perpetual moving average method versus the results of using the periodic weighted average method. In a period of rising prices, the periodic weighted average method will yield the lower ending inventory figure (the ending weighted average unit cost for the perpetual system will be higher than the weighted average unit cost for the period for the periodic system). Then think about the results of applying the lower-of-cost-or-market rule to individual items versus the results of applying it to the total inventory. The individual item approach gives the most conservative valuation for balance sheet purposes. When categories or total inventory is used, situations caused by products whose replacement cost is higher than original cost are allowed to offset situations where replacement cost is lower than original cost. When an item-by-item approach is used, all possible declines in utility are recognized and not offset by inventory items whose replacement cost exceeds original cost. Combine the results of these analyses to get the final answer. (Solution = c.)

QUESTION

2. (L.O. 1) Peachy Products has an item in inventory with a cost of $85. Current replacement cost is $75. The expected selling price is $100, estimated selling costs are $18, and the normal profit is $5. Using the lower-of-cost-or-market rule, the item should be included in the inventory at:
    a. $75.
    b. $77.
    c. $82.
    d. $85.

Approach and Explanation: Write down the two steps in determining LCM and follow them:
    (1)   Find market: Three possibilities:
                            Ceiling ($100 - $18) = $82
                            Floor ($82 - $5) = $77
                            Replacement cost = $75
            Choose the middle value of these three: $77 = market
    (2)   Compare market with cost and choose the lower.
            Market of $77 versus cost of $85. Lower = $77   (Solution = b.)

QUESTION

3. (L.O. 1) In applying the lower-of-cost-or-market rule to inventories at December 31, 2010, Xavier Corporation wrote the inventory down from $500,000 to $420,000. Using the indirect method of recording inventory at market, this writedown should be reported:
   a. as a prior period adjustment of $80,000.
   b. as an operating expense in 2010.
   c. as an extraordinary item on the 2010 income statement.
   d. as a part of cost of goods sold expense.
   e. immediately after cost of goods sold or immediately after gross profit on the 2010 income statement.

Explanation: Using the indirect method of recording inventory at market when the market is lower than cost, the $80,000 loss will be shown separately from cost of goods sold (below cost of goods sold) in the income statement; it is not an extraordinary item. The direct method of recording inventory at market would include the $80,000 loss as an unidentifiable part of cost of goods sold. (Solution = e.)

QUESTION

4. (L.O. 4) In 2010, Lucas Manufacturing signed a noncancelable contract with a supplier to purchase raw materials in 2011 for $700,000. Before the December 31, 2010 balance sheet date, the market price for these materials dropped to $510,000. The journal entry to record this situation at December 31, 2010 will result in a credit that should be reported:
   a. as a valuation account to Inventory on the balance sheet.
   b. as a current liability.
   c. as an appropriation of retained earnings.
   d. on the income statement.

Approach and Explanation: Draft the entry referred to in the question. Think about the classification of each account in the entry. Focus on the credit part addressed in the stem of the question. The journal entry is:

Unrealized Holding Loss on Purchase Commitments	190,000	
Estimated Liability on Purchase Commitments		190,000

The loss would be reported on the income statement under Other Expenses and Losses. The liability is reported as a current liability because the contract is to be executed within the year that immediately follows the balance sheet date. (Solution = b.)

This entry is made to comply with the conservatism constraint. The entry is made because the noncancelable contract price is greater than the market price and the buyer expects that losses will occur when the purchase is effected. The buyer should recognize losses in the period during which such declines in market prices take place related to purchase commitments. When Lucas purchases the materials in the next accounting period, Purchases (or Inventory) will be debited for $510,000, Estimated Liability on Purchase Commitments will be debited for $190,000, and Cash will be credited for $700,000.

QUESTION

5. (L.O. 5) The following information pertains to the Godfrey Company for the six months ended June 30 of the current year:

Merchandise inventory, January 1	$ 700,000
Purchases	5,000,000
Freight-in	400,000
Sales	6,000,000

Gross profit is normally 25% of sales. What is the estimated amount of inventory on hand at June 30?
   a. $100,000
   b. $1,600,000
   c. $2,100,000
   d. $4,600,000

Approach and Explanation: Use the following steps to solve a gross profit inventory method question:

(1)   **Compute the gross profit percentage on selling price:**
Gross profit is 25% of cost (given).

> | TIP: | This problem was simple because the gross profit percentage given in the problem is stated in terms of sales. When the gross margin percentage is expressed in terms of cost (such as in cases where a "markup" percentage is given), that percentage must first be converted to the equivalent percentage of selling price before the other computations can be performed. |
> |---|---|

(2)   **Compute estimated gross** profit by multiplying net sales by the gross profit percentage.

Sales	$6,000,000
Gross profit percentage	25%
Estimated gross profit	$1,500,000

(3)   **Compute estimated cost of goods sold** by subtracting gross profit from net sales.

Sales	$6,000,000
Estimated gross profit	(1,500,000)
Estimated cost of goods sold	$4,500,000

(4)   **Compute estimated ending inventory** by subtracting cost of goods available for sale.

Beginning inventory	$ 700,000
Purchases	5,000,000
Freight-in	400,000
Cost of goods available for sale	6,100,000
Estimated cost of goods sold	(4,500,000)
Estimated ending inventory	$1,600,000

(Solution = b.)

QUESTION

6.   (L.O. 5) The cost of goods available for sale for 2010 for Storey Corporation was $2,700,000. The gross profit rate was 20% of sales. Sales for the year amounted to $2,400,000. The ending inventory is estimated to be:
   a. $0.
   b. $480,000.
   c. $540,000.
   d. $780,000.

Explanation: Step 1:   Compute the gross profit percentage on selling price:
Gross profit is 20% of sales.

Step 2:   Compute estimated gross profit:

Sales	$2,400,000
Gross profit percentage	X 20%
Estimated gross profit	$ 480,000

Step 3:   Compute estimated cost of goods sold:

Sales	$2,400,000
Estimated gross profit	(480,000)
Estimated cost of goods sold	$1,920,000

Step 4:   Compute estimated ending inventory:

Cost of goods available for sale	$2,700,000
Estimated cost of goods sold	(1,920,000)
Estimated ending inventory (at cost)	$ 780,000

(Solution = d.)

QUESTION
7.   (L.O. 5) If gross profit is 25% of cost, then gross profit as a percentage of sales equals:
a.   80%.
b.   75%.
c.   33 2/3%.
d.   20%.

Explanation: Sales (S) - Cost of Goods Sold (CGS) = Gross Profit (GP)
If GP = 25% of cost, then cost of goods sold = 100%.
S - 100% = 25%.
S = 125%.
Expressing gross profit (GP) as a percentage of sales (S) we get:
    25%   125% = 20%.
Thus, gross profit = 20% of sales.

(Solution = d.)

QUESTION
8.   (L.O. 6) A company uses the retail method to estimate ending inventory for interim reporting purposes. If the retail method is used to approximate a lower-of-average-cost-or-market valuation, which of the following describes the proper treatment of net markups and net markdowns in the cost-to-retail ratio calculation?

	Net Markups	Net Markdowns
a.	Include	Include
b.	Include	Exclude
c.	Exclude	Include
d.	Exclude	Exclude

Approach and Explanation: First notice that the lower-of-average-cost-or-market approach to the retail method is often referred to as the conventional retail method. Recall that using a lower-of-cost-or-market figure is an application of the principle of conservatism. Also recall that the retail method involves multiplying the ending inventory at retail by a ratio. The lower the ratio, the lower the computed inventory value. Including the net markups (increases in retail prices) but excluding the net markdowns (decreases in retail prices) gives the highest denominator possible for the ratio calculation which yields the lowest ratio possible. (Note: Net markups are often called net additional markups.) (Solution = b.)

QUESTION

9.   (L.O. 6) The following data relate to the merchandise inventory of the Hofma Company:

Beginning inventory at cost	$ 13,800
Beginning inventory at selling price	20,000
Purchases at cost	31,000
Purchases at selling price	50,000

What is the cost to retail ratio?
a.   156%.
b.   145%.
c.   69%.
d.   64%.

Explanation:

Ratio	=	Cost ÷ Retail
Ratio	=	($13,800 + $31,000) ÷ ($20,000 + $50,000)
Ratio	=	$44,800 ÷ $70,000
Ratio	=	64% (Solution = d.)

QUESTION

10.   (L.O. 6) The Ruffier Department Store uses the conventional retail inventory method. The following information is available at December 31, 2010:

	Cost	Retail
Beginning inventory	$ 37,800	$ 60,000
Purchases	200,000	290,000
Freight-in	7,200	
Sales		275,000

What is the estimated cost of the ending inventory?
a. $47,250.
b. $52,500.
c. $53,586.
d. $192,500.

Computations:

	Cost	Retail
Beginning inventory	$ 37,800	$ 60,000
Purchases	200,000	290,000
Freight-in	7,200	
Cost of goods available for sale	$ 245,000	350,000
Sales		(275,000)

Step 1: Ending inventory at retail $ 75,000
Step 2: Cost to retail ratio = $245,000 ÷ $350,000 = 70%
Step 3: Estimated cost of ending inventory = $75,000 x 70% = $ 52,500

Approach and Explanation: Think about how the conventional retail method of inventory estimation works. An estimate of the ending inventory at retail is made by deducting sales from the retail value of goods available for sale, and the ending inventory at retail is converted to a cost value by applying an appropriate ratio which is an expression of the relationship between inventory cost and its retail value. Apply the following steps to compute the amount required:

Step 1:   **Compute the ending inventory at retail.** Deduct net sales from the retail price of all of the goods available for sale during the period. Arrive at $75,000.

Step 2:   **Compute the cost to retail ratio.** Divide the cost of the goods available for sale ($245,000) by the retail value of those same goods ($350,000). Arrive at 70%.

Step 3:   **Determine the estimated cost of the ending inventory.** Apply the cost to retail ratio (70%) to the ending inventory at retail ($75,000). Arrive at $52,500. (Solution = b.)

QUESTION

11.   (L.O. 7) Which of the following statements is **false** regarding an assumption of inventory cost flow?

    a.   The cost flow assumption need not correspond to the actual physical flow of goods.

    b.   The assumption selected may be changed each accounting period.

    c.   The FIFO assumption uses the earliest acquired prices to cost the items sold during a period.

    d.   The LIFO assumption uses the earliest acquired prices to cost the items on hand at the end of an accounting period.

Explanation: Once a method is selected from acceptable alternative methods, the entity must consistently apply that method for successive periods. The reason for this **consistency concept** is that **comparability** of financial statements is reduced or lost if methods are changed from period to period. However, an entity may change a method if it becomes evident that another method is more appropriate. (Solution = b.)

QUESTION

12.   (L.O. 8) The Billy Dial Department Store uses a calendar year and the LIFO retail inventory method (assuming stable prices). The following information is available at December 31, 2010:

	Cost	Retail
Beginning inventory	$ 37,200	$ 60,000
Purchases	200,000	290,000
Freight-in	4,000	
Net markups		30,000
Net markdowns		20,000
Sales		285,000

What is the ending inventory at LIFO cost?

    a. $46,763.

    b. $47,400.

    c. $47,603.

    d. $50,250.

Computations:	**Cost**	**Retail**
Beginning inventory	$ 37,200	$ 60,000
Purchases	200,000	290,000
Freight-in	4,000	
Goods available for sale	241,200	350,000
Net markups		30,000
Subtotals	$ 241,200	380,000
Net markdowns		(20,000)
Sales		(285,000)
Ending inventory at retail		$ 75,000

Ending inventory:	**Retail**	**Ratio**	**Cost**
Beginning layer	$ 60,000		$ 37,200
Added layer	15,000	68%*	10,200
Ending inventory	$ 75,000		$ 47,400

*$204,000ª ÷ $300,000ᵇ = 68%

ª$200,000 + $4,000 = $204,000
ᵇ$290,000 Purchases + $30,000 Markups - $20,000 Markdowns = $300,000

Approach and Explanation: Think about how LIFO works. If the ending inventory is greater than the beginning inventory, the ending inventory is comprised of the beginning inventory plus a new layer; if the ending inventory is less than the beginning inventory, the ending inventory is comprised of a remaining portion of the beginning inventory layer. Think about how the retail method of inventory estimation works. An estimate of the ending inventory at retail is made by deducting sales from the retail value of goods available for sale and the ending inventory at retail is converted to a cost or to a lower-of-cost-or-market value by applying an appropriate ratio which is an expression of the relationship between inventory cost and its retail value. Apply the following steps to compute the amount required:

Step 1:   **Compute the ending inventory at retail.** Arrive at $75,000.
Step 2:   **Compute the cost-to-retail ratio.** Comparing ending inventory at retail ($75,000) with beginning inventory at retail ($60,000) indicates a layer was added during 2007. Therefore, a ratio is needed to cost the layer which was added during 2007. The ratio for the new layer should exclude the beginning inventory. The ratio should include both net markups and net markdowns to approximate a cost (rather than a LCM valuation).
Step 3:   **Determine the ending inventory at an approximate LIFO cost.** Use the beginning layer ($37,200 at LIFO cost) and apply the purchases' cost-to-retail ratio (68%) to the added layer at retail ($15,000). (Solution = b.)

QUESTION
13.   (L.O. 7) The inventory turnover ratio is a measure of the liquidity of the inventory. This ratio is computed by dividing:
a.   the cost of goods sold by 365 days.
b.   the cost of goods sold by the average amount of inventory on hand.
c.   net credit sales by the average amount of inventory on hand.
d.   365 days by the cost of goods sold.

Approach and Explanation: Write down the formula to compute the inventory turnover ratio. Think about the logic of each of the computation's components. The formula is as follows:

$$\frac{\text{Inventory}}{\text{Turnover ratio}} = \frac{\text{Cost of Goods Sold}}{\text{Average Inventory}}$$

The cost of goods sold figure is a cost figure whereas net credit sales is a figure reflecting the selling prices of items sold. The cost of an inventory item is reflected in the Inventory account until such time when the item is sold; then, the cost is transferred to the Cost of Goods Sold account. If an item is sold on credit, the selling price of the item is recorded in the Accounts Receivable account. Hence, the accounts receivable turnover ratio uses net credit sales and average accounts receivable balance; whereas, the inventory turnover ratio uses cost of goods sold and the average inventory balance for its computation. A variant of the inventory turnover ratio is the **average days to sell inventory.** (Solution = b.)

QUESTION

14.   (L.O. 7) The average days to sell inventory is computed by dividing:
   a.   365 days by the inventory turnover ratio.
   b.   the inventory turnover ratio by 365 days.
   c.   net sales by the inventory turnover ratio.
   d.   365 days by cost of goods sold.

Explanation: The **average days to sell inventory** is a variant of the inventory turnover ratio. It is computed by dividing 365 days by the inventory turnover ratio. It measures the average number of days an item remains in inventory before it is sold. (Solution = a.)

CHAPTER 10

ACQUISITION AND DISPOSITION OF PROPERTY, PLANT, AND EQUIPMENT

OVERVIEW

Assets that have physical existence and that are expected to be used in revenue-generating operations for more than one year or operating cycle, whichever is longer, are classified as long-term tangible assets. Some problems may arise in determining the acquisition cost of a fixed asset, such as: the initial acquisition may be the result of several expenditures, a plant asset may be obtained in exchange for the issuance of stock, one fixed asset may be exchanged for another fixed asset, a plant asset may be obtained on a deferred payment plan, or additional expenditures may be involved subsequent to acquisition. These and other issues and their related accounting procedures are examined in this chapter.

SUMMARY OF LEARNING OBJECTIVES

1. **Describe property, plant, and equipment.** The major characteristics of property, plant, and equipment are: (1) They are acquired for use in operations and not for resale, (2) they are long-term in nature and usually subject to depreciation, and (3) they possess physical substance.

2. **Identify the costs included in the initial valuation of land, buildings, and equipment.**
    Cost of land: Includes all expenditures made to acquire land and to ready it for use. Land costs typically include (1) the purchase price; (2) closing costs, such as title to the land, attorney's fees, and recording fees; (3) costs incurred in getting the land in condition for its intended use, such as grading, filling, draining, and clearing; (4) assumption of any liens, mortgages or encumbrances on the property; (5) any additional land improvements that have an indefinite life; and (6) cost to remove unwanted building (less scrap proceeds) on newly acquired land.
    Cost of buildings: Includes all expenditures related directly to their acquisition or construction. Costs related to constructed assets include (1) materials, labor, overhead costs, and avoidable interest cost incurred during construction and (2) professional fees and building permits.
    Cost of equipment: Includes (1) the purchase price, (2) freight and handling charges incurred, (3) insurance on the equipment while in transit, (4) cost of special foundations if required, (5) assembling and installation costs, and (6) costs of conducting trial runs.

3. **Describe the accounting problems associated with self-constructed assets.** The assignment of indirect costs of manufacturing creates special problems because companies cannot trace these costs directly to work and material orders related to the fixed assets constructed. Companies might handle these costs in one of two ways: (1) Assign no fixed overhead to the cost of the constructed asset, or (2) assign a portion of all overhead to the construction process. The second method is used extensively in practice.

4. **Describe the accounting problems associated with interest capitalization.** Only avoidable actual interest (with modifications) incurred during the acquisition period should be capitalized. The rationale for this approach is that during construction, the asset is not generating revenue and therefore companies should defer (capitalize) interest cost. Once construction is completed,

the asset is ready for its intended use and revenues can be earned. Any interest cost incurred in purchasing an asset that is ready for its intended use should be expensed.

5.   **Understand accounting issues related to acquiring and valuing plant assets.** The following issues relate to acquiring and valuing plant assets: (1) *Cash discounts:* Whether taken or not, they are generally considered a reduction in the cost of the asset. The real cost of the asset is the cash or cash equivalent price of the asset. (2) *Deferred-payment contracts:* Companies account for assets purchased on long-term credit contracts at the present value of the consideration exchanged between the contracting parties. (3) *Lump sum purchase:* Allocate the total cost among the various assets on the basis of their relative fair values. (4) *Issuance of stock:* If the stock is being actively traded, the market value of the stock issued is a fair indication of the cost of the property acquired; if the market value of the capital stock exchanged is not determinable, establish the fair value of the property and use as the basis for recording the asset and issuance of the capital stock. (5) *Exchanges of nonmonetary assets:* The accounting for exchanges of nonmonetary assets depends on whether the exchange has commercial substance. See **Illustration 10-1** for a summary of how to account for exchanges of nonmonetary assets. (6) *Contributions:* A contribution is a nonreciprocal transfer. A nonreciprocal transfer is to be recorded at the fair value of the asset received or given. In general, contributions received are to be recorded by a credit to revenue. Contributions given are recorded by a debit to Contribution Expense.

6.   **Describe the accounting treatment for costs incurred subsequent to acquisition.** **Illustration 10-2** summarizes how to account for costs subsequent to acquisition.

7.   **Describe the accounting treatment for the disposal of property, plant, and equipment.** Regardless of the time of disposal, companies take depreciation up to the date of disposition, and then remove all accounts related to the retired asset. Gains or losses on the retirement of plant assets should be shown in the income statement along with other items that arise from customary business activities. If an asset is scrapped or abandoned without any cash recovery, a loss should be recognized equal to the asset's book value. If scrap value or insurance proceeds exist, the gain or loss that occurs is the difference between the proceeds and the asset's book value. Gains or losses on involuntary conversions may be reported as extraordinary items.

TIPS ON CHAPTER TOPICS

TIP: **Property, plant, and equipment** is a classification that is often referred to as **fixed assets** or **plant assets**. Included in this section should be long-lived tangible assets that are currently being used in operations to generate goods and services for customers. Two exceptions to this guideline are: (1) Construction of Plant in Process, and (2) Deposits on Machinery. In each of these cases, the asset is not yet being used in operations but an expenditure has been made which is to be classified in the property, plant, and equipment section of the balance sheet. Idle fixed assets are to be classified as Investments or as Other Assets and plant assets no longer used and held for sale are to be classified either as Current Assets or Other Assets, depending on whether they are expected to be sold within the next year or not. Land held by a land developer is classified as Inventory.

TIP: In determining the **cost of a plant asset,** keep in mind the same guideline we had for inventory. The cost includes all costs necessary to get the item to the location and condition for its intended use.

TIP: In determining the cost of a plant asset, keep in mind the historical cost principle. **Cost** is measured by the cash or the fair value of the noncash consideration given or the fair value of the consideration received, whichever is the more objectively determinable. Fair value refers to cash equivalent value. When cash is given to acquire an asset, it is a relatively simple matter to determine the asset's cost. However, when a noncash asset is given in exchange or when a deferred payment plan is involved, more thought is required to determine the asset's cost. Pay close attention to these areas as they are often the subjects from which discriminating exam questions are derived.

TIP: When one noncash asset is exchanged for another noncash asset, it is important to determine if the exchange has commercial substance. An exchange has **commercial substance** if the future cash flows change significantly as a result of the transaction. That is, if the company is in the same economic position as before the exchange, the exchange lacks commercial substance. If the asset exchange lacks commercial substance **and** if a gain is experienced on the disposal of the old asset, then we are to depart from the historical cost principle in determining the cost of the new asset; the entire gain or a portion of the gain (depending on whether boot is received) is to be deferred.

TIP: In the context of accounting for property, plant, and equipment, the term **"capitalize"** means to record and carry forward into one or more periods expenditures from which benefits or proceeds will be realized; thus, a balance sheet account is debited.

TIP: In accounting for the many expenditures related to the operation and maintenance of property, plant, and equipment, the accountant must determine whether to record these individual expenditures by a debit to the income statement or by a debit to the balance sheet. In making this determination, keep in mind that expenditures benefiting the company for more than the current accounting period should be capitalized in order to properly match expenses with revenues (through the process of depreciation) over successive accounting periods; expenditures for items that do not yield benefits beyond the current accounting period should be expensed.

TIP: In the context of the topic of property, plant, and equipment, the term **carrying value** refers to the amount derived by deducting the balance in the Accumulated Depreciation account from the balance in the related asset account. Synonymous terms are: **book value**, net asset value, undepreciated value, and **carrying amount**. Book value may be very different from fair value. Fair value is often referred to as fair market value or market value. The computation of book value is **not** affected by the estimated residual value or salvage value.

TIP: The net cost (cost less scrap proceeds) of tearing down an old building should be charged (debited) to the Land account if the building was someone else's old building and recently acquired along with the land as a site to be used for another structure. (The cost is charged to Land because it was necessary to get the land in the condition for its intended purpose—to provide space upon which to erect a new building.) The cost of tearing down an old building should be charged to Loss on Disposal of Building if the building has been used in the entity's operations and is now demolished to make way for another building or an alternative use of the land. Therefore, the cost of tearing down an old building is **never** charged to the Building account.

TIP: A **nonreciprocal transfer** (transfer of assets in one direction) of a nonmonetary asset is to be recorded at the fair value of the asset at the date of transfer. Property donated to an entity is an example of this type of transaction and results in a credit to Revenue. Some companies subscribe to the approach whereby a donation from a government entity is recorded by a credit to Donated Capital (Additional Paid-in Capital). The party making the donation records an expense (contributions expense) in the amount of the fair value of the asset given.

TIP: Sometimes a company will promise to donate (pledge) some type of asset in the future. If the promise is **unconditional** (such as when the passage of time is what triggers the gifting), the company should report the contribution expense and the related payable immediately, using the fair value of the related asset to measure the amount. If the promise is **conditional,** the company recognizes expense when it transfers the asset.

TIP: In cases where land is held as an investment (such as land held for speculation or land held for future plant site), the related property taxes, insurance, and other direct costs incurred while holding the land are often capitalized until such time the investment begins to generate revenue. Such costs are no longer capitalized once the asset begins to generate revenue.

TIP: Property, plant and equipment assets are usually carried on the books at undepreciated cost. The use of fair value to measure property, plant and equipment is usually unacceptable as it would require the recognition of gains or losses prior to disposition of the assets. However, if the fair value of the property is less than its carrying amount, the asset may be written down. These situations occur when the asset is impaired (discussed in **Chapter 11**) or where the asset is being held for sale. A long-lived asset classified as held for sale should be measured at the lower of its carrying amount or fair value less cost estimated to sell it. A long-lived asset is not depreciated if it is classified as held for sale; this is because such assets are not being used to generate revenues.

CASE 10-1

Purpose: (L.O. 2, 6) This case will review the costs to be capitalized for property, plant, and equipment.

Property, plant, and equipment generally represents a large portion of the total assets of a company. Accounting for the acquisition and usage of such assets is, therefore, an important part of the financial reporting process.

Instructions

(a)   Distinguish between a revenue expenditure and a capital expenditure. Explain why its distinction is important.

(b)   Identify at least six costs that should be capitalized as the cost of land. Assume that land with an existing building is acquired for cash and that the existing building is to be removed immediately in order to provide space for a new building on that site.

(c)   Identify at least five costs that should be capitalized as the cost of a building.

(d)   Identify at least six costs that should be capitalized when equipment is acquired for cash.

(e)   Describe the factors that determine whether expenditures relating to property, plant, and equipment already in use should be capitalized.

(AICPA Adapted)

Solution to Case 10-1

(a)   A **capital expenditure** is expected to yield benefits either in all future accounting periods (acquisition of land) or in a limited number of accounting periods (acquisition of buildings and equipment). Capital expenditures are capitalized, that is, recorded as assets, and, if related to assets of limited life, amortized over the periods which will be benefited. A **revenue expenditure** is an expenditure for which the benefits are **not** expected to extend beyond the current period. Hence, they benefit only the current period (recorded as an expense) or they benefit no period at all (recorded as a loss).

The distinction between capital and revenue expenditures is of significance because it involves the timing of the recognition of expense and, consequently, the determination of periodic earnings. This distinction also affects the costs reflected in the asset accounts which will be recovered from future periods' revenues.

If a revenue expenditure is improperly capitalized, net income of the current period is overstated, assets are overstated, and future earnings are understated for all the periods to which the improperly capitalized cost is amortized. If the cost is not amortized, future earnings will not be affected, but assets and retained earnings will continue to be overstated for as long as the cost remains on the books. If a nonamortizable capital expenditure is improperly expensed, current earnings are understated and assets and retained earnings are understated for all foreseeable periods in the future. If an amortizable capital expenditure is improperly expensed, net income of the current period is understated, assets and retained earnings are understated, and net income is overstated for all future periods to which the cost should have been amortized.

(b)   The cost of land may include:
(1)   purchase price.
(2)   survey fees.
(3)   title search fees.
(4)   escrow fees.
(5)   delinquent property taxes assumed by buyer.
(6)   broker's commission.
(7)   legal fees.
(8)   recording fee.
(9)   unpaid interest assumed by buyer.
(10)   cost of clearing, grading, landscaping, and subdividing (less salvage).
(11)   cost of removing old building (less salvage).
(12)   special assessments such as lighting or sewers if they are permanent in nature.
(13)   landscaping of permanent nature.
(14)   any other cost necessary to acquire the land and get it in the condition necessary for its intended purpose.

TIP: Typically, the cost of land includes the cost of elements that occur prior to excavation for a new building. Costs related to the foundation of the building are elements of building cost.

(c)   The cost of a building may include:
(1)   purchase price or construction costs (including an allocation of overhead if self-constructed).
(2)   excavation fees.
(3)   architectural fees.
(4)   building permit fee.
(5)   cost of insurance during construction (if paid by property owner).
(6)   property taxes during construction.
(7)   interest during construction (only interest actually incurred).
(8)   cost of temporary buildings.
(9)   any other cost necessary to acquire the building and get it in the location and condition for its intended purpose.

(d)   The cost of equipment may include:
(1)   purchase price (less discounts allowed).
(2)   sales tax.
(3)   installation charges.
(4)   freight charges during transit.
(5)   insurance during transit.
(6)   cost of labor and materials for test runs.
(7)   cost of special platforms.
(8)   ownership search.
(9)   ownership registration.
(10)   breaking-in costs.
(11)   other costs necessary to acquire the equipment and get it to the location and condition for its intended use.

(e)   The factors that determine whether expenditures relating to property, plant, and equipment already in use should be capitalized are as follows:
(1)   Expenditures are material.

     (2)   They are nonrecurring in nature.

     (3)   They benefit future periods in some way such as by doing one of the following:

          a.   They extend the useful life of a plant asset.

          b.   They enhance the quality of existing services.

          c.   They add new asset services.

          d.   They reduce future operating costs of existing assets.

          e.   They are required to meet environmental concerns and regulations.

Approach:

1.   Scan all requirements before you begin on the first question. Sometimes the latter requirements will help you to see more clearly what is really being requested in the earlier requirements. Sometimes the solution to one requirement appears to overlap with the solution to another part of the question.

2.   Prepare a key word outline before you begin writing detailed answers. This outline should very briefly list the concepts you want to cover in your paragraph(s). This outline will help you to organize your thoughts before you begin writing sentences.

EXERCISE 10-1

Purpose: (L.O. 2, 6) This exercise will help you identify which expenditures related to property, plant, and equipment should be capitalized and which should be expensed.

> **TIP:**   Remember that expenditures which benefit the company for more than the current accounting period should be capitalized in order to properly match expenses with revenues over successive accounting periods. Expenditures for items that do not yield benefits beyond the current accounting period should be expensed.

Instructions

Assume all amounts are material. For each of the following independent items, indicate by use of the appropriate letter if it should be:

C = Capitalized   or   E = Expensed

_____   1.   Invoice price of drill press.

_____   2.   Sales tax on computer.

_____   3.   Costs of permanent partitions constructed in an existing office building.

_____   4.   Installation charges for new conveyer system.

_____   5.   Costs of trees and shrubs planted in front of office building.

_____   6.   Costs of surveying new land site.

_____   7.   Costs of major overhaul of delivery truck.

_____   8.   Costs of building new counters for show room.

_____   9.   Costs of powders, soaps, and wax for office floors.

_____   10.   Cost of janitorial services for office and show room.

_____   11.   Costs of carpets in a new office building.

_____   12.   Costs of annual termite inspection of warehouse.

_____   13.   Insurance charged for new equipment while in transit.

_____   14.   Property taxes on land used for parking lot.

_____   15.   Cost of a fan installed to help cool old factory machine.

_____   16.   Cost of exterminator's services.

_____   17.   Costs of major redecorating of executives' offices.

_____   18.   Cost of fertilizers for shrubs and trees.

_____   19.   Cost of labor services for self-constructed machine.

_____   20.   Costs of materials used and labor services expended during trial runs of new machine.

Solution to Exercise 10-1

1.	C	6.	C	11.	C	16.	E
2.	C	7.	C	12.	E	17.	C
3.	C	8.	C	13.	C	18.	E*
4.	C	9.	E*	14.	E	19.	C
5.	C	10.	E	15.	C	20.	C

*This answer assumes the products were consumed during the current period. Material amounts of unused supplies on hand at the balance sheet date should be reported as a prepaid expense.

> **TIP:** As used in this chapter, the term **capital expenditure** refers to one which is expected to benefit more than one period; hence, it is initially recorded as an asset and should be expensed over the periods benefited. A **revenue expenditure** is one which is expected **not** to be of benefit to any period beyond the current period; hence, it is recorded by a debit to either an expense account or to a loss account in the period incurred.

EXERCISE 10-2

Purpose: (L.O. 2) This exercise will give you practice in identifying capital versus revenue expenditures.

Hughes Supply Company, a newly formed corporation, incurred the following expenditures related to Land, to Buildings, and to Machinery and Equipment.

Cash paid for land and dilapidated building thereon		$ 300,000
Removal of old building	$ 60,000	
Less salvage	16,500	43,500
Surveying before construction to determine best		
position for building		1,110
Interest on short-term loans during construction		22,200
Excavation before construction for basement		57,000
Fee for title search charged by abstract company		1,560
Architect's fees		8,400
Machinery purchased (subject to 2% cash discount,		
which was not taken)		165,000
Freight on machinery purchased		4,020
Storage charges on machinery, necessitated by noncompletion		
of building when machinery was delivered on schedule		6,540
New building constructed (building construction took 8 months		
from date of purchase of land and old building)		1,500,000
Assessment by city for sewers (a one-time assessment)		4,800
Transportation charges for delivery of machinery from storage		
to new building		1,860
Installation of machinery		6,000
Trees, shrubs, and other landscaping after completion of building		
(permanent in nature)		16,200

Instructions
(a)   Identify the amounts that should be debited to Land.
(b)   Identify the amounts that should be debited to Buildings.
(c)   Identify the amounts that should be debited to Machinery and Equipment.
(d)   Indicate how the costs above **not** debited to Land, Buildings, or Machinery and Equipment should be recorded.

Solution to Exercise 10-2

	(a) Land	(b) Bldgs.	(c) M&E	(d) Other
Cash paid for land & old bldg.	$300,000			
Removal of old building ($60,000 - $16,500)	43,500			
Surveying before construction		$ 1,110		
Interest on loans during construction		22,200		
Excavation before construction		57,000		
Abstract fees for title search	1,560			
Architect's fees		8,400		
Machinery purchased			$161,700	$ 3,300 Misc. Exp. (Int. Exp.)
Freight on machinery			4,020	
Storage charges caused by noncompletion of building				6,540 Misc. Exp. (Loss)
New building construction		1,500,000		
Assessment by city	4,800			
Transportation charges— machinery				1,860 Misc. Exp. (Loss)
Installation—machinery			6,000	
Landscaping	16,200			
Totals	$366,060	$1,588,710	$171,720	$11,700

> **TIP:** The purchase price of the machine is the **cash equivalent price** at the date of acquisition which is the $165,000 reduced by the 2% cash discount allowed ($3,300), whether or not the discount is taken. The additional outlay of $3,300 is due to extending the time for payment which is equivalent to interest (time value of money). The cost of the machine does **not** include the $6,540 storage charges and $1,860 transportation charges out of storage because these costs were not planned costs necessary to get the equipment to the location intended for use; rather they were caused by the lack of completing the building on schedule (hence, a loss or miscellaneous expense).

CASE 10-2

Purpose: (L.O. 5) This case will review the rules for determining a plant asset's cost when the asset is acquired on a deferred payment plan or in a nonmonetary exchange.

A company often acquires property, plant, and equipment by means other than immediate cash payment.

Instructions

(a) Explain how to determine a plant asset's cost if it is acquired on a deferred payment plan.

(b) Explain how to determine a plant asset's cost if it is acquired in exchange for a nonmonetary asset when the transaction has commercial substance.

(c) Explain how to determine a machine's cost if it is acquired in exchange for a similar machine, a small cash payment is made, and the transaction lacks commercial substance.

Solution to Case 10-2

(a)   A plant asset acquired on a deferred-payment plan should be recorded at an equivalent cash price excluding interest. If a fair rate of interest is not stated in the sales contract, an imputed interest rate should be determined. The asset should then be recorded at the contract's present value, which is computed by discounting the payments at the stated or imputed interest rate. The interest portion (stated or imputed) of the contract price should be charged to interest expense over the life of the contract.

(b)   An exchange has commercial substance when the future cash flows (timing and amounts) generated by the new asset are expected to differ significantly from the future flows expected to be generated by the old asset if it were retained. When the exchange has commercial substance, a plant asset acquired in exchange for another nonmonetary asset should be recorded at the fair value (cash equivalent value) of the consideration given or the fair value of the consideration received, whichever is more clearly determinable. This is an application of the historical cost principle. Any gain or loss on the exchange of the old asset should be recognized. (An exchange has commercial substance if the future cash flows change materially as a result of the transaction.)

(c)   In an exchange lacking commercial substance, when exchanging an old machine and paying cash for a new machine, the new machine should be recorded at the amount of monetary consideration (cash) paid plus the undepreciated cost of the nonmonetary asset (old machine) surrendered if there is no indicated loss. If a loss is indicated, it should be recognized. This would reduce the recorded amount of the new machine. An experienced loss is indicated when the old asset's market value is less than its carrying value at the date of exchange; a gain is indicated if the asset's market value exceeds its carrying value. No experienced gain, however, should be recognized by the party paying monetary consideration in an exchange lacking commercial substance.

> **TIP:**   In an exchange lacking commercial substance, when cash is paid in an exchange of similar assets and the market value of the asset to be exchanged is less than its book value (an experienced loss), the historical cost principle is followed in determining the cost of the new asset. Additionally, the loss on the old asset is recognized in total. When cash is paid in an exchange of similar assets and the market value of the asset to be exchanged is greater than its book value (a gain), there is a departure from the historical cost principle in determining the cost of the new asset and the gain is **not** recognized.

EXERCISE 10-3

Purpose: (L.O. 4) This exercise will provide an example of the capitalization of interest cost incurred during construction.

Marvel Company engaged Invention Company to construct a special purpose machine to be used in its factory. The following data pertain:

1. The contract was signed by Marvel on August 30, 2010. Construction was begun immediately and was completed on December 1, 2010.
2. To aid in the financing of this construction, Marvel borrowed $600,000 from Bank of Okahumpa on August 30, 2010 by signing a $600,000 note due in 3 years. The note bears an interest rate of 12% and interest is payable each August 30.
3. Marvel paid Invention $200,000 on August 30, 2010, and invested the remainder of the note's proceeds ($400,000) in 5% government securities until December 1.
4. On December 1, Marvel made the final $400,000 payment to Invention.
5. Aside from the note payable to the Bank of Okahumpa, Marvel's only outstanding liability at December 31, 2010 is a $60,000, 9%, 5-year note payable dated January 1, 2007, on which interest is payable each December 31.

Instructions

(a)   Calculate the weighted-average accumulated expenditures, interest revenue, avoidable interest, total interest incurred, and interest cost to be capitalized during 2007. Round all computations to the nearest dollar.

(b)   Prepare the journal entries needed on the books of Marvel Company at each of the following dates: August 30, 2010; December 1, 2010; and December 31, 2010.

Solution to Exercise 10-3

(a)   **Computation of Weighted-Average Accumulated Expenditures:**

Expenditures			Capitalization		Weighted-Average
Date	Amount	x	Period	=	Accumulated Expenditures
August 30	$200,000		3/12		$50,000
December 1	400,000		0		0
					$50,000

Interest Revenue: $400,000 x 5% x 3/12 = $5,000

Avoidable Interest:

	Weighted-Average			
	Accumulated Expenditures	x	Interest Rate	= Avoidable Interest
	$50,000		12%	$6,000

Total Interest Incurred:

$600,000 x 12% x 4/12	=	$ 24,000
$60,000 x 9%	=	5,400
		$ 29,400

Interest to be capitalized: $6,000

(b)   8/30   Cash   600,000
                Notes Payable   600,000

             Machine...   200,000
             Short-term Investments   400,000
                Cash.   600,000

      12/1   Cash   405,000
                Interest Revenue
                   ($400,000 x 5% x 3/12)...........................   5,000
                Short-term Investments   400,000

             Machine...   400,000
                Cash.   400,000

      12/31 Machine [computed in part (a)]............................   6,000
             Interest Expense ($29,400 - $6,000).....................   23,400
                Cash ($60,000 x 9%)...................................   5,400
                Interest Payable
                   ($600,000 x 12% x 4/12)...........................   24,000

Explanation: Paragraphs 6 and 7 of *SFAS No. 34* state:
   "The historical cost of acquiring an asset includes the costs necessarily incurred to bring it to the condition and location for its intended use. If an asset requires a period of time in which to carry out the activities necessary to bring it to that condition and location, the interest cost incurred during that period as a result of expenditures for the asset is a part of the historical cost of acquiring the asset. The objectives of capitalizing interest are (a) to obtain a measure of acquisition cost that more closely reflects the enterprise's total investment in the asset and (b) to charge a cost that relates to the acquisition of a resource that will benefit future periods against the revenues of the periods benefited."

Examples of assets that qualify for interest capitalization are: (1) assets that an enterprise constructs for its own use (such as facilities), and (2) assets intended for sale or lease that are constructed as discrete projects (such as ships or real estate projects). Interest cannot be capitalized for inventories that are routinely manufactured or otherwise produced in large quantities on a repetitive basis. Marvel's machine is a qualifying asset.

The amount to be capitalized is that portion of the interest cost incurred during the asset's acquisition period that theoretically could have been avoided (for example, by avoiding additional borrowings or by using the funds expended for the asset to repay existing borrowings) if expenditures for the asset had not been made.

Avoidable interest is determined by applying an appropriate interest rate(s) to the weighted-average amount of accumulated expenditures for the asset during the period. The appropriate rate is that rate associated with a specific new borrowing, if any. If average accumulated expenditures for the asset exceed the amount of a specific new borrowing associated with the asset, the capitalization rate to be applied to such excess shall be a weighted average of the rates applicable to other borrowings of the enterprise.

(Alternatively, the FASB does allow that the interest rate to be used may rely exclusively on an average rate of all borrowings, if desired.)

The weighted-average amount of accumulated expenditures for the asset represents the average investment tied up in the qualifying asset during the period. For Marvel, a $200,000 balance in Machine for the three-month capitalization period (date of expenditures to the date the asset is ready for use) means an equivalent (average) investment of $50,000 on an annual basis. Marvel uses only the 12% rate applicable to the specific new borrowing to compute the avoidable interest because the specific borrowing ($600,000) exceeds the weighted-average accumulated expenditures.

The amount of interest to be capitalized is not to exceed the actual interest costs incurred. Thus, Marvel compares its avoidable interest of $6,000 and its actual interest incurred of $29,400 and chooses the lower amount to capitalize. Any interest amounts earned on funds borrowed which are temporarily in excess of the company's needs are to be reported as interest revenue rather than be used to offset the amount of interest to be capitalized. Thus, Marvel will report $5,000 as interest revenue and that $5,000 will not affect the amount of interest to be capitalized.

EXERCISE 10-4

Purpose: (L.O. 5) This exercise will give you practice in accounting for the acquisition of a plant asset on a deferred payment plan.

Starstruck, Inc. purchased a computer network on December 31, 2010 for $200,000, paying $50,000 down and agreeing to pay the balance in five equal installments of $30,000 payable each December 31 beginning in 2011. An assumed interest rate of 10% is implicit in the purchase price and is the market rate of interest.

Instructions (Round to the nearest cent)
(a)   Prepare the journal entry(ies) at the date of purchase.
(b)   Prepare an amortization schedule for the installment agreement.
(c)   Prepare the journal entry(ies) at December 31, 2011, to record the cash payment and the applicable interest expense (assume the effective interest method is employed).
(d)   Prepare the journal entry(ies) at December 31, 2012, to record the cash payment and the applicable interest expense (assume the effective interest method is employed).

Solution to Exercise 10-4

(a)   Time diagram:

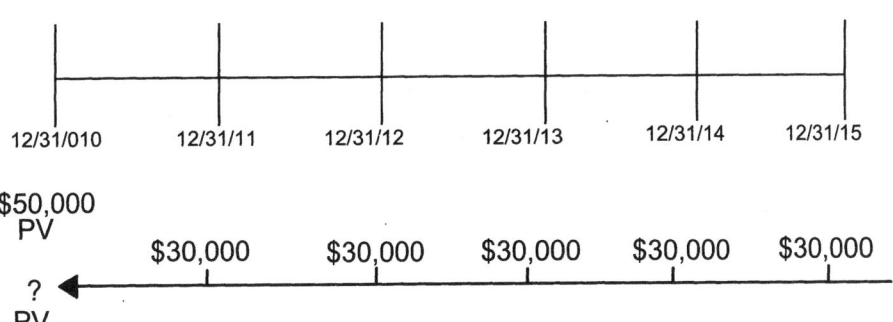

Entry:

Equipment 163,723.70*
Discount on Notes Payable.. 36,276.30
    Cash. 50,000.00
    Notes Payable ($30,000 x 5)...................................   150,000.00

*PV of a $30,000 ordinary annuity @ 10% for 5 years
    ($30,000 x 3.79079) $ 113,723.70
Down payment   50,000.00
Capitalized value of equipment $ 163,723.70

(b)

Date	Cash Payment	10% Interest Expense	Reduction of Principal	Liability Balance
12/31/10				$113,723.70
12/31/11	$ 30,000.00	$ 11,372.37	$ 18,627.63	95,096.07
12/31/12	30,000.00	9,509.61	20,490.39	74,605.68
12/31/13	30,000.00	7,460.57	22,539.43	52,066.25
12/31/14	30,000.00	5,206.63	24,793.37	27,272.88
12/31/15	30,000.00	2,727.12*	27,272.88	-0-
Totals	$ 150,000.00	$ 36,276.30	$113,723.70	

*This is a plug figure, which includes a rounding error of $0.17.

(c)   **December 31, 2011**

Notes Payable...30,000.00
Interest Expense (see schedule).......................................11,372.37
    Cash. 30,000.00
    Discount on Notes Payable 11,372.37

(d)   **December 31, 2012**

Notes Payable	30,000.00	
Interest Expense (see schedule)	9,509.61	
Cash		30,000.00
Discount on Notes Payable		9,509.61

> **TIP:** For each entry in (c) and (d), two entries could replace the one compound entry. For example, the two equivalent entries for (c) would be:
>
> | | | |
> |---|---|---|
> | Notes Payable | 30,000.00 | |
> | Cash | | 30,000.00 |
> | | | |
> | Interest Expense | 11,372.37 | |
> | Discount on Notes Payable | | 11,372.37 |
>
> **TIP:** When a deferred payment plan is involved in the acquisition of a noncash asset, pay careful attention to whether a fair rate of interest is stated in the agreement. When an unreasonably low stated interest rate is present, interest must be imputed so that the effective amount of interest reported reflects the market rate of interest.

EXERCISE 10-5

Purpose: (L.O. 5) This exercise reviews the computations involved in a lump-sum purchase of plant assets.

The Eliason Company paid $750,000 cash for a package of plant assets. The package consisted of the following:

	Seller's Book Value	Market Value
Land	$ 60,000	$ 300,000
Building	120,000	400,000
Equipment	220,000	250,000
Tools	100,000	50,000
Total	$ 500,000	$ 1,000,000

Instructions
(a) Prepare the journal entry for Eliason to record the acquisition of these assets on the company's books.
(b) Why must you allocate the total cost to separate accounts for the individual assets? Why can't you simply use "Plant Assets" as an account and record the total cost to that account? Explain.

Solution to Exercise 10-5

(a)	Land	225,000	
	Building	300,000	
	Equipment	187,500	
	Tools	37,500	
	Cash		750,000

Approach and Explanation: The total cost ($750,000) is to be allocated to the individual assets based on the relative market values of these assets. The formula that can be used to accomplish this objective is as follows:

$$\frac{\text{Market Value of One Item in Group}}{\text{Market Value of All items in Group}} \times \frac{\text{Amount to be}}{\text{Allocated}} = \frac{\text{Amount to be Assigned to Item Designated in the Numerator}}{}$$

Land:	($300,000 ÷ $1,000,000) x $750,000 =	$225,000
Building:	($400,000 ÷ $1,000,000) x $750,000 =	$300,000
Equipment:	($250,000 ÷ $1,000,000) x $750,000 =	$187,500
Tools:	($50,000 ÷ $1,000,000) x $750,000 =	$37,500

TIP: Sum the four answers obtained by using the formula. They should total to the amount you set out to allocate ($750,000, in this case).

(b) The total cost must be allocated to the individual assets because land is not subject to the process of depreciation, and the depreciable assets normally are subject to different service lives and maybe even different depreciation methods.

TIP: There are several areas in accounting which utilize the formula to allocate a single sum between two or more items based on the relative fair market values of the items involved. That formula is as follows:

$$\frac{\text{Market Value of One Item in Group}}{\text{Market Value of All Items in Group}} \times \frac{\text{Amount to be}}{\text{Allocated}} = \frac{\text{Amount to be Assigned to Item Designated in the Numerator}}{}$$

This formula is used in **Chapter 10** to allocate one lump-sum amount of cost to the individual assets acquired in a **lump sum purchase** (often called a **basket purchase**). The formula will also be used in volume two of this book in **Chapter 15** to allocate the proceeds from the issuance of several classes of securities, in **Chapter 16** to allocate the proceeds from the issuance of bonds with detachable warrants, and in **Chapter 17** to allocate the cost of an investment. The formula is also useful in the managerial accounting arena such as in the case where there are joint costs to be allocated to joint products. The same formula was used in **Chapter 8** to allocate the cost of certain inventory items to units based on their relative sales values.

ILLUSTRATION 10-1
SUMMARY OF REQUIREMENTS FOR RECOGNIZING GAINS AND LOSSES ON EXCHANGES OF NONMONETARY ASSETS (L.O. 5)

1.   Compute the total gain or loss experienced on the transaction, which is equal to the difference between the fair value of the asset given up and the book value of the asset given up. An excess of fair value over book value indicates an experienced gain; an excess of book value over fair value indicates an experienced loss.

2.   If a loss is computed in 1, always recognize the entire loss.

3.   If a gain is computed in 1,
    (a)   and the exchange has commercial substance, the entire gain is recognized.
    (b)   and the exchange lacks commercial substance,
        (1)   and no cash is involved, no gain is recognized.
        (2)   and some cash is given, no gain is recognized.
        (3)   and some cash is received, the following portion of the gain is recognized:

$$\frac{\text{Cash Received (Boot)}}{\text{Cash Received (Boot) + Fair Value of Other Assets Received}} \times \text{Total Gain Experienced}$$

TIP:	An exchange has commercial substance if the future cash flows (timing and amounts) are expected to change significantly because of the transaction.
TIP:	When cash is received in a nonmonetary exchange where a gain on the old asset is evident, the amount of cash received can affect the portion of the gain to be recognized. If the amount of cash received is 25% or more of the total fair value of the exchange, the **entire** gain is to be recognized.
TIP:	"Boot" is a term used to describe monetary consideration (such as cash or a receivable which is a claim for cash) given or received in an exchange of nonmonetary assets. When boot is **received** in an exchange that lacks commercial substance, a portion of the fair value of the old asset exchanged is converted to a more liquid asset and a **proportionate** amount of the gain is recognized by the party receiving the boot if a gain has been experienced.
TIP:	Recall that it is the conservatism constraint that requires **all losses to be recognized** rather than deferred to future periods. Also if a loss on the old asset was not recorded, the new asset would be recorded at an amount in excess of its fair value (cash equivalent price) which would overstate assets.
TIP:	A trade-in allowance is usually not a good estimate of the fair value of a used asset because it often includes a price concession off of the list price of the new asset.
TIP:	The rules stated here for recognition of gain or loss pertain to reporting on general purpose financial statements. These rules differ from the treatment called for on an income tax return.

TIP: The rules above can also be summarized by the type of exchange as follows:

Type of Exchange	Accounting Rule
Exchange has commercial substance	Recognize gains immediately
	Recognize losses immediately
Exchange lacks commercial substance— no cash (boot) received	Defer gains Recognize losses immediately
Exchange lacks commercial substance— cash (boot) is received	Recognize partial gain Recognize losses immediately

Note: If cash is 25% or more of the fair value of the exchange, recognize the entire gain because **both** parties should consider the transaction a monetary exchange and thereby rely solely on fair value for the asset measurements.

TIP: Often the party receiving boot is a dealer and therefore, the asset they are giving up is considered to be inventory. As a result, the dealer records sales revenue and related cost of goods sold. The used machine is received by the dealer and is recorded at fair value. This type of transaction almost always has commercial substance to the dealer.

EXERCISE 10-6

Purpose: (L.O. 5) This exercise will allow you to practice recording the exchange of nonmonetary assets.

Thien Le Company exchanged equipment used in its manufacturing operations plus $15,000 in cash for similar equipment used in the operations of Peggy Gunshanan Company. The following information pertains to the exchange:

	Thien Le Co.	Peggy Gunshanan Co.
Equipment (cost)	$ 84,000	$ 84,000
Accumulated depreciation	66,000	30,000
Fair value of equipment	31,500	46,500
Cash given up	15,000	

Instructions
(a)   Prepare the journal entries to record the exchange on the books of both companies assuming the exchange lacks commercial substance.
(b)   Prepare the journal entries to record the exchange on the books of both companies assuming the fair value of Thien Le Co.'s old asset is $16,500 (rather than $31,500) and the fair value of Peggy Gunshanan's old equipment is $31,500 (rather than $46,500). Assume the exchange lacks commercial substance.
(c)   Prepare the journal entries to record the exchange on the books of both companies, assuming the fair value of Thien Le Co.'s old asset is $46,500 (rather than $31,500) and the fair value of Peggy Gunshanan's old equipment is $61,500 (rather than $46,500). Assume the exchange lacks commercial substance.

Solution to Exercise 10-6

(a)   **Thien Le Company:**

Equipment (New)	33,000	
Accumulated Depreciation	66,000	
Equipment (Old)		84,000
Cash . . .		15,000

Computation of book value:
Cost of old asset	$ 84,000
Accumulated depreciation	(66,000)
Book value of old asset	$ 18,000

Computation of gain:
Fair value of equipment given	$ 31,500
Book value of equipment given	(18,000)
Gain experienced on old asset	$ 13,500

Valuation of new equipment:
Book value of equipment given	$18,000
Boot given	15,000
Cost of new equipment	$33,000

OR

Fair value of equipment received	$46,500	
Gain deferred	(13,500)	
Cost of new equipment	$33,000	

Peggy Gunshanan Company:

Cash	15,000	
Equipment (New)	31,500	
Accumulated Depreciation	30,000	
Loss on Disposal of Plant Asset.	7,500	
Equipment (Old)		84,000

Computation of book value:

Cost of old asset	$84,000
Accumulated depreciation	(30,000)
Book value of old asset	$54,000

Computation of loss:

Fair value of equipment given	$ 46,500
Book value of equipment given	(54,000)
Loss experienced on old asset	$ (7,500)

Valuation of new equipment:

Book value of equipment given	$54,000
Loss recognized on disposal	(7,500)
Fair value of equipment given	46,500
Boot received	(15,000)
Cost of new equipment	$31,500

Approach and Explanation: Refer to **Illustration 10-1** which summarizes the rules for recognizing gains and losses experienced on exchanges of nonmonetary assets.

Thien Le has experienced a gain of $13,500 on the old asset. It is an exchange of similar productive assets in an exchange that lacks commercial substance. Boot is given; therefore, the gain is not recognized. Rather than crediting a gain, the gain is reflected in the cost of the new asset by reducing what otherwise would have been recorded as the new asset's cost. Thus, the gain is deferred and there is a departure from the historical cost principle in determining the cost of the new asset.

Peggy Gunshanan has experienced a loss. A loss is always recognized, regardless of whether the exchange has or lacks commercial substance and regardless of whether boot is given or received. (Think about the conservatism constraint here to help you to remember this.) The historical cost principle is followed in determining the amount to record for the equipment received.

> **TIP:** The parties will bargain so that the total fair value given equals the total fair value received. Therefore, since Peggy Gunshanan is giving up equipment worth $46,500, but Thien Le's equipment is only worth $31,500, Thien Le is also giving $15,000 cash to Peggy Gunshanan.

(b)   **Thien Le Company:**

Equipment (New)	31,500	
Accumulated Depreciation	66,000	
Loss on Disposal of Plant Asset.............................	1,500	
Equipment (Old)		84,000
Cash.		15,000

Computation of loss:

Fair value of equipment given	$16,500
Book value of equipment given	(18,000)
Loss experienced on old asset	$ (1,500)

Valuation of new equipment:

Book value of equipment given	$18,000
Loss recognized on disposal	(1,500)
Boot given	15,000
Cost of new equipment	$31,500

OR

Fair value of equipment given	$16,500
Boot given	15,000
Cost of new equipment	$31,500

Peggy Gunshanan Company:

Cash	15,000	
Equipment (New)	16,500	
Accumulated Depreciation	30,000	
Loss on Disposal of Plant Asset.............................	22,500	
Equipment (Old)		84,000

Computation of loss:

Fair value of equipment given	$ 31,500
Book value of equipment given	(54,000)
Loss experienced on old asset	$ (22,500)

Valuation of new equipment:

Book value of equipment given	$ 54,000
Loss recognized on disposal	(22,500)
Fair value of equipment given	31,500
Boot received	(15,000)
Cost of new equipment	$16,500

Explanation: Both Thien Le and Peggy Gunshanan experienced losses on the disposal of their old plant assets. A loss is always to be recognized (because of conservatism). The historical cost principle is followed in determining the cost of the new plant asset.

(c) **Thien Le Company:**

Equipment (New)	33,000	
Accumulated Depreciation	66,000	
Equipment (Old)		84,000
Cash.		15,000

Computation of gain:

Fair value of equipment given	$46,500
Book value of equipment given	(18,000)
Gain experienced on old asset	$ 28,500

Valuation of new equipment:

Book value of equipment given	$18,000
Boot given	15,000
Cost of new equipment	$33,000

OR

Fair value of equipment given	$46,500
Gain deferred	(28,500)
Boot given	15,000
Cost of new equipment	$33,000

Peggy Gunshanan Company:

Cash	15,000	
Equipment (New)	40,830	
Accumulated Depreciation	30,000	
Equipment (Old)		84,000
Gain on Disposal of Plant Asset.............................		1,830

Computation of gain experienced:

Fair value of equipment given	$61,500
Book value of equipment given	(54,000)
Gain experienced on old asset	$ 7,500

Computation of gain recognized:

    [$15,000 ÷ ($15,000 + $46,500)] x $7,500 = $1,830

> **TIP:** The cash received is less than 25% of the total fair value of the exchange [$15,000 ($15,000 + $46,500) = 24.39% which is less than 25%]. Thus, only a portion of the gain is recognized on Peggy Gunshanan's books.

Valuation of new equipment:

Book value of equipment given	$54,000
Fair value of boot received	(15,000)
Gain recognized	1,830
Cost of new equipment	$40,830

OR

Fair value of equipment given	$61,500
Boot received	(15,000)
Gain deferred ($7,500 - $1,830)	(5,670)
Cost of new equipment	$40,830

Explanation: Thien Le's entire gain is deferred (**not** recognized currently) because Thien Le is giving boot in an exchange of nonmonetary assets in an exchange that lacks commercial substance. The "gain" serves to reduce the recorded value of the new asset. Peggy Gunshanan's gain is partially recognized because boot is being **received** in an exchange of similar productive assets in an exchange that lacks commercial substance. The portion of the gain recognized is determined by a ratio of the boot received to the total fair value of the consideration received. The portion of the gain experienced but not recognized reduces what otherwise would have been recorded as the cost of the new equipment.

ILLUSTRATION 10-2
EXPENDITURES SUBSEQUENT TO ACQUISITION (L.O. 6)

A plant asset often requires expenditures subsequent to acquisition. Generally, four major types of expenditures may be incurred relative to existing plant assets; they are as follows:

Additions. Increase or extension of existing assets.
Improvements and Replacements. Substitution of an improved asset for an existing one.
Rearrangement and Reinstallation. Movement of assets from one location to another.
Repairs. Expenditures that maintain assets in condition for operation.

Costs that are incurred subsequent to acquisition are to be capitalized (by a debit to an asset account or to an accumulated depreciation account, depending on the circumstances) if they are material, nonrecurring in nature, and benefit future periods in some manner such as by doing one or more of the following:

a. They extend the useful life of a plant asset.
b. They enhance the quality of existing services.
c. They add new asset services.
d. They reduce future operating costs of existing assets.
e. They are required to meet governmental regulations (such as for environmental reasons).
f. They facilitate future production.

The accounting treatment appropriate for various costs incurred subsequent to the acquisition of capitalized assets is summarized as follows:

ILLUSTRATION 10-2 (Continued)

Type of Expenditure	Normal Accounting Treatment
Additions	Capitalize cost of addition to asset account.

Improvements and Replacements	(a) **Carrying value of old asset known:** Remove cost of and accumulated depreciation on old asset, recognizing any gain or loss. Capitalize cost of improvement/replacement.
	(b) **Carrying value of old asset unknown:**
	  1. If the asset's useful life is extended, debit accumulated depreciation for cost of improvement/replacement.
	  2. If the quantity or quality of the asset's productivity is increased, capitalize cost of improvement/replacement to asset account.

Rearrangement and Reinstallation	(a) If original installation cost is **known**, account for cost of rearrangement/reinstallation as a replacement (carrying value known). (b) If original installation cost is **unknown** and rearrangement/reinstallation cost is **material** in amount and benefits future periods, capitalize as an asset. (c) If original installation cost is **unknown** and rearrangement/reinstallation cost is **not material or future benefit is questionable**, expense the cost when incurred.
Repairs	(a) **Ordinary:** Expense cost of repairs when incurred. (b) **Major:** As appropriate, treat as an addition, improvement, or replacement.

TIP: Does an expenditure increase future service potential of the asset? If so, capitalize the expenditure. Does an expenditure merely maintain the existing level of service? If so, expense the expenditure in the period incurred.

CASE 10-3

Purpose: (L.O. 6) This case will provide a few examples of the accounting for costs subsequent to the acquisition of fixed assets.

Hardent Resources Group has been in its plant facility for twenty years. Although the plant is quite functional, numerous repair costs are incurred to maintain it in sound working order. The company's plant asset book value is currently $750,000, as indicated below:

Original cost	$ 1,350,000
Accumulated depreciation	(600,000)
Book value	$ 750,000

During the current year, the following expenditures were made involving the plant facility:
(a)   The entire plant was repainted at a cost of $26,000.
(b)   The roof was an asbestos cement slate; for safety purposes, it was removed and replaced with a new and better quality roof at a cost of $62,000. Book value of the old roof was $31,000.
(c)   Because of increased demands for its product, the company increased its plant capacity by building a new addition at a cost of $315,000.
(d)   The plumbing system was completely updated at a cost of $53,000. The cost of the old plumbing system was not known. It is estimated that the useful life of the building will not change as a result of this updating.
(e)   A series of major repairs were made at a cost of $50,000, because parts of the wood structure were rotting. The cost of the old wood structure was not known. These extensive repairs are estimated to increase the useful life of the building.

Instructions
Indicate how each of these transactions would be recorded in the accounting records.

Solution to Case 10-3

(a)   Expenditures that do not increase the service benefits of the asset are expensed. Painting costs are considered ordinary repairs because they maintain the existing condition of the asset or restore it to normal operating efficiency.

(b)   The approach to follow is to remove the old book value of the roof and substitute the cost of the new roof. It is assumed that the expenditure increases the future service potential of the asset. Recognize a loss equal to the book value of the old roof removed.

(c)   Any addition to plant assets is capitalized because a new asset has been created. This addition increases the service potential of the plant.

(d) Conceptually the book value of the old plumbing system should be removed. However, in practice, it is often difficult if not impossible to determine this amount. In this case, one of two approaches is followed. One approach is to capitalize the cost of the replacement on the theory that sufficient depreciation was taken on the item to reduce the carrying amount to almost zero. A second approach is to debit accumulated depreciation on the theory that the replacement extends the useful life of the asset and thereby recaptures some or all of the past depreciation. In our present situation, the problem specifically states that the useful life is not extended and therefore debiting accumulated depreciation is inappropriate. Thus, this expenditure should be added to the cost of the plant facility.

(e) See discussion in (d) above. In this case, because the useful life of the asset has increased, a debit to accumulated depreciation would appear to be the most appropriate treatment.

EXERCISE 10-7

Purpose: (L.O. 7) This exercise will (1) illustrate several different ways in which you may dispose of property, and (2) discuss the appropriate accounting procedures for each.

Presented below is a schedule of property dispositions for Friedlander Co.

Schedule of Property Dispositions

	Cost	Accumulated Depreciation	Cash Proceeds	Fair Market Value	Nature of Disposition
Land	$ 80,000	---	$ 64,000	$ 64,000	Condemnation
Building	30,000	---	7,200	---	Demolition
Warehouse	130,000	---	148,000	148,000	Destruction by fire
Machine	16,000	$22,000	3,600	14,400	Trade-in
Furniture	20,000	6,400	---	5,600	Contribution
Automobile	16,000	15,700	5,920	5,920	Sale
		6,920			

The following additional information is available:

Land. On January 7, a condemnation award was received as consideration for unimproved land held primarily as an investment, and on April 7, another parcel of unimproved land to be held as an investment was purchased at a cost of $70,000.

Building. On May 4, land and building were purchased at a total cost of $150,000, of which 20% was allocated to the building on the corporate books. The real estate was acquired with the intention of demolishing the building, and this was accomplished during the month of August. Cash proceeds received in August represent the net proceeds from demolition of the building.

Warehouse. On January 2, the warehouse was destroyed by fire. The warehouse was purchased January 2, 1998, and had been depreciated $22,000. On June 15, part of the insurance proceeds was used to purchase a replacement warehouse at a cost of $130,000.

Machine. On October 31, the machine was exchanged for another similar machine having a fair market value of $10,800 and cash of $3,600 was received. The exchange lacked commercial substance.

Furniture. On July 2, furniture was contributed to a qualified charitable organization. No other contributions were made or pledged during the year.

Automobile. On December 31, the automobile was sold to Dee Dee Burgess, a stockholder.

Instructions
Indicate how these items would be reported on the income statement of Friedlander Co.

(AICPA adapted)

Solution to Exercise 10-7

The following accounting treatment appears appropriate for these items:

Land. The loss on the condemnation of the land of $16,000 ($80,000 - $64,000) should be reported as an extraordinary item on the income statement. A condemnation comes about from a government unit exercising its right of eminent domain. *Eminent domain* is defined as "expropriation of assets by a government." Expropriation of assets was given as an example of an extraordinary item in *APB Opinion 30*. The $70,000 land purchase has no income statement effect.

Building. There is no recognized gain or loss on the demolition of the building. The entire purchase cost ($30,000), decreased by the demolition proceeds ($7,200), is allocated to land.

Warehouse. The gain on the destruction of the warehouse should be reported in the "other revenues and gains" section of the income statement. A fire can happen in any environment; therefore, it is not an extraordinary item. The gain is computed as follows:

Insurance proceeds		$148,000
Cost	$130,000	
Accumulated depreciation	(22,000)	(108,000)
Realized gain		$ 40,000

Some contend that a portion of this gain should be deferred because the proceeds are reinvested in similar assets. Deferral of the gain in this situation is not permitted under GAAP.

Machine. The recognized gain on the exchange would be computed as follows:

Fair market value of old machine		$14,400
Cost	$16,000	
Accumulated depreciation	(6,400)	(9,600)
Total gain experienced		$ 4,800

Total gain recognized = $4,800 x [$3,600 ÷ ($3,600 + $10,800)] = $1,200

This gain would probably be reported in the "other revenues and gains" section. It might be considered an unusual item, but it would usually not be infrequent. The cost of the new machine would be capitalized at $7,200:

Carrying value of old asset	
($16,000 - $6,400)	$9,600
Boot received	(3,600)
Gain recognized	1,200
Cost of new machine	$7,200

OR

Fair market value of new machine		$10,800
Gain experienced	$4,800	
Gain recognized	(1,200)	
Gain deferred		(3,600)
Cost of new machine		$ 7,200

Furniture. The contribution of the furniture to a charitable organization would be reported as a contribution expense of $5,600 with a related gain on disposition of furniture of $1,300 [$5,600 - ($20,000 - $15,700)]. The contribution expense and the related gain may be netted, if desired, for reporting purposes.

Automobile. The loss on sale of the automobile of $3,160 [$5,920 - ($16,000 - $6,920)] should probably be reported in the "other expenses and losses" section. This is a related party transaction; such transactions require special disclosure.

TIP: The receipt of the condemnation award (January 7) represents an **involuntary conversion of nonmonetary assets to monetary assets**. Any gain or loss related to the transaction shall be recognized even though the enterprise reinvests or is obligated to reinvest the monetary assets in replacement nonmonetary assets. The receipt of insurance proceeds due to the destruction of the warehouse is also an involuntary conversion of nonmonetary assets to monetary assets. The conditions surrounding a condemnation are usually unusual and infrequent and thus cause the related gain or loss to be classified as an extraordinary item.

TIP:	The sale of property, plant, and equipment for cash should be accounted for as follows:
	(1) The carrying value at the date of the sale (cost of the property, plant, and equipment less the accumulated depreciation) should be removed from the accounts.
	(2) The excess of cash from the sale over the carrying value removed is accounted for as a gain on the sale, while the excess of carrying value removed over cash from the sale is accounted for as a loss on the sale.
TIP:	When a plant asset is disposed of, the accumulated depreciation must be updated before the gain or loss can be computed. The discussions above assume that updating has taken place.

ANALYSIS OF MULTIPLE-CHOICE TYPE QUESTIONS

QUESTION

1. (L.O. 2) Jacobson Manufacturing Company purchased a machine for $65,000 on January 2, 2010. At the date of purchase, Jacobson incurred the following additional costs:

Loss on sale of old machine	$ 2,000
Freight-in	900
Installation cost	1,500
Breaking-in costs	650

The amount to record for the acquisition cost of the new machine is:
   a. $65,000.
   b. $67,400.
   c. $68,050.
   d. $69,400.

Approach and Explanation: Apply the guideline: The cost of a plant asset includes all costs required to get the item to the location and condition for its intended purpose.

Purchase price	$ 65,000
Freight-in	900
Installation cost	1,500
Breaking-in costs	650
Total acquisition cost	$ 68,050

The loss on sale of the old machine should be charged to an income statement account so it will not impact the new asset's value. (Solution = c.)

QUESTION

2. (L.O. 2) Buena Vista Hotel purchases Embassy Hotel with the intention of demolishing the Embassy Hotel and building a new high-rise hotel on the site. The cost of the Embassy Hotel should be:
   a.   capitalized as part of the cost of the land.
   b.   capitalized as part of the cost of the new hotel.
   c.   written off as a loss when it is torn down.
   d.   depreciated over the life of the new hotel structure.

Explanation: The cost of the land should include all costs necessary to acquire it and prepare it for its intended use by the buyer—which is to provide a site for a new building. (Solution = a.)

QUESTION

3. (L.O. 2) The Jupiter Company purchased a parcel of land to be used as the site of a new office complex. The following data pertain to the purchase of the land and the beginning of construction for the new building:

Purchase price of land	$200,000
Attorney's fees for land transaction	1,000
Title insurance cost	2,000
Survey fees to determine the boundaries of the lot	800
Excavation costs for the building's foundation	8,000
Costs of clearing and grading the land	1,400

The total acquisition cost of the land is:
a. $213,200.
b. $205,200.
c. $203,800.
d. $202,400.
e. $200,000.

Approach and Explanation: Think about how the cost of land is determined: an asset's cost includes all costs necessary to acquire the asset and get it to the location and condition for its intended purpose. When land has been purchased for the purpose of constructing a building, all costs incurred up to the excavation for the new building are considered land costs. Think of the common components of land cost (refer to the listing in the **Solution to Case 10-1).** The cost is computed as follows:

Purchase price	$200,000
Attorney's fees	1,000
Title insurance	2,000
Survey fees	800
Costs of clearing and grading	1,400
Total cost of land	$205,200

The $8,000 excavation costs for the building's foundation should be charged (debited) to the Building account. (Solution = b.)

QUESTION

4. (L.O. 2) The Venus Company hired an architect to design plans and a construction firm to build a new office building on a parcel of land it owns. The following data relates to the building:

Price paid to the construction firm	$320,000
Architect fees	18,000
Permit fees	1,200
Property taxes during the construction period	800
Insurance premium for first year of operations	3,000
Property taxes during the first year of operations	6,000

The total acquisition cost of the new building is:
a. $349,000.
b. $340,000.
c. $338,000.
d. $320,000.

Approach and Explanation: Think about how the cost of a building is determined: an asset's cost includes all costs necessary to acquire the asset and get it to the location and condition for its intended purpose. Think of the common components of building cost (refer to the listing in the **Solution to Case 10-1).** The cost is computed as follows:

Price paid to construction firm	$320,000
Architect fees	18,000
Permit fees	1,200
Property taxes during construction	800
Total cost of building	$340,000 (Solution = b.)

QUESTION

5. (L.O. 2) The Patty Company purchased a piece of office equipment to be used in operations. The following expenditures and other data relate to the equipment:

Invoice price excluding sales tax	$12,000
Sales tax	600
Delivery charges	200
Installation costs	300
Cost of a special platform	400
Cost of supplies used in testing	80
Insurance premium for first year of use	60

The total acquisition cost of this piece of equipment is:
a. $13,640.
b. $13,580.
c. $13,100.
d. $12,700.

Approach and Explanation: Apply the cost principle: the cost of equipment includes all costs necessary to acquire the equipment, transport it to the place where it will be used, and prepare it for use. Thus, all costs related to equipment incurred prior to use in regular operations are charged to the Equipment account. Recurring costs (such as for insurance and maintenance) incurred after the equipment is ready for use should be expensed in the period incurred. Refer to the list of common elements of equipment cost in the **Solution to Case 10-1.** The cost of the equipment is determined as follows:

Invoice price	$12,000
Sales tax	600
Delivery charges	200
Installation costs	300
Costs of special platform	400
Costs of supplies used in testing	80
	$13,580 (Solution = b.)

QUESTION

6. (L.O. 3) A manufacturing company decides to build its own factory equipment. The cost of self-constructed plant assets may include which of the following:

	Materials	Labor	Mfg. Overhead
a.	Yes	Yes	Yes
b.	Yes	Yes	No
c.	Yes	No	No
d.	No	Yes	No

Explanation: In addition to the materials and labor used to build a plant asset, the manufacturer should assign a pro rata portion of the manufacturing overhead to obtain the asset's cost. However, the asset should not be recorded for more than its fair value (the total amount that would be charged by an outside independent producer). (Solution = a.)

QUESTION

7.   (L.O. 4) Herndon Inc. has a fiscal year ending October 31. On November 1, 2009, Herndon borrowed $20,000,000 at 15% to finance construction of a new plant. Repayments of the loan are to commence the month following completion of the plant. During the year ending October 31, 2010, expenditures for the partially completed structure totaled $12,000,000. These expenditures were incurred evenly through the year. Interest earned on the unexpended portion of the loan amounted to $800,000 for the year. What amount of interest should be capitalized as of October 31, 2010?

   a. $0.
   b. $100,000.
   c. $900,000.
   d. $2,200,000.

Explanation: The situation is one which qualifies for the capitalization of interest. The following steps should help to compute the amount:

   (1)   **Find the weighted-average accumulated expenditures** for the period:

Total expenditures at beginning of the period	$ 0
Total expenditures at end of the period	12,000,000
Sum	$ 12,000,000

   $12,000,000 ÷ 2 = average of $6,000,000

   (2)   **Determine the interest rate to use.** Because the amount of a specific borrowing ($20,000,000) exceeds the weighted-average accumulated expenditures ($6,000,000), use the interest rate for that specific borrowing (15%).

   (3)   **Compute the avoidable interest** by multiplying the appropriate interest rate (15% from Step 2) by the weighted-average accumulated expenditures ($6,000,000 from Step 1).

   $6,000,000 x 15% = $900,000 Avoidable interest

   (4)   **Determine the amount of interest to capitalize** by selecting the lower of the actual interest incurred (15% x $20,000,000 = $3,000,000) or the amount of avoidable interest ($900,000 from Step 3). The lower in this case is the $900,000 avoidable interest. (Solution = c.)

TIP: The interest earned ($800,000) is to be reported as revenue on the income statement and should not be used to offset the interest to be capitalized.

QUESTION

8.   (L.O. 5) A large plot of land was donated by the City of Moberly to the Dupont Corporation to entice the company to build a plant and provide new jobs in the community. The land should be recorded on Dupont's books at:

   a.   the cost of the attorney's fees involved in handling the transaction.
   b.   the value assigned by Dupont's board of directors.
   c.   the land's market value.
   d.   no more than one dollar because the land was obtained for no cost.

Explanation: A donation (contribution) is a **nonreciprocal transfer** (value goes in only one direction rather than in both directions as happens in an exchange transaction). A nonreciprocal transfer is to be recorded at the fair value of the property, goods, or services involved. Although contributions received are normally credited to revenue, a donation from a governmental entity to a for-profit entity to entice the business to its community is sometimes credited to Donated Capital (an element of additional paid-in capital on the balance sheet). Contributions of property from governmental entities are excluded from the scope of the FASB's pronouncement on contributions which in general requires contributions received to be recognized as revenue. (Solution = c.)

QUESTION

9. (L.O. 5) The Holstrum Corporation intends to acquire some plant assets from Bailey Corporation by issuing common stock in exchange. The cost of the assets should be measured by:
   a. the par value of the stock.
   b. the market value of the stock.
   c. the book value of the stock.
   d. Bailey's carrying value of the assets.

Explanation: Cost is measured by the fair market value (cash equivalent) of the consideration given (the stock in this case), or the fair market value of the consideration received (the plant assets in this case), whichever is the more objectively determinable. If the market value of the common stock is not determinable, the fair market value of the plant assets should be used. (Solution = b.)

> **TIP:** If treasury stock is used to acquire a new plant asset, the same rule applies: record the asset at the fair value (market value) of the treasury stock or at the fair value of the asset, whichever is the more objectively determinable.

QUESTION

10. (L.O. 5) In January 2010, Barbie Company entered into a contract to acquire a new machine for its factory. The machine, which had a cash price of $300,000, was acquired in exchange for the following:

Down payment	$ 30,000
Note payable in 24 equal monthly installments	240,000
500 shares of Barbie common stock, with	
an agreed value of $100 per share	50,000
Total	$ 320,000

Prior to the machine's use, installation costs of $8,000 were incurred. The amount to record for the acquisition cost of the machine is:
   a. $300,000.
   b. $308,000.
   c. $320,000.
   d. $328,000.

Approach and Explanation: Any time you have a question regarding the acquisition cost of a plant asset, write down (or mentally review) the two rules regarding asset cost: (1) Cost is measured by the fair market value (cash equivalent) of the consideration given or the fair market value of the consideration received, whichever is the more objectively determinable; and (2) An asset's cost includes all costs necessary to get it to the location and condition for its intended purpose. Then apply the rules to the situation given.

The cash equivalent of the machine acquired is $300,000 (cash price). The cash equivalent of the consideration given is the cash down payment of $30,000 plus the fair value of the stock ($50,000) plus the present value of the note payable (something less than $240,000). Because no information is given about the market value of the note or the appropriate interest rate for the note, but the cash equivalent price is given for the asset received, the more objectively determinable figure is the $300,000. The $8,000 installation cost must be added to get the total acquisition cost. (Solution = b.)

QUESTION

11.   (L.O. 5) Two home builders agree to exchange tracts of land that each holds for purposes of development. An appraiser was hired and the following information is available:

	Batson	Beamer
Book value of land	$ 50,000	$ 72,000
Fair value of land	80,000	100,000
Cash paid	20,000	

The future cash flows are **not** expected to change materially for either party. In recording this exchange should a gain be recognized by Batson, Beamer, or both parties?

	Batson	Beamer
a.	Yes	Yes
b.	Yes	No
c.	No	Yes
d.	No	No

Approach and Explanation:

(1)   **Determine if the exchange has commercial substance.** One tract of land for another to use for the same purpose where the future cash flows are not expected to change materially for either party is an exchange that **lacks** commercial substance.

(2)   **Determine if a gain or loss is experienced.** Fair value exceeds book value for both parties so both have experienced a gain.

(3)   **Determine if boot is given or received.** Batson is giving boot; Beamer is receiving boot.

(4)   **Write down the rules for recognition of gain in an exchange lacking commercial substance.** The party giving boot (Batson) is not to recognize any gain. The party receiving boot is to recognize a portion of the gain experienced. In this case, the receipt of cash by Beamer represents a partial sale of the land, thus converting a portion of the old asset's fair value to cash. (Solution = c.)

QUESTION

12.   (L.O. 5) Refer to the facts of **Question 11.** The amount to be recorded by Batson for the acquisition cost of the new tract of land is:
   a. $50,000.
   b. $70,000.
   c. $72,000.
   d. $80,000.
   e. $100,000.

Approach and Explanation: When boot is given in an exchange lacking commercial substance, no gain is to be recognized. The cost of the new asset is equal to the recorded value (book value) of the old asset, reduced for any impairment (minus any loss recognized), plus the boot given. There was no loss in this case; therefore, $50,000 book value + $20,000 boot = $70,000 cost. A journal entry approach can also be used (the debit to the new asset account is a plug figure): (Solution = b.)

Land (New)..	70,000	**Plug last.**
Land (Old)	50,000	**Do second.**
Cash..	20,000	**Do first.**

The cost of the new tract of land can also be determined as follows:

Fair market value of asset given	$ 80,000
Cash given	20,000
Cost of new before deferral of gain on old	100,000
Gain on old to be deferred	(30,000)a
Cost of new asset	$ 70,000 (Solution = b.)

aFair market value of old asset	$80,000
Book value of old asset	(50,000)
Gain on old asset experienced but not recognized	$30,000

QUESTION

13. (L.O. 5) The King-Kong Corporation exchanges one plant asset for a similar plant asset and gives cash in the exchange. The exchange is **not** expected to cause a material change in the future cash flows for either entity. If a gain on the disposal of the old asset is indicated, the gain will:
   a.   be reported in the Other Revenues and Gains section of the income statement.
   b.   effectively reduce the amount to be recorded as the cost of the new asset.
   c.   effectively increase the amount to be recorded as the cost of the new asset.
   d.   be credited directly to the owner's capital account.

Explanation: The payer of cash in an exchange of nonmonetary assets in an exchange lacking commercial substance is **not** to recognize any gain on the disposal of the old asset. The gain is deferred by way of reduction (credit) to the cost of the new asset received in the exchange. The gain is thus spread over future periods by way of lower depreciation charges (because of a lower cost figure for the new asset). (Solution = b.)

QUESTION

14. (L.O. 7) A van has an original cost of $42,000 and accumulated depreciation of $11,000. It is sold for $27,000 cash. The journal entry to record the sale will include a:
   a.   debit to Loss on Disposal of Plant Assets for $4,000.
   b.   credit to Gain on Disposal of Plant Assets for $4,000.
   c.   credit to Vans for $27,000.
   d.   debit to Loss on Disposal of Plant Assets for $15,000.

Approach and Explanation: Prepare the journal entry to record the sale. Begin with the cash received so debit Cash. Remove the old asset from the books; credit Vans for $42,000 and debit Accumulated Depreciation for $11,000. Examine the entry and determine what is needed to balance the entry; a debit balancing figure represents a loss or a credit balancing figure represents a gain.

In this case, a debit of $4,000 is needed to balance; hence, a loss of $4,000 is recorded. (Solution = a.)

Cash...	27,000	
Accumulated Depreciation Vans	11,000	
Loss on Disposal of Plant Assets..	4,000	
Vans		42,000

QUESTION

15. (L.O. 6) In accounting for plant assets, which of the following outlays made subsequent to acquisition should be fully expensed in the period the expenditure is made?

    a. Expenditure made to increase the efficiency or effectiveness of an existing asset.

    b. Expenditure made to extend the useful life of an existing asset beyond the time frame originally anticipated.

    c. Expenditure made to maintain an existing asset so that it can function in the manner intended.

    d. Expenditure made to add new asset services.

Explanation: If an expenditure benefits future periods, it should be capitalized (debited to a balance sheet account); if the expenditure does not yield benefits to a future period, it should be recorded by a debit to an income statement account. An expenditure made to maintain an existing asset in good working condition does not provide any benefits other than those that were in potential when the original asset was acquired; hence, it should be expensed. Answer selections "a," "b," and "d" all represent future economic benefits; hence, they should be debited to an asset account or to an accumulated depreciation account, depending on whether or not an asset's life is increased by the expenditure subsequent to acquisition. (Solution = c.)

CHAPTER 11

DEPRECIATION, IMPAIRMENTS, AND DEPLETION

OVERVIEW

Expenses arise from the cost of goods or services that are consumed in the process of generating revenue. When a long-term tangible asset is acquired, it actually represents a bundle of future asset services. The total cost of these services equals the acquisition cost of the asset **minus** the asset's expected (estimated) market value at the end of its useful life. As a productive asset is used, services (benefits) are consumed; therefore, a portion of the original asset cost should be charged to expense in order to comply with the matching principle. The process of allocating (expensing) the cost of long-term tangible assets over the accounting periods during which the asset is used is called **depreciation**. The process of allocating the costs of natural resources to inventory (and later to cost of goods sold) is called **depletion**. Depreciation and depletion are discussed in this chapter.

SUMMARY OF LEARNING OBJECTIVES

1. **Explain the concept of depreciation.** Depreciation is the accounting process of allocating the cost of long-lived tangible assets to expense in a systematic and rational manner to those periods expected to benefit from the use of the asset.

2. **Identify the factors involved in the depreciation process.** Three factors involved in the depreciation process are: (1) determining the depreciation base for the asset, (2) estimating the service life, and (3) selecting a method of cost apportionment (depreciation).

3. **Compare activity, straight-line, and decreasing-charge methods of depreciation.** (1) *Activity method:* Assumes that depreciation is a function of use or productivity instead of the passage of time. The life of the asset is considered in terms of either the output it provides, or an input measure such as the number of hours it works. (2) *Straight-line method:* Considers depreciation a function of time instead of a function of usage. The straight-line procedure is often the most conceptually appropriate when a decline in usefulness is constant from period to period. (3) *Decreasing-charge method:* Provides for a higher depreciation charge in the earlier years and lower charges in later periods. The main justification for this approach is that the asset is the most productive and suffers the greatest loss of services in the earlier years.

4. **Explain special depreciation methods.** Two special depreciation methods are: (1) *Group and composite methods:* The term "group" refers to a collection of assets that are similar in nature; "composite" refers to a collection of assets that are dissimilar in nature. The group method is frequently used where the assets are fairly homogeneous (similar in nature) and have approximately the same useful lives. The composite approach may be used when the assets are heterogeneous (dissimilar) and have different lives. (2) *Hybrid or combination methods:* These methods may combine straight-line/activity approaches.

5. **Explain the accounting issues related to asset impairment.** The process to determine an impairment loss is as follows: (1) Review events and changes in circumstances for possible impairment. (2) If events or changes suggest impairment, determine if the sum of the expected future net cash flows from the long-lived asset is less than the carrying amount of the asset. If less, measure the impairment loss. (3) The impairment loss is the amount by which the carrying amount of the asset is greater than the fair value of the asset. After a company records an

impairment loss, the reduced carrying amount of the long-lived asset is now considered its new cost basis. An impairment loss may not be restored for an asset held for use. If the asset is expected to be disposed of, the impaired asset should be reported at the lower of cost or net realizable value. It is not depreciated. An impaired asset held for disposal can be continuously written up or down in future periods as long as the write-up is never greater than the carrying amount before impairment.

6. **Explain the accounting procedures for depletion of natural resources.** To account for depletion of natural resources, companies: (1) establish the depletion base, and (2) write off resource cost. Four factors are involved in establishing the depletion base: (a) Acquisition costs, (b) Exploration costs, (c) Development costs, and (d) Restoration costs. Companies normally compute depletion on the units of production method. Thus, depletion is a function of the number of units withdrawn during the period. In adopting this approach, the total cost of the natural resource less salvage value is divided by the number of units estimated to be in the resource deposit to obtain a cost per unit of product. This cost per unit is multiplied by the number of units extracted to compute depletion.

7. **Explain how to report property, plant, and equipment and natural resources.** The basis of valuation for property, plant, and equipment and for natural resources should be disclosed along with pledges, liens, and other commitments related to these assets. Companies should not offset any liability secured by property, plant, and equipment or by natural resources against these assets, but should report it in the liabilities section. Property, plant, and equipment not currently employed as producing assets in the business should be segregated from assets used in operations. When assets are depreciated, a valuation account normally called Accumulated Depreciation is credited. When assets are depleted, an accumulated depletion account may be used or the depletion may be credited directly to the natural resource account. Companies engaged in significant oil and gas producing activities must provide significant additional disclosures about these activities. Analysis may be performed to evaluate the asset turnover ratio, profit margin on sales, and the rate of return on assets.

*8. **Describe income tax methods of depreciation.** Congress enacted a Modified Accelerated Cost Recovery System (MACRS) in the Tax Reform Act of 1986. It applies to depreciable assets placed in service in 1987 and later. The computation of depreciation under MACRS differs from the computation under GAAP in three respects: (1) a mandated tax life, which is generally shorter than the economic life; (2) cost recovery on an accelerated basis; and (3) an assigned salvage value of zero.

 *This material is covered in Appendix 11A in the text.

TIPS ON CHAPTER TOPICS

TIP: **Residual value** is often referred to as **salvage value**, and sometimes it is called estimated **scrap value**.

TIP: Residual value is used in the computation of depreciation for the early years of life of an asset whenever the straight-line method or the sum-of-the-years'-digits method or an activity method is used. Salvage value is **not** a factor in determining depreciation for the early years of life if a declining-balance method is used; however, salvage value can effect the amount computed for depreciation in the last year(s) of an asset's life. An asset should **not** be depreciated below its salvage value.

TIP: The **activity method** is often called the **variable charge** approach or the **units of output** or the **units of production method**.

TIP: The **declining-balance depreciation method** applies a constant rate to a declining book value to calculate depreciation. The rate used is often twice the straight-line rate, in which case the method is then referred to as the **200% declining-balance method** or the **double declining-balance method**. Sometimes the rate is one and one-half times the straight-line rate, in which case the method is called the **150% declining-balance method**.

TIP: The **book value** of a plant asset is determined by deducting the balance of accumulated depreciation from the balance of the related asset account. The balance in the related asset account is generally the asset's original cost. Thus, the estimated residual value does not directly affect the book value computation. Book value is often called **carrying value, carrying amount, net asset value,** or **undepreciated value**. An asset's book value at a given date may be far different than its market (fair) value at the same date.

TIP: **Depreciable cost** or **depreciation base** is a term that refers to the total amount to be depreciated over the life of the asset. It is determined by deducting the estimated residual value from the cost of the asset.

TIP: When an asset being depreciated by a group or composite depreciation method is disposed of, no gain or loss is recorded; the difference between the original cost of the asset and the proceeds from disposal is charged to Accumulated Depreciation.

TIP: Companies can use either the full-cost approach or the successful-efforts approach to account for exploration costs in the oil and gas industry.

Those who favor the **full-cost concept** argue that the cost of drilling a dry hole is a cost needed to find the commercially profitable wells and therefore should be capitalized. Those who favor the successful-efforts concept believe that companies should capitalize only the costs of successful projects (i.e., only the costs directly related to a successful project gets charged to that project; any remaining costs are treated as period charges (expenses).

TIP: Fair-value information is required for supplemental disclosures for gas and oil producers. Revenue recognition accounting (RRA) has been suggested for those companies but is not a generally accepted method. Under RRA, as soon as a company discovers oil, it would report the value of the oil on the balance sheet and in the income statement. Thus, RRA is a fair-value approach, in contrast to full-costing and successful-efforts concepts which are historical cost approaches.

CASE 11-1

Purpose: (L.O. 1, 2) This case examines the process of matching the cost of fixed assets with the revenues which the assets help to generate.

Plant assets provide services for two or more periods. There is a cost to the services consumed; this cost should be matched with the periods benefited.

Instructions
(a)   Briefly define depreciation as used in accounting.
(b)   Identify the factors that are relevant in determining the annual depreciation and explain whether these factors are determined objectively or whether they are based on judgment.

(AICPA Adapted)

Solution to Case 11-1

(a)   Depreciation is the accounting process of allocating an asset's historical cost (recorded amount) to the accounting periods benefited by the use of the asset. It is a process of cost allocation, not valuation. Depreciation is not intended to provide funds for an asset's replacement; it is merely an application of the matching principle.

(b)   The factors relevant in determining the annual depreciation for a depreciable asset are the initial recorded amount (acquisition cost and any subsequent capitalized costs), estimated salvage value, estimated useful life, and deprecation method.

Assets are typically recorded at their acquisition cost, which is in most cases objectively determinable. But cost assignments in other cases—"basket purchases" and selection of an implicit interest rate in asset acquisition under deferred-payment plans—may be quite subjective and involve considerable judgment.

The salvage value is an estimate of an amount potentially realizable when the asset is retired from service. It is initially a judgment factor and is affected by the length of the asset's useful life to the enterprise.

The useful life is also a judgment factor. It involves selecting the "unit" of measure of service life and estimating the number of such units embodied in the asset. Such units may be measured in terms of time periods or in terms of activity (for example, years or machine hours). When selecting the life, one should select the lower (shorter) of the physical life or the economic life to the user. Physical life involves wear and tear and casualties; economic life involves such things as technological obsolescence and inadequacy.

Selecting the depreciation method is generally a judgment decision; but, a method may be inherent in the definition adopted for the units of service life, as discussed earlier. For example, if such units are machine hours, the method is a function of the number of machine hours used during each period. A method should be selected that will best measure the portion of services expiring each period. Once a method is selected, it may be applied by using a predetermined, objectively derived formula.

EXERCISE 11-1

Purpose: (L.O. 3) This exercise will give you practice in computing depreciation for three successive periods for three commonly used methods.

Hudspeth Company purchases equipment on January 1, Year 1, at a cost of $645,000. The asset is expected to have a service life of 12 years and a salvage value of $60,000.

Instructions
(a)   Compute the amount of depreciation for each of Years 1 through 3 using the straight-line depreciation method.
(b)   Compute the amount of depreciation for each of Years 1 through 3 using the sum-of-the-years'-digits method.
(c)   Compute the amount of depreciation for each of Years 1 through 3 using the double-declining balance method. (In performing your calculations, round the constant percentage to the nearest one-hundredth of a percentage point and round final answers to the nearest dollar.)

Solution to Exercise 11-1

(a) $\dfrac{\$645,000 - \$60,000}{12} = \underline{\$48,750}$ Depreciation for each of Years 1 through 3 using the straight-line method.

(b) $\dfrac{12 \times 13}{2} = 78$

$12/78 \times (\$645,000 - \$60,000) = \underline{\$90,000}$ depreciation Year 1
$11/78 \times (\$645,000 - \$60,000) = \underline{\$82,500}$ depreciation Year 2
$10/78 \times (\$645,000 - \$60,000) = \underline{\$75,000}$ depreciation Year 3

(c) $\dfrac{100\%}{12} \times 2 = 16.67\%$

$\$645,000 \times 16.67\% =$ $\underline{\$107,522}$ depreciation Year 1
$(\$645,000 - \$107,522) \times 16.67\% =$ $\underline{\$\ 89,598}$ depreciation Year 2
$(\$645,000 - \$107,522 - \$89,598)$
$\quad \times 16.67\% =$ $\underline{\$\ 74,662}$ depreciation Year 3

EXERCISE 11-2

Purpose: (L.O. 3) This exercise will provide an illustration of the computations for depreciation of partial periods using three common methods.

Kalidas Company purchased a new plant asset on April 1, 2010, at a cost of $345,000. It was estimated to have a service life of 20 years and a salvage value of $30,000. Kalidas uses the calendar year as its accounting period.

Instructions (Round all final answers to the nearest dollar.)

(a)   Compute the amount of depreciation for this asset for 2010 and 2011 using the straight-line method.

(b)   Compute the amount of depreciation for this asset for 2010 and 2011 using the sum-of-the-years'-digits method.

(c)   Compute the amount of depreciation for this asset for 2010 and 2011 using the double-declining balance method.

Solution to Exercise 11-2

(a) $\dfrac{\$345,000 - \$30,000}{20 \text{ years}} \times 9/12 = \underline{\$11,813}$ depreciation for 2010

$\dfrac{\$345,000 - \$30,000}{20 \text{ years}} = \underline{\$15,750}$ depreciation for 2011

Approach and Explanation: Write down and apply the formula for straight-line depreciation. Multiply the annual depreciation amount by the portion of the asset's first year of service that falls in the given accounting period.

$$\frac{\text{Cost - Salvage Value}}{\text{Estimated Service LIfe}} = \text{Depreciation Charge}$$

(b) $\dfrac{20 \,(20 + 1)}{2} = 210$

$$
\begin{array}{lcl}
9/12 \times 20/210 \times (\$345,000 - \$30,000) & = & \underline{\$22,500} \text{ depreciation for 2010} \\
3/12 \times 20/210 \times (\$345,000 - \$30,000) & = & \$\ 7,500 \\
+\ 9/12 \times 19/210 \times (\$345,000 - \$30,000) & = & \underline{\ 21,375} \\
& & \underline{\$28,875} \text{ depreciation for 2011}
\end{array}
$$

Approach and Explanation: Write down and apply the formula for sum-of-the-years'-digits depreciation. Apportion the depreciation for the given asset year between the two accounting periods involved. The first nine months of the asset's first year of life fall in the 2010 calendar year. The last three months of the asset's first year of life and the first nine months of the asset's second year of life fall in the 2011 calendar year. There is no shortcut to the two-part computation of depreciation for 2011, as illustrated above.

Formula: $\dfrac{n\,(n + 1)}{2} = \text{Sum of the Years}$

$$\frac{\substack{\text{No. of Years Remaining at} \\ \text{Beginning of Asset Year}}}{\text{Sum of the Years}} \times (\text{Cost - Salvage}) = \text{Depreciation for Full Asset Year}$$

(c)   Straight-line rate $\frac{100\%}{20}$ = 5%;   5% x 2 = 10%

10% x $345,000 = $34,500 depreciation for asset's first year
10% x ($345,000 - $34,500) = $31,050 depreciation for asset's second year

9/12 x $34,500 = $25,875 depreciation for 2010

3/12 x $34,500 =	$ 8,625	
+ 9/12 x $31,050 =	23,288	
	$ 31,913	depreciation for 2011

Approach and Explanation: Write down and apply the formula for the declining balance method. Apportion the depreciation for a given **asset year** between the two accounting periods involved.

Constant Percentage x   Book Value at Beginning of Asset Year   = Depreciation for Asset Year

An alternative approach is as follows:
After the first partial year, calculate depreciation for a full **accounting year** by multiplying the constant percentage by the book value of the asset at the beginning of the accounting period.
Thus, the computation for 2008 would be as follows:
10% x ($345,000 - $25,875) = $31,913.

EXERCISE 11-3

Purpose: (L.O. 3) This exercise is designed to test your ability to solve for missing data by applying your knowledge regarding depreciation computations.

Dunlap Company acquired a plant asset at the beginning of Year 1. The asset has an estimated service life of 5 years. An employee has prepared depreciation schedules for this asset using three different methods to compare the results of using one method with the results of using other methods. You are to assume that the following schedules have been correctly prepared for this asset using (1) the straight-line (SL) method, (2) the sum-of-the-years'-digits (SYD) method, and (3) the double-declining balance (DDB) method (switching to the straight-line method after the mid-life of the asset).

Year	Straight-line	Sum-of-the-Years'-Digits	Double-declining Balance
1	$ 6,000	$ 10,000	$ 14,400
2	6,000	8,000	8,640
3	6,000	6,000	5,184
4	6,000	4,000	888
5	6,000	2,000	888
Total	$ 30,000	$ 30,000	$ 30,000

Instructions

Answer the following questions:

(a)   What is the cost of the asset being depreciated?

(b)   What amount, if any, was used in the depreciation calculations for the salvage value of this asset?

(c)   Which method will produce the highest charge to income in Year 1?

(d)   Which method will produce the highest charge to income in Year 4?

(e)   Which method will produce the highest book value for the asset at the end of Year 3?

(f)   If the asset is sold at the end of Year 3, which method would yield the highest gain (or lowest loss) on disposal of the asset?

Solution to Exercise 11-3

(a)   If there is any salvage value and the amount is unknown (as is the case here), the cost would have to be determined by looking at the data for the double-declining balance method.

$$100\% \div 5 = 20\%; \quad 20\% \times 2 = 40\%$$
$$\text{Cost} \times 40\% = \$14,400; \quad \$14,400 \div .40 = \underline{\$36,000} \text{ cost of asset}$$

Approach: Write down the formula for each of the depreciation methods mentioned. Fill in the data given for Year 1. Examine what remains to be solved.

(Cost - Salvage Value) ÷ Estimated Service Life = St.-line Depreciation
(Cost - Salvage Value) ÷ 5 = $6,000

(# of Years Remaining at Beginning of Asset Year ÷ Sum of the Years)
  x (Cost - Salvage Value) = SYD Depreciation
5 ÷ 15 x (Cost - Salvage Value) = $10,000

Constant Percentage x Cost = DDB Depreciation
40% x Cost = $14,400

There are two variables (cost and salvage value) unknown for each of the first two methods, and there is no way to solve for either of them. However, cost can easily be determined for the third method (DDB). Once you solve for cost, it is a simple matter to solve for salvage value.

(b) $36,000 cost (answer a) - $30,000 total depreciation = <u>$6,000</u> salvage value

Approach: The difference between the answer to part (a) and the total depreciation per the schedule ($30,000) is the salvage value used.

(c)   The highest charge to income for Year 1 will be yielded by the double-declining balance method.

Approach: Examine the depreciation schedules. Notice the method that results in the highest depreciation amount for Year 1.

(d)   The highest charge to income for Year 4 will be yielded by the straight-line method.

Approach: Examine the depreciation schedules given. Notice the method that results in the highest depreciation amount for Year 4.

(e)   The method to yield the highest book value at the end of Year 3 would be the method that yields the lowest accumulated depreciation at the end of Year 3 which is the straight-line method. Computations:

SL   = $36,000 - ($6,000 + $6,000 + $6,000)
        = $18,000 book value at the end of Year 3.
SYD   = $36,000 - ($10,000 + $8,000 + $6,000)
        = $12,000 book value at the end of Year 3.
DDB   = $36,000 - ($14,400 + $8,640 + $5,184)
        = $7,776 book value at the end of Year 3.

Approach: Write down the formula to compute book value: Cost - Accumulated Depreciation = Book Value. To obtain a high book value, you need a low accumulated depreciation. Examine the depreciation schedules to determine the method that would yield the lowest total depreciation for the first three years.

(f)   The method that will yield the highest gain (or lowest loss) if the asset is sold at the end of Year 3 is the method which will yield the lowest book value at the end of Year 3. In this case, it is the double-declining balance method.

Approach: Write down the formula to compute gain or loss on disposal: Selling Price - Book Value = Gain (Loss). To obtain a high gain, you need a low book value. Examine the formula for book value. To get a low book value, you need high depreciation charges. Use the depreciation schedules to determine the method that would yield the highest accumulated depreciation balance at the end of three years.

EXERCISE 11-4

Purpose: (L.O. 4) This exercise will enable you to practice working with the composite method for computing depreciation.

Presented below is information related to the Lori Demro Corporation (all assets are acquired at the beginning of Year 1):

Asset	Cost	Estimated Scrap	Estimated Life (in years)
A	$60,750	$8,250	10
B	50,400	7,200	9
C	54,000	4,800	8
D	28,500	2,250	7
E	35,250	3,750	6

Instructions
(a)   Compute the rate of depreciation per year to be applied to the plant assets under the composite method.
(b)   Compute the composite life.
(c)   Prepare the adjusting entry necessary at the end of the year to record depreciation for Year 1.
(d)   Prepare the entry at the end of Year 6 to record the sale of fixed asset D for cash of $7,500. It was used for 6 years, and depreciation was recorded under the composite method.

Solution to Exercise 11-4

(a)

Asset	Cost	Estimated Scrap	Depreciable Cost	Estimated Life	Depreciation Per Year
A	$ 60,750	$ 8,250	$ 52,500	10	$ 5,250
B	50,400	7,200	43,200	9	4,800
C	54,000	4,800	49,200	8	6,150
D	28,500	2,250	26,250	7	3,750
E	35,250	3,750	31,500	6	5,250
	$228,900	$26,250	$202,650		$25,200

Composite rate = $25,200 ÷ $228,900; or <u>11.009%</u>

Approach and Explanation: Steps to compute the composite rate:

1.   Compute what would be the amount of annual straight-line depreciation for each asset by dividing each asset's **depreciable cost** by its estimated service life. Sum these amounts ($25,200).

2.   Compute the composite rate by dividing the total depreciation per year (results of Step 1—$25,200) by the amount of **original cost** ($228,900).

(b)   Composite life = $202,650 ÷ $25,200; or <u>8.04 years</u>

Approach and Explanation: Compute the composite life by dividing the total depreciable cost ($202,650) by the total annual depreciation charge ($25,200).

(c)   **End of Year 1**

Depreciation Expense on Plant Assets   25,200

     Accumulated Deprecation on Plant Assets   25,200

      ($228,900 x 11.009% = $25,200)

Approach and Explanation: Compute the depreciation for any given year by multiplying the balance in the asset account by the composite rate (results of Step 2). The balance in the asset account will change over time due to the acquisition of new assets and the disposal of old assets.

(d)   **End of Year 6**

Cash   7,500

Accumulated Depreciation on Plant Assets   21,000

     Plant Assets   28,500

Approach and Explanation: When using the group or composite method, no gain or loss on disposition is recorded. The difference between the proceeds (if any) on disposal and the original cost of the asset is debited (or credited) to the Accumulated Depreciation account. Thus, if an asset is retired before, or after, the average service of the group is reached, the resulting gain or loss is buried in the Accumulated Depreciation account.

EXERCISE 11-5

Purpose: (L.O. 4) This exercise will provide you with an illustration of how to account for a change in the estimated service life and salvage value of a plant asset due to an expenditure subsequent to acquisition.

The Russell Company purchased a machine on January 1, 2000 for $105,000. The machine was being depreciated using the straight-line method over an estimated life span of 20 years, with a $15,000 salvage value. At the beginning of 2010, when the machine had been in use for 10 years, the company paid $25,000 to overhaul the machine. As a result of this improvement, the company estimated that the useful life of the machine would be extended an additional 5 years and the salvage value would be reduced to $10,000.

Instructions
Compute the depreciation charge for 2010.

Solution to Exercise 11-5

Cost	$ 105,000
Accumulated depreciation at 1/1/10	(45,000)[a]
Book value at 1/1/10	60,000
Additional expenditure capitalized	25,000
Revised book value	85,000
Current estimate of salvage value	(10,000)
Remaining depreciable cost at 1/1/10	75,000
Remaining years of useful life at 1/1/10	÷ 15[b]
Depreciation expense for 2010	$ 5,000

[a]Cost	$105,000
Original estimate of salvage value	(15,000)
Original depreciable cost	90,000
Original service life in years	÷ 20
Original depreciation per year	4,500
Number of years used	x 10
Accumulated depreciation at 1/1/10	$ 45,000

[b]Original estimate of life in years	20
Number of years used	(10)
Additional years	5
Remaining years of useful life at 1/1/10	15

> **TIP:** A change in the estimated useful life and/or salvage value of an existing depreciable asset is to be accounted for prospectively (in current and/or future periods). Therefore, the book value at the beginning of the period of change, less the current estimate of salvage value, is to be allocated over the remaining periods of life, using the appropriate depreciation method. The book value at the beginning of the period of change is calculated using the original estimates of service life and salvage value.

> **TIP:** The $25,000 cost of overhaul is capitalized in this case because the cost benefits future periods by extending the useful life of the machine.

Approach: Whenever you have a situation that involves a change in the estimated service life and/or salvage value of a depreciable asset, use the format shown above to compute the remaining depreciable cost and allocate that amount over the remaining useful life using the given depreciation method.

EXERCISE 11-6

Purpose: (L.O. 3) This exercise will allow you to practice using various depreciation methods and it will also give you the opportunity to compare the results of using one method to the results of using another method.

On January 1, 2010, Irish Company, a machine-tool manufacturer, acquires a piece of new industrial equipment for $1,000,000. The new equipment has a useful life of five years and the salvage value is estimated to be $100,000. Irish estimates that the new equipment can produce a total of 40,000 units and expects it to produce 10,000 units in its first year. Production is then estimated to decline by 1,000 units per year over the remaining useful life of the equipment.

The following depreciation methods may be used:

Double declining-balance
Straight-line
Sum-of-the-years'-digits
Units-of-output

Instructions

(a)   Identify which depreciation method would result in the maximization of profits for financial statement reporting for the **three**-year period ending December 31, 2012. Prepare a schedule showing the amount of accumulated depreciation at December 31, 2012, under the method selected. Show supporting computations in good form. Ignore present value and income tax considerations in your answer.

(b)   Identify which depreciation method would result in the minimization of profits for the **three**-year period ending December 31, 2012. Prepare a schedule showing the amount of accumulated depreciation at December 31, 2012, under the method selected. Show supporting computations in good form. Ignore present value and income tax considerations in your answer.

(AICPA Adapted)

Solution to Exercise 11-6

(a) The straight-line method of depreciation would result in the maximization of profits for financial statement reporting for the three-year period ending December 31, 2012.

Irish Company
ACCUMULATED DEPRECIATION USING STRAIGHT-LINE METHOD
December 31, 2012

(Cost - Salvage Value)   Estimated Service Life

($1,000,000 - $100,000)   5 years = $180,000

Year	Depreciation Expense	Accumulated Depreciation
2010	$ 180,000	$ 180,000
2011	180,000	360,000
2012	180,000	540,000
	$ 540,000	

(b) The double declining balance method of depreciation would result in the minimization of profits for the three-year period ending December 31, 2012.

Irish Company
ACCUMULATED DEPRECIATION USING
DOUBLE DECLINING-BALANCE METHOD
December 31, 2012

Straight-line rate is 5 years, or 20%. Double declining-balance rate is 40% (20% x 2). Ignore salvage value.

Year	Book Value at Beginning of Year	Depreciation Expense	Accumulated Depreciation
2010	$1,000,000	$400,000	$400,000
2011	600,000	240,000	640,000
2012	360,000	144,000	784,000
		$784,000	

Other supporting computations:

Irish Company
ACCUMULATED DEPRECIATION USING
SUM-OF-THE-YEARS'-DIGITS METHOD
December 31, 2012

$[n \times (n + 1)] \div 2 = [5 \times (5 + 1)] \div 2 = 15$

5/15 X ($1,000,000 - $100,000) = $300,000
4/15 x ($1,000,000 - $100,000) = $240,000
3/15 X ($1,000,000 - $100,000) = $180,000

Year	Depreciation Expense	Accumulated Depreciation
2010	$ 300,000	$ 300,000
2011	240,000	540,000
2012	180,000	720,000
	$ 720,000	

Irish Company
ACCUMULATED DEPRECIATION USING
UNITS-OF-OUTPUT METHOD
December 31, 2012

(Cost - Salvage Value)   Total Units of Output =
($1,000,000 - $100,000)   40,000 =
$22.50 Depreciation per Unit

10,000 x $22.50 = $225,000
9,000 x $22.50 = $202,500
8,000 x $22.50 = $180,000

Year	Depreciation Expense	Accumulated Depreciation
2010	$ 225,000	$ 225,000
2011	202,500	427,500
2012	180,000	607,500
	$ 607,500	

EXERCISE 11-7

Purpose: (L.O. 6) This exercise will give you practice in computing depletion.

During 2010, Alston Corporation acquired a mineral mine for $2,700,000, of which $450,000 is attributable to the land value after the mineral has been removed. Engineers estimate that 15 million units of mineral can be recovered from this mine. During 2010, 1,200,000 units were extracted and 800,000 units were sold.

Instructions
Compute the depletion for 2010.

Solution to Exercise 11-7

($2,700,000 - $450,000) ÷ 15,000,000 = $.15

$.15 x 1,200,000 = $180,000 Depletion for 2010

Approach and Explanation: Write down the formula to compute depletion, enter the data given, and solve.

$$\frac{\text{Acquisition Cost } + \text{ Costs to Explore and Develop} - \text{Residual Value of Land } + \text{Costs to Restore Land to Alternative Use}}{\text{Number of Units to be Extracted}} = \frac{\text{Depletion Cost Per}}{\text{Recoverable Unit}}$$

$$\begin{array}{ccccc}\text{Depletion Cost} & & \text{Units Extracted} & & \text{Depletion} \\ \text{Per Recoverable} & \text{x} & \text{During} & = & \text{for the} \\ \text{Unit} & & \text{Period} & & \text{Period}\end{array}$$

TIP:	The depletion charge for the period is the amount to be removed from the property, plant, and equipment classification ($180,000 in this case). It is based on the units **extracted** from the earth during the period. The portion of this $180,000 which gets to the income statement is dependent upon the number of units **sold**. When the number of units extracted exceed the number sold, as in this exercise, a portion of the depletion costs goes into the Inventory account on the balance sheet.

ILLUSTRATION 11-1
ACCOUNTING FOR IMPAIRMENTS (L.O. 5)

A summary of the key concepts in accounting for impairments is presented below:

A **recoverability test** is used to determine whether an impairment has occurred: If the sum of the expected future net undiscounted cash flows (from the use of the asset and its eventual disposition) is less than the carrying amount of the asset, the asset has been impaired.

If the recoverability test indicates that an impairment has occurred, a loss is computed. The impairment loss is the amount by which the carrying amount of the asset exceeds its fair value. The fair value of an asset is measured by its market value (if an active market exists) or by the present value of expected future net cash flows (if an active market does not exist). If an asset is to be disposed of instead of held for use, the asset's net realizable value (fair value less cost to sell) is used as a measure of the net cash flows that will be received from this asset.

Subsequent to recognizing the loss from impairment, the following guidelines are to be followed:

1. If the asset is to be held for use, it will be depreciated based on the new cost basis.
2. If the asset is to be sold, no more depreciation is taken once the asset is no longer used.
3. Restoration of the impairment loss is not permitted for an asset which is held for use.
4. Restoration of the impairment loss is allowed for an asset held for sale. Because assets held for disposal will be recovered through sale rather than through use in operations, they are continually revalued. Each period they are reported at the lower of cost or net realizable value. Thus, an asset held for disposal can be written up or down in future periods, as long as the write-up does not produce a new carrying value greater than the carrying amount of the asset before an adjustment was made to reflect a decision to dispose of the asset.

TIP:	Losses or gains related to impaired assets should be reported as part of income from continuing operations. Thus, they are **not** classified as extraordinary items.
TIP:	International accounting standards permit write-ups for subsequent recoveries of impairments back up to the original amount before the impairment. U.S. GAAP prohibits those write-ups, except for assets to be disposed of.

ANALYSIS OF MULTIPLE-CHOICE TYPE QUESTIONS

QUESTION
1. (L.O. 2) The term "depreciable cost," or "depreciable base," as it is used in accounting, refers to:
    a.   the total amount to be charged (debited) to expense over an asset's useful life.
    b.   cost of the asset less the related depreciation recorded to date.
    c.   the estimated market value of the asset at the end of its useful life.
    d.   the acquisition cost of the asset.

Approach and Explanation: Write down a definition of depreciable cost **before** you read any of the answer selections. **Depreciable cost** or **depreciable base** is the total amount of asset cost that can be expensed over the life of the asset; thus, it is original cost less estimated residual (salvage) value. Answer selection "b" describes the term book value. Answer selection "c" describes salvage value or residual value. Selection "d" represents the total cost of the asset. (Solution = a.)

QUESTION
2. (L.O. 2) A machine is purchased by the Dunnagin Company for $18,000. Dunnagin pays $6,000 in cash and gives a note payable for $12,000 that is payable in installments over a four-year period. Dunnagin estimates that the machine could physically last for 12 years, even though Dunnagin expects to use it in its business for only 9 years. The period of time to be used by Dunnagin for depreciation purposes is:
    a.   4 years.
    b.   5 years.
    c.   9 years.
    d.   12 years.

Approach and Explanation: Think about the objective of the depreciation process—to allocate an asset's cost to the periods benefited. The asset should be depreciated over its useful life, which is the length of time the asset will be of service to the entity using it. (Solution = c.)

QUESTION
3. (L.O. 3) A machine with an estimated service life of five years and an expected salvage value of $5,000 was purchased on January 1, 2010 for $50,000. The amount to be recorded for depreciation for 2010, 2011, and 2012, respectively, using the sum-of-the-years'-digits method will be:
    a. $20,000; $12,000; $7,200.
    b. $16,667; $13,333; $10,000.
    c. $15,000; $12,000; $9,000.
    d. $15,000; $8,000; $4,400.

Approach and Explanation: Write down the formula to compute SYD depreciation. Enter the data given and solve.

$$\frac{n\ (n\ +\ 1)}{2} = \text{Sum of the Years} \qquad\qquad \frac{5\ (6)}{2} = 15$$

$$\frac{\text{\# of Years Life Remaining at Beginning of Asset Year}}{\text{Sum of the Years}} \times (\text{Cost - Salvage}) = \text{Depreciation for Full Asset Year}$$

2010:	($50,000 - $5,000) x 5/15 =	$ 15,000	
2011:	($50,000 - $5,000) x 4/15 =	$ 12,000	
2012:	($50,000 - $5,000) x 3/15 =	$ 9,000	(Solution = c.)

QUESTION
4. (L.O. 3) A machine with an estimated service life of five years and an expected salvage value of $5,000 was purchased on January 1, 2010, for $50,000. The amount to be recorded for depreciation for years 2010, 20011, and 2012, respectively, using the 200% declining-balance method will be:
    a. $20,000; $12,000; $7,200.
    b. $18,000; $10,800; $6,480.
    c. $16,667; $13,333; $10,000.
    d. $10,000; $8,000; $6,400.

Approach and Explanation: Write down the formula for the declining-balance method. Enter the data given and solve.

Book Value at Beginning of Year x Constant Percentage = Depreciation

Constant Percentage = 2 x (100% ÷ Life) = 2 x (100% ÷ 5) = 40%

2010:	$50,000 x 40% =	$20,000
2011:	($50,000 - $20,000) x 40% =	$12,000
2012:	($50,000 - $20,000 - $12,000) x 40% =	$ 7,200

(Solution = a.)

QUESTION
5. (L.O. 3) Salvage (residual) value may or may not be used in computing depreciation expense in the early years of an asset's life. Net income is understated if, in the first year, estimated salvage value is excluded from the depreciation computation when using the:

	Units of Output Method	Sum-of-the-Years'-Digits Method
a.	Yes	Yes
b.	No	No
c.	No	Yes
d.	Yes	No

Approach and Explanation: Before looking at the methods addressed directly in the question, think about how salvage value affects the depreciation computation under various methods. In considering the common depreciation methods such as straight-line, activity methods, sum-of-the-years'-digits, and declining-balance methods, the declining-balance methods are the only methods that do not use the residual value in computing depreciation in the early years of the asset's life. However, the residual value may affect the computations with the declining-balance method in the latter years of the asset's life because the asset should not be depreciated below its residual value. The units-of-output method is an activity method. (Solution = a.)

QUESTION
6. (L.O. 3, 7) A machine was purchased for $8,000,000 on January 1, 2010. It has an estimated useful life of 8 years and a residual value of $800,000. Depreciation is being computed using the sum-of-the-years'-digits method. What amount should be shown for this machine, net of accumulated depreciation, in the company's December 31, 2011 balance sheet?
    a. $4,200,000
    b. $5,000,000
    c. $6,300,000
    d. $6,600,000

Approach and Explanation: Write down the formula to compute book value and the formula to compute depreciation using the sum-of-the-years'-digits method. Fill in the data from the scenario at hand and solve. Be careful that you don't get so involved with the computation for depreciation that you lose sight of the question—and that is, to compute the book value of the equipment. It would be helpful to underline the middle of the last sentence of the stem of the question in order to keep your focus on what is being asked.

Cost - Accumulated Depreciation = Book Value

$$\frac{\text{No. of Years Remaining Life}}{\text{Sum of the Years}} \times (\text{Cost - Salvage}) = \text{Depreciation Charge}$$

$$\frac{n\,(n + 1)}{2} = \text{Sum of the Years} \qquad\qquad \frac{8\,(8 + 1)}{2} = 36$$

8/36 x ($8,000,000 - $800,000) = $1,600,000 depreciation for 2010.
7/36 x ($8,000,000 - $800,000) = $1,400,000 depreciation for 2011.

Depreciation for 2010	$ 1,600,000
Depreciation for 2011	1,400,000
Accumulated depreciation at 12/31/11	$ 3,000,000

Cost	$ 8,000,000
Accumulated depreciation	(3,000,000)
Book value at 12/31/11	$ 5,000,000 (Solution = b.)

QUESTION

7. (L.O. 3, 4) Tammy Corporation purchased a machine on July 1, 2010 for $900,000. The machine has an estimated life of five years and a salvage value of $120,000. The machine is being depreciated by the 150% declining-balance method. What amount of depreciation should be recorded for the year ended December 31, 2011?

   a. $229,500
   b. $198,900
   c. $189,000
   d. $163,800

Approach and Explanation: Write down the formula to use for the declining-balance approach. (Notice the facts indicate there is a partial period for the first year (2010) and the question asks for the depreciation for the 2008 reporting period.) Compute the rate that is 150% of the straight-line rate. Apply the formula to the facts given. Remember that salvage value is not used with this method in computing depreciation in the early years of the asset's life.

Constant Percentage x Book Value at Beginning of the Year = Depreciation

$$\frac{100\%}{\text{Life}} = \frac{100\%}{5 \text{ years}} = 20\% \qquad 20\% \times 150\% = 30\% \text{ constant percentage}$$

30% x $900,000 = $270,000 First year of life
30% x (900,000 - $270,000) = $189,000 Second year of life
   1/2 x $270,000 = $135,000 for 2010
   (1/2 x $270,000) + (1/2 x $189,000) = $229,500 for 2011
OR
   30% x ($900,000 - $135,000) = $229,500 for 2011   (Solution = a.)

QUESTION
8. (L.O. 3, 4) A plant asset with a five-year estimated useful life and no salvage value is sold during the second year of the asset's life. How would the use of the straight-line method of depreciation instead of an accelerated depreciation method affect the amount of gain or loss on the sale of the plant asset?

	Gain	Loss
a.	Increase	Decrease
b.	Decrease	Increase
c.	No Effect	Increase
d.	No Effect	No Effect

Approach and Explanation: An accelerated method would result in more accumulated depreciation and, therefore, a lower book value. In contrast, the straight-line method results in less accumulated depreciation and a higher book value. This means a lower gain or a higher loss is computed if the asset is sold and the straight-line method is in use. One way you can prove this to yourself is to make up a set of facts (cost, service life, accelerated method to use) and assume the asset is sold for a given amount at the end of the second year. Compare that gain or loss with the gain or loss that would result if the straight-line method is used. (Solution = b.)

QUESTION
9. (L.O. 4) Roberts Truck Rental uses the group depreciation method for its fleet of trucks. When it retires one of its trucks and receives cash from a salvage company, the carrying value of property, plant, and equipment will be decreased by the:
   a. original cost of the truck.
   b. original cost of the truck less the cash proceeds.
   c. cash proceeds received.
   d. cash proceeds received and original cost of the truck.

Approach and Explanation: Write down the journal entry to record the disposal of the truck and analyze its effect. Remember that no gain or loss is recorded on the disposal when the group or composite method is used.

Cash	Proceeds	
Accumulated Depreciation...	**Plug**	
Truck	Original Cost	

In analyzing the entry's net effect on the book value (carrying amount) of property, plant, and equipment we find the following: (1) The decrease in Truck will reduce PP&E by the truck's original cost. (2) The debit to Accumulated Depreciation will increase PP&E by the excess of the truck's original cost over the proceeds from disposal. (3) Therefore, the net effect is to decrease PP&E by the amount of the cash proceeds from the sale. (Solution = c.)

QUESTION
10. (L.O. 4) Which of the following uses a straight-line depreciation calculation?

	Group Depreciation	Composite Depreciation
a.	Yes	Yes
b.	Yes	No
c.	No	Yes
d.	No	No

Explanation: Both the group and composite depreciation methods use a straight-line method calculation. Both methods perform one calculation for a group of assets. The group method is used for a collection of similar assets; whereas, the composite method is used for a group of dissimilar assets. Each method involves the computation of a total depreciable cost for all the assets included in one asset account and of an estimated weighted-average useful life. (Solution = a.)

QUESTION

11. (L.O. 4) The Schoen Company purchased a piece of equipment at the beginning of 2000 for $60,000. The equipment was being depreciated using the straight-line method over an estimated life of 20 years, with no salvage value. At the beginning of 2010, when the equipment had been in use for 10 years, the company paid $10,000 to overhaul the equipment. As a result of this improvement, the company estimates that the useful life of the equipment will be extended an additional five years. What should be the depreciation expense for this equipment in 2010?

a. $2,000
b. $2,667
c. $3,000
d. $1,867

Approach and Explanation: Write down the model or format to compute depreciation whenever there has been a change in the estimated service life and/or salvage value. Fill in the data of the case at hand and solve.

Cost	$ 60,000
Accumulated depreciation at 1/1/10	(30,000)[a]
Book value (before overhaul) at 1/1/10	30,000
Additional expenditure capitalized (if any)	10,000
Revised book value (after overhaul)	40,000
Current estimate of salvage value	0
Remaining depreciable cost at 1/1/10	40,000
Remaining years of useful life at 1/1/10	÷ 15[b]
Depreciation expense for 2010	$ 2,667
	(Solution = b.)

[a]Cost	$ 60,000
Original estimate of salvage	(0)
Original depreciable cost	60,000
Original service life in years	÷ 20
Original depreciation per year	3,000
Number of years used	x 10
Accumulated depreciation at 1/1/10	$ 30,000

[b]Original estimate of life in years	20
Number of years used	(10)
Additional years	5
Remaining years of useful life at 1/1/10	15

TIP:	Be careful when computing the length of time between two dates. The length of time between the beginning of 2000 and the beginning of 2010 is 10 years; whereas, the length of time between the end of 2000 and the beginning of 2010 is nine years. It is a common mistake to deduct one year from the other (2010 - 2000 = 10 years). As you can see from the foregoing, that will not always work. It is wise to write down the years that fall between the two dates and then count those years on your list. For example, the length of time between the end of 2007 and the beginning of 2010 is two years and is determined as follows:
	2008 1
	2009 2

QUESTION
12.   (L.O. 5) As the result of certain changes in circumstances indicating that the carrying amount of plant assets may not be recoverable, Timberlake Company reviewed the assets at the end of 2010 for impairment. The company estimates that it will receive net future cash inflows of $85,000 (undiscounted) as a result of continuing to hold and use these assets. The fair value of the assets at December 31, 2010 is estimated to be $75,000. The assets were acquired two years ago at a cost of $500,000 and have been depreciated using the straight-line method and a five-year service life. The loss from impairment to be reported at the end of 2010 is:
   a. $0.
   b. $215,000.
   c. $225,000.
   d. $300,000.

Explanation: The carrying amount of the asset at the end of 2010 is $300,000 [$500,000 cost less (2 years X $500,000 X 20%)], but the recoverable amount is only $85,000. Thus, the test for recognition of an impairment loss has been met according to SFAS 121. The impairment loss is measured by the excess of the carrying amount ($300,000) over the fair value ($75,000). Therefore, Timberlake should recognize a loss of $225,000 ($300,000 - $75,000 = $225,000). (Solution = c.)

QUESTION
13.   (L.O. 7) The book value of a plant asset is:
   a.   the fair market value of the asset at a balance sheet date.
   b.   the asset's acquisition cost less the total related depreciation recorded to date.
   c.   equal to the balance of the related accumulated depreciation account.
   d.   the assessed value of the asset for property tax purposes.

Approach and Explanation: Write down the definition for the term book value: **book value** is the asset's original cost (acquisition cost) less accumulated depreciation. Look for the answer selection that agrees with your definition. (Solution = b.)

QUESTION
14.   (L.O. 7) The rate of return on assets (ROA) can be computed by which of the following computations?

1. $\dfrac{\text{Net income}}{\text{Net sales}}$

2. $\dfrac{\text{Net sales}}{\text{Average total assets}}$

3.   Profit margin on sales x Asset turnover

4. $\dfrac{\text{Net income}}{\text{Average total assets}}$

   a.   Formula 1.
   b.   Formula 2.
   c.   Formula 3.
   d.   Formula 4.
   e.   Formula 3 or 4.

Explanation: Formula 1 above measures the rate of return on sales (**profit margin on sales ratio**). Formula 2 computes the **asset turnover ratio**. Formula 3 is one of two ways to compute the **rate of return on total assets**; Formula 4 is the second of two ways to compute the **rate of return on total assets.** (Solution = e.)

CHAPTER 12

INTANGIBLE ASSETS

OVERVIEW

The balance sheet classification for intangible assets is used to report assets which lack physical existence and are not financial instruments. For instance (1) bank deposits and accounts receivable both are intangible by a legal definition but are financial instruments and are properly classified as current assets for accounting purposes, and (2) investment in stock (or bonds) is intangible in nature but is a financial instrument and should be classified as either a current asset or a long-term investment for accounting purposes. Assets such as patents, trademarks, copyrights, franchises, trade names, subscription lists, licenses, and goodwill are intangible in nature and are classified in the Intangible Assets section of a balance sheet. Intangible assets derive their value from the rights and privileges granted to the company using the assets and are discussed in this chapter.

SUMMARY OF LEARNING OBJECTIVES

1. **Describe the characteristics of intangible assets.** Intangible assets have two main characteristics: (1) They lack physical existence, and (2) they are not financial instruments. In most cases, intangible assets provide services over a period of years. As a result, they are normally classified as long-term assets.

2. **Identify the costs to include in the initial valuation of intangible assets.** Intangibles are recorded at cost. Cost includes all costs of acquisition and expenditures necessary to make the intangible asset ready for its intended use. If intangibles are acquired in exchange for stock or other assets, the cost of the intangible is the fair value of the consideration given or the fair value of the intangible received, whichever is more clearly evident. When a company buys several intangibles, or a combination of intangibles and tangibles, in a "basket purchase, " it should allocate the cost on the basis of relative fair values.

3. **Explain the procedure for amortizing intangible assets.** Intangibles have either a limited useful life or an indefinite useful life. Companies amortize limited-life intangible assets. They do not amortize indefinite life intangible assets. Limited-life intangibles should be amortized by systematic charges to expense over their useful life. The useful life should reflect the period over which these assets will contribute to cash flows. The amount to report for amortization expense should reflect the pattern in which a company consumes or uses up the asset, if it can reliably determine that pattern. Otherwise use a straight-line approach.

4. **Describe the types of intangible assets.** Major types of intangibles are: (1) *marketing-related intangibles,* used in the marketing or promotion of products or services; (2) *customer-related intangibles,* resulting from interactions with outside parties; (3) *artistic-related intangibles,* giving ownership rights to such items as plays and literary works; (4) *contract-related intangibles,* representing the value of rights that arise from contractual arrangements; (5) *technology-related intangible* assets, relating to innovations or technological advances; and (6) *goodwill,* arising from business combinations.

5. **Explain the conceptual issues related to goodwill.** Unlike receivables, inventories, and patents that a company can sell or exchange individually in the marketplace, goodwill can be identified only with the business as a whole. Goodwill is a "going-concern" valuation and is recorded only when an entire business is purchased. A company should not capitalize (record in the accounts) goodwill generated internally. The future benefits of goodwill may have no

relationship to the costs incurred in the development of that goodwill. Goodwill may exist even in the absence of specific costs to develop it. Costs to maintain and restore goodwill are **not** capitalized.

6. **Describe the accounting procedures for recording goodwill.** To record goodwill, a company compares the fair value of the net tangible and identifiable intangible assets with the purchase price of the acquired business. The difference is considered goodwill. Goodwill is the residual. Goodwill is often identified on the balance sheet as the excess of cost over the fair value of the net assets acquired.

7. **Explain the accounting issues related to intangible-asset impairments.** Impairment of a long-lived asset occurs when the carrying amount of the asset is not recoverable. Companies use a recoverability test and a fair value test to determine impairments for limited-life intangible assets. They use only a fair value test for indefinite-life intangibles. Goodwill impairments require a two-step process: First, test the fair value of the reporting unit, then do the fair value test on implied goodwill.

8. **Identify the conceptual issues related to research and development costs.** R & D costs are not in themselves intangible assets, but research and development activities frequently result in the development of something a company patents or copyrights. The difficulties in accounting for R & D expenditures are: (1) identifying the costs associated with particular activities, projects, or achievements, and (2) determining the magnitude of the future benefits and length of time over which a company may realize such benefits. Because of these latter uncertainties, companies are required to expense all research and development costs when incurred.

9. **Describe the accounting for research and development costs and other similar costs.** The costs associated with R & D activities and the accounting treatment accorded them are as follows: (1) **Materials, equipment, and facilities:** Expense the entire costs, unless the items have alternative future uses (in R & D activities or otherwise), then carry materials as inventory (and allocate to R & D expense as consumed) and capitalize equipment and facilities (and depreciate as used). (2) **Personnel:** Salaries, wages, and other related costs of personnel engaged in R & D should be expensed as incurred. (3) **Purchased intangibles:** Expense the entire cost, unless the items have alternative future uses, then capitalize and amortize. (4) **Contract services:** The costs of services performed by others in connection with the reporting company's R & D should be expensed as incurred. (5) **Indirect costs:** A reasonable allocation of indirect costs (except for general and administrative costs, which must be related to be included) are included in R & D costs and expensed. Many costs have characteristics similar to R & D costs. Examples are start-up costs, initial operating losses, and advertising costs. For the most part, these costs are expensed as incurred, similar to the accounting for R & D costs.

10. **Indicate the presentation of intangible assets and related items.** On the balance sheet all intangible assets other than goodwill can be reported as a single separate item. Contra accounts are not normally shown separately for intangibles. If goodwill is present, it should be reported as a separate item. On the income statement, companies should report amortization expense and impairment losses for intangible assets as part of continuing operations. Goodwill impairment losses should be presented as a separate line item in the continuing operations section, unless the goodwill impairment is associated with a discontinued operation. The notes to the financial statements have additional detailed information. Financial statements must disclose the total R & D costs charged to expense each period for which an income statement is presented.

*11.   **Understand the accounting treatment for computer software costs.** Costs incurred in creating a software product should be charged to R & D expense when incurred until technological feasibility has been established for the product. Subsequent costs should be capitalized and amortized to current and future periods. Software that a company purchases for sale or lease to third parties and has alternative future uses may be capitalized and amortized using the greater of the percent-of-revenue approach or the straight-line approach.

*This material is covered in Appendix 12A in the text.

TIPS ON CHAPTER TOPICS

TIP:	A corporation's intangible items such as quality of management, customer loyalty, information infrastructure, trade secrets, knowledge, intellectual capital, and computer programming know-how often provide more value to a corporation than its "hard" assets (like buildings and equipment), and yet they are normally not reported on the company's balance sheet. These "soft" assets are all part of goodwill if and when they are purchased by another corporation as a part of the whole business in a business combination.
TIP:	The costs incurred to create intangibles are generally expensed as incurred. The only internal costs capitalized are direct costs incurred in obtaining the intangible, such as legal costs. Thus, even though a company may incur substantial research and development costs to create a product for which they obtain a patent, these costs are expensed. Only the legal costs to obtain the patent, the fees charged by the government for obtaining the patent, and any other direct costs of obtaining the patent are capitalized and charged to the Patent account.
TIP:	The systematic allocation of the cost of intangible assets to expense over the periods benefited is called **amortization**. Usually the straight-line method is employed. Each intangible with a limited life should be amortized over its useful life. The greater the uncertainty regarding an asset's useful life, the shorter is the amortization period. If an intangible becomes impaired or worthless, the asset should be written down or written off immediately to expense (or loss).
TIP:	When an intangible asset is amortized, the charge (debit) should be reported as an expense and the credit is made to the appropriate asset account. A separate accumulated amortization account may be used but usually the asset account is credited directly.
TIP:	In the event that the estimated life of a limited-life intangible asset is revised, the remaining carrying amount should be amortized over the remaining useful life.
TIP:	If no legal, regulatory, contractual, competitive, or other factors limit the useful life of an intangible asset, a company considers its useful life to be indefinite. **Indefinite** means that there is no foreseeable limit on the period of time over which the asset is expected to provide cash flows.
TIP:	Research and development (R & D) costs are to be expensed in the period incurred. The FASB established this guideline after a study revealed that very few R & D projects ever culminate in a successfully marketed product. When great uncertainty exists, the conservatism constraint (or principle) dictates that we choose the alternative with the **least** favorable effect on net income and on assets.
TIP:	To record goodwill when a business is acquired, the total fair market value of the net tangible and identifiable intangible assets is compared with the purchase price of the acquired business. The difference is considered goodwill, which is why goodwill is sometimes referred to as a "master valuation" account. Goodwill is the residual: the excess of cost over fair value of the identifiable net assets acquired.

> **TIP:** A manufacturing company has a patent on a manufacturing process and another patent on the finished product it is manufacturing. The periodic amortization of the patents will be classified as a cost of manufacturing and will become a part of the cost of the finished goods inventory. At the point of sale of the product, the cost of the product sold becomes cost of goods sold expense.

CASE 12-1

Purpose: (L. O. 1, 2, 3, 4) This case will review the six major categories of intangible assets and will discuss the guidelines for determining the cost of an intangible asset.

A classified balance sheet will report a company's curent assets followed by long-term investments, property, plant and equipment, and intangible assets.

Required:
(a)   Describe the two main characteristics of an asset to be classified as an intangible asset on the balance sheet.
(b)   List and describe the six major categories of intangible assets. Give examples of each.
(c)   Explain how the cost of an intangible asset is determined.
(d)   Explain how to determine whether an intangible asset is to be amortized or not amortized.

Solution to Case 12-1

(a)   Intangible assets have two main characteristics which are:
   1.   **They lack physical existence.** Unlike tangible assets such as property, plant, and equipment, intangible assets derive their value from the rights and privileges granted to the company using them.
   2.   **They are not a financial instrument.** Assets such as bank deposits, accounts receivable, and long-term investments in bonds and stocks lack physical substance, so they are intangible by nature; however, they are not classified as intangible assets for accounting purposes. These assets are financial instruments and derive their value from the right (claim) to receive cash or cash equivalents in the future.

(b)   There are many different types of intangibles, and they are often classified into the following six major categories.
   1.   **Marketing-related intangible assets** are those assets primarily used in the marketing or promotion of products or services. Examples are trademarks or trade names, newsprint mastheads, Internet domain names, and noncompetition agreements.

      A **trademark** or **trade name** is a word, phrase, or symbol that distinguishes or identifies a particular enterprise or product. Under common law, the right to use a trademark or trade name, whether it is registered or not, rests exclusively with the original user as long as the original user continues to use it. Registration with the U.S. Patent and Trademark Office provides legal protection for a number of renewals for periods of ten years each; therefore, you may properly consider the trademark or trade name to have an indefinite life (therefore, its cost is not amortized).

2. **Customer-related intangible assets** occur as a result of interactions with outside parties. Examples are customer lists, order or production backlogs, and both contractual and noncontractual customer relationships.

3. **Artistic-related intangible assets** involve ownership rights to plays, literary works, musical works, pictures, photographs, and video and audiovisual material. These ownership rights are protected by copyrights.

    A **copyright** is a federally granted right that all authors, painters, musicians, sculptors, and other artists have in their creations and expressions. A copyright is granted for the life of the creator plus 70 years. It gives the owner, or heirs, the exclusive right to reproduce and sell an artistic or published work. Copyrights are not renewable; thus they have a limited life and must be amortized.

4. **Contract-related intangible assets** represent the value of rights that arise from contractual arrangements. Examples are franchise and licensing agreements, construction permits, broadcast rights, and service or supply contracts.

    A **franchise** is a contractual arrangement under which the franchisor grants the franchisee the right to sell certain products or services, to use certain trademarks or trade names, or to perform certain functions, usually within a designated geographical area.

    Another type of franchise is the arrangement commonly entered into by a municipality (or other governmental body) and a business enterprise that uses public property. In such cases, a privately owned enterprise is permitted to use public property in performing its services. Examples are the use of public land for telephone or electric lines, the use of public waterways for a ferry service, or the use of the airwaves for radio or TV broadcasting. Such operating rights, obtained through agreement with governmental units or agencies, are frequently referred to as **licenses** or **permits.**

5. **Technology-related intangible assets** relate to innovations or technological advances. Examples are patented technology and trade secrets. Patents are granted by the U.S. Patent and Trademark Office. The two principal kinds of patents are **product patents** (which cover actual physical products) and process patents (which govern the process by which products are made). A **patent** gives the holder exclusive right to use, manufacture, and sell a product or process for a period of **20 years** without interference or infringement by others.

6. **Goodwill** is an excess of cost over the fair value of net identifiable assets acquired in a business combination. The cost (purchase price) of an acquired business is assigned where possible to the identifiable tangible and identifiable intangible net assets; the remainder is recorded in an unidentifiable intangible asset account called **Goodwill.** The only way goodwill can be sold is to sell the business. Goodwill acquired in a business combination is considered to have an indefinite life and therefore should **not** be amortized.

(c) The guidelines used in determining the cost of an intangible asset are similar to those you have already learned for determining the cost of inventory and property, plant, and equipment items. The cost of an intangible asset includes all costs of acquisition and expenditures necessary to make the intangible asset ready for its intended use for example, purchase price, legal fees, and other incidental costs. The cost of the intangible is measured by the fair market value (cash equivalent value) of the consideration given or by the fair market value of the intangible asset received, whichever is more clearly evident. When several intangibles, or a combination of intangibles and tangibles are bought in a "basket purchase," the total cost should be allocated to the individual items on the basis of their fair market values or on the basis of the relative sales values of the items. Thus, essentially the accounting treatment for purchased intangibles closely parallels that followed for purchased tangible assets.

TIP:	If a patent or trademark (or trade name) is acquired from another entity, its capitalization cost is the purchase price. If the product for which a patent is obtained is developed by the enterprise itself or if a trademark or trade name is developed internally, the capitalizable cost includes attorney fees, registration fees, consulting fees, design costs (for the trademark or trade name); successful legal defense costs, and other expenditures directly related to securing it (excluding research and development costs). When the total cost of a trademark, trade name, patent or any other intangible is insignificant, it can be expensed rather than capitalized.
TIP:	Legal fees and other costs incurred in successfully defending a patent lawsuit are debited to Patents, an asset account, because such a suit establishes the legal rights of the holder of the patent. Such costs should be amortized along with acquisition cost over the remaining useful life of the patent.

(d) An intangible asset has either a limited (finite) useful life or an indefinite useful life. An intangible asset with a limited life is amortized; an intangible asset with an indefinite life is **not** amortized. Limited-life intangibles should be amortized by systematic charges to expense over their useful lives. The useful life of an intangible asset should reflect the periods over which the assets will contribute to cash flows.

TIP:	**Indefinite** means that there is no foreseeable limit on the period of time over which the intangible asset is expected to provide cash flows.
TIP:	If the estimate of the useful life of an intangible asset changes, the remaining carrying amount should be amortized over the remaining useful life.
TIP:	The life of a trademark or trade name is generally indefinite; therefore, its cost is **not** amortized.
TIP:	The useful life of a patent or copyright is often less than its legal life. The costs of the patent or copyright should be allocated to the years in which the benefits are expected to be received.
TIP:	Franchises and licenses may be for a definite period of time, for an indefinite period of time, or perpetual. The enterprise securing the franchise or license carries an intangible account titled Franchise or License on its books only when there are costs (such as a lump sum payment in advance or legal fees and other expenditures) that are identified with the acquisition of the operating right. The cost of a franchise (or license) with a limited life should be amortized as operating expense over the life of the franchise. A franchise with an indefinite life, or a perpetual franchise, should be carried at cost and not amortized. Annual payments made under a franchise agreement (sometimes called royalty payments) should be reported as operating expenses in the period in which they are incurred because they do not represent an asset since they do not relate to future rights to use property.

EXERCISE 12-1

Purpose: (L.O. 2, 9) This exercise will give you practice in identifying items that are to be classified as costs associated with various intangible assets.

The Redskins Corporation incurred the following costs during January 2010:
1. Attorneys' fees in connection with organization of the corporation
2. Meetings of incorporators, state filing fees, and other organization costs to begin corporation
3. Improvements to leased offices prior to occupancy
4. Costs to design and construct a prototype
5. Testing of prototype
6. Troubleshooting breakdowns during commercial production
7. Fees paid to engineers and lawyers to prepare patent application; patent granted January 22
8. Payment of six months rent on leased facilities
9. Stock issue costs
10. Payment for a copyright
11. Materials purchased for future research and development projects; materials have alternative future use
12. Costs to advertise new business
13. Costs for one-time activities to start a new operation.

Instructions
(a)   For each item above, identify what account should be debited to record the expenditure.
(b)   Indicate in which classification the related account will be reported in the financial statements.

Solution to Exercise 12-1

(a) Account Debited	(b) Classification
1. Organization Cost	Operating Expense
2. Organization Cost	Operating Expense
3. Leasehold Improvements	Property, Plant, and Equipment (or Intangible Asset)
4. Research and Development Expense	Operating Expense
5. Research and Development Expense	Operating Expense
6. Factory Overhead	Allocated to Inventory and Cost of Goods Sold
7. Patent	Intangible Asset
8. Prepaid Rent	Current Asset
9. Organization Cost	Operating Expense
10. Copyright	Intangible Asset
11. Raw Materials Inventory	Current Asset
12. Advertising Expense	Operating Expense
13. Start-up costs	Operating Expense

EXERCISE 12-2

Purpose: (L.O. 2, 3) This exercise will review the accounting guidelines related to three types of intangible assets—patent, franchise, and trademark.

Information concerning Linda Heckenmueller Corporation's intangible assets follows:

1.   Heckenmueller incurred $85,000 of experimental and development costs in its laboratory to develop a patent which was granted on January 2, 2010. Legal fees and other costs associated with registration of the patent totaled $16,000. Heckenmueller estimates that the useful life of the patent will be 8 years; the legal life of the patent is 20 years.

2.   On January 1, 2010, Heckenmueller signed an agreement to operate as a franchisee of Cluck-Cluck Fried Chicken, Inc. for an initial franchise fee of $117,400. The agreement provides that the fee is not refundable and no future services are required of the franchisor. The agreement also provides that 5% of the revenue from the franchise must be paid to the franchisor annually. Heckenmueller's revenue from the franchise for 2010 was $1,800,000. Heckenmueller estimates the useful life of the franchise to be 10 years.

3.   A trademark was purchased from Wolfe Company for $64,000 on July 1, 2007. Expenditures for successful litigation in defense of the trademark totaling $16,000 were paid on July 1, 2010. Heckenmueller estimates that the trademark will have an indefinite life.

Instructions

(a)   Prepare a schedule showing the intangible asset section of Heckenmueller's balance sheet at December 31, 2010. Show supporting computations in good form.

(b)   Prepare a schedule showing all expenses resulting from the transactions that would appear on Heckenmueller's income statement for the year ended December 31, 2010. Show supporting computations in good form.

(AICPA adapted)

Solution to Exercise 12-2

(a)

Linda Heckenmueller Corporation
INTANGIBLE ASSETS
December 31, 2010

Patent, net of accumulated amortization of $2,000 (Schedule 1)	$ 14,000
Franchise, net of accumulated amortization of $11,740 (Schedule 2)	105,660
Trademark (Schedule 3)	80,000
Total intangible assets	$ 199,660

Schedule 1: Patent

Cost of securing patent on 1/2/10	$ 16,000
2010 amortization ($16,000 x 1/8)	(2,000)
Cost of patent, net of amortization	$ 14,000

Schedule 2: Franchise

Cost of franchise on 1/1/10	$ 117,400
2010 amortization ($117,400 x 1/10)	(11,740)
Cost of franchise, net of amortization	$ 105,660

Schedule 3: Trademark

Cost of trademark on 7/1/07	$ 64,000
Cost of successful legal defense on 7/1/10	16,000
Cost of trademark	$ 80,000

(b)

Linda Heckenmueller Corporation
EXPENSES RESULTING FROM SELECTED INTANGIBLES TRANSACTIONS
For the Year Ended December 31, 2010

Patent amortization (Schedule 1)	$ 2,000
Franchise amortization (Schedule 2)	11,740
Franchise royalty fee ($1,800,000 x 5%)	90,000
Total expenses	$103,740

> **TIP:** The $85,000 of research and development costs incurred in developing the patent would have been expensed prior to 2010 (per *SFAS No. 2*).

Approach: The ideal approach would be to prepare the journal entries associated with the facts given and post them to T-accounts to determine the balances to be reported on the income statement for the year ending December 31, 2010 and on the balance sheet at December 31, 2010. Under some circumstances (such as exam conditions), time may not permit these additional steps. You should at least think about and visualize the flow of the information through the accounts. This will greatly aid the successful completion of the schedules required.

Explanation:

1. Research and development costs are to be expensed in the period incurred. Thus, the $85,000 of experimental and development costs incurred in developing the patent would have been expensed prior to 2010. Legal fees and other costs associated with obtaining the patent should be matched with each of the eight years estimated to be benefited; therefore, the $16,000 of legal fees and registration costs should be capitalized and amortized.

2. The franchise rights will benefit future periods. Therefore, the costs associated with obtaining those rights should be capitalized and amortized over future periods. The acquisition cost is determined by the cash given ($117,400). The fact that "the fee is not refundable and no future services are required of the franchisor" has no impact on how the franchisee accounts for the franchise. The provision in the agreement which calls for the franchisee to pay 5% of the annual revenue from the franchise to the franchisor does not initially require any accounting treatment; an expense accrues as revenues are earned from use of the franchise. The capitalized franchise costs are to be amortized over the useful period of 10 years.

3. The purchase price of the trademark ($64,000) was capitalized in mid-2007 when the trademark was acquired. Expenditures of $16,000 for successful litigation in defense of the trademark rights are to be charged to the Trademark account because such a suit establishes the legal rights of the holder of the trademark (which benefits future periods). The cost of the trademark is not being amortized becasue the trademark is estimated to have an indefinite life.

EXERCISE 12-3

Purpose: (L.O. 5, 6) This exercise will review the procedure for determining the recorded value for purchased goodwill.

Sharon Gilkey, owner of Montana Designs, is negotiating with Chris Buffet for the purchase of Hospitality Galleries. The condensed balance sheet of Hospitality is given in abbreviated form below.

Hospitality Galleries
Balance Sheet
As of December 31, 2009

Assets		Liabilities and Stockholders' Equity		
Cash	$150,000	Accounts payable		$ 75,000
Land	100,000	Long-term notes payable		450,000
Building (net)	300,000	Total liabilities		525,000
Equipment (net)	275,000	Common stock	$300,000	
Copyright (net)	40,000	Retained earnings	40,000	340,000
Total assets	$865,000	Total liabilities and stockholders' equity		$865,000

Sharon and Chris agree that:
1. The fair value of the land exceeds its book value by $70,000.
2. The fair value of the equipment is less than its book value by $15,000.

Chris agrees to sell Hospitality Galleries for $530,000.

Instructions
(a) Prepare the entry to record the purchase of the gallery on Sharon's books.
(b) Prepare the entry to record the amortization of goodwill for 2010.

Solution to Exercise 12-3

(a) Journal Entry:

Cash	150,000	
Land	170,000	
Building	300,000	
Equipment	260,000	
Copyright	40,000	
Goodwill	135,000	
Accounts Payable		75,000
Long-term Note Payable		450,000
Cash		530,000

Approach and Explanation: Goodwill is the excess of the purchase price ($530,000) over the fair market value of the net identifiable assets. Net assets equal assets minus liabilities. Identifiable assets include all tangible and intangible assets other than goodwill. Thus, to compute goodwill; sum the fair values of the assets being conveyed, deduct the fair value of the liabilities being assumed, and compare the fair value of the net identifiable assets with the purchase price. The fair value of an asset is assumed to be equal to its book value unless the parties agree otherwise.

Computation:

Cash	$150,000
Land	170,000
Building, net	300,000
Equipment, net	260,000
Copyright, net	40,000
Accounts payable	(75,000)
Long-term note payable	(450,000)
Fair market value of net identifiable assets	$395,000
Purchase price	530,000
Value assigned to goodwill	$135,000

(b) There is no journal entry to record the amortization of goodwill for 2010. Goodwill acquired in the acquisition of a business is considered to have an indefinite life; therefore, the goodwill should **not** be amortized.

TIP: In a few cases (e.g. a forced liquidation or distressed sale due to the death of a company founder), the purchaser in a business combination pays **less than** the fair value of the identifiable net assets. That is, assets are worth more if sold individually than as a total package. Such a situation is referred to as a **bargain purchase** and the excess amount of fair value of identifiable net assets over purchase price is recorded as a gain (**not** extraordinary) by the purchaser.

ILLUSTRATION 12-2
ACCOUNTING FOR IMPAIRMENTS OF PROPERTY, PLANT AND EQUIPMENT AND LIMITED LIFE INTANGIBLES (L.O. 7)

A summary of the key concepts in accounting for impairments is presented below:

A **recoverability test** is used to determine whether an impairment has occurred: If the sum of the expected future net undiscounted cash flows (from the use of the asset and its eventual disposition) is less than the carrying amount of the asset, the asset has been impaired.

If the recoverability test indicates that an impairment has occurred, a loss is computed. The **impairment loss** is the amount by which the carrying amount of the asset exceeds its fair value. The fair value of an asset is measured by its market value (if an active market exists) or by the present value of expected future net cash flows (if an active market does not exist). If an asset is to be disposed of instead of held for use, the asset's net realizable value (fair value less cost to sell) is used as a measure of the net cash flows that will be received from this asset.

Subsequent to recognizing the loss from impairment, the following guidelines are to be followed:

1.   If the asset is to be held for use, it will be depreciated based on the new cost basis.
2.   If the asset is to be sold, no more depreciation is taken once the asset is no longer used.
3.   Restoration of the impairment loss is not permitted for an asset which is held for use.
4.   Restoration of the impairment loss is allowed for an asset held for sale. Because assets held for disposal will be recovered through sale rather than through use in operations, they are continually revalued. Each period they are reported at the lower of cost or net realizable value. Thus, an asset held for disposal can be written up or down in future periods, as long as the write-up does not produce a new carrying value greater than the carrying amount of the asset before an adjustment was made to reflect a decision to dispose of the asset.

TIP: Losses or gains related to impaired assets should be reported as part of income from continuing operations (generally in the "other expenses and losses" section). Thus, they are **not** classified as extraordinary items.

TIP: The impairment rule for goodwill is a two-step process. First, the fair value of the reporting unit should be compared to its carrying amount including goodwill. If the fair value of the reporting unit is greater than the carrying amount, goodwill is considered not to be impaired. However, if the fair value of the reporting unit is less than the carrying amount of the net assets, then a second step must be performed to determine whether impairment has occurred. In the second step, the fair value of the goodwill must be determined (implied value of goodwill) and compared to its carrying amount to determine if an impairment has occurred.

TIP: Companies should test indefinite-life intangibles for impairment at least annually.

TIP: The impairment test for an indefinite-life asset other than goodwill is a fair value test. This test compares the fair value of the asset with the asset's carrying amount. If the fair value of the asset is less than the carrying amount, an impairment loss is recognized. Companies use this one-step test because many indefinite-life assets easily meet the recoverability test (because cash flows may extend many years into the future). As a result, the recoverability test is not used.

CASE 12-2

Purpose: (L.O. 7) This case will examine the accounting for impairments.

In some cases, the carrying amount of a long-lived asset (property, plant, and equipment or intangible asset) is not recoverable, and therefore a write-off is needed.   This write-off is referred to as an impairment.

For each type of long-lived asset listed below, indicate the impairment test suitable for that kind of asset.

Type of Long-Lived Asset	Impairment Test
Property, plant, and equipment	_____
Limited-life intangible	_____
Indefinite-life intangible other than goodwill	_____
Goodwill	_____

Solution to Case 12-2

Type of Long-Lived Asset	Impairment Test
Property, plant, and equipment	Recoverability test, then fair value test
Limited-life intangible	Recoverability test, then fair value test
Indefinite-life intangible other than goodwill	Fair value test
Goodwill	Fair value test on reporting unit, then fair value test on implied goodwill

EXERCISE 12-4

Purpose: (L.O. 7) This exercise will illustrate the accounting for impairment of an intangible asset with a limited-life.

The following information relates to a patent owned by Pulido Company:

Cost	$4,300,000
Carrying amount	2,100,000
Expected future net cash flow	1,900,000
Fair value	1,500,000

Instructions

(a) Prepare the journal entry (if any) to record the impairment of the asset at December 31, 2009, assuming Pulido will continue to use the asset in the future.

(b) Using the same assumption as part (a) above, prepare the journal entry to record amortization expense for 2010 assuming the asset has a remaining useful life of 4 years at the beginning of 2010.

(c) Using the same assumption as part (a) above, prepare the journal entry (if any) at December 31, 2010, assuming the fair value of the asset has increased to $2,400,000.

(d) Prepare the journal entry (if any) to record the impairment of the asset at December 31, 2009, assuming Pulido ceased using the patent at the end of 2009 and intends to dispose of the patent in the coming year. Pulido expects to incur a $12,000 cost of disposal.

(e) Using the same assumption as part (d) above, prepare the journal entry at December 31, 2010 for amortization for 2010, assuming the asset has not been sold at that time.

(f) Using the same assumption as part (d) above, prepare the journal entry at December 31, 2010 assuming the asset has not been sold at that time and the fair value of the asset has increased to $2,400,000.

(g) Indicate the income statement classification of the account, Loss on Impairment.

Solution to Exercise 12-4

(a) Loss on Impairment... 600,000
          Patent (or Accumulated Patent Amortization).................   600,000

Approach and Explanation: Follow the guidelines in **Illustration 12-2:**

Recoverability test: The expected future net undiscounted cash flows from the use of the asset and its eventual disposition amount to $1,900,000 which is **less than** the carrying amount (book value) of the asset of $2,100,000; hence, the recoverability test indicates that an impairment has occurred.

Impairment loss: The impairment loss ($600,000) is the amount by which the carrying amount of the asset ($2,100,000) exceeds its fair value ($1,500,000).

(b) Amortization of Patent Expense.. 375,000
          Patent...   375,000

Explanation: After an impairment is recognized, the reduced carrying amount of the patent is its new cost basis. The patent's new cost should be amortized over its remaining useful life (which may be shorter but not longer than its remaining legal life).

(c) No journal entry is to be recorded at December 31, 2010 due to the increase in fair value of the patent. Restoration of a previously recognized impairment loss is not permitted when the asset is expected to be held and used by the company in the future.

(d) Loss on Impairment.. 612,000
          Patent...   612,000

Approach and Explanation: Follow the guidelines in **Illustration 12-2:**

Recoverability test: The expected future net undiscounted cash flows from the asset's expected disposition is measured by the asset's net realizable value (fair value less cost to sell) which is $1,500,000 less $12,000 equals $1,488,000. The expected future net cash flows of $1,488,000 is less than the carrying amount of the asset ($2,100,000); hence, the recoverability test indicates that an impairment has occurred.

Impairment loss: The impairment loss ($612,000) is the amount by which the carrying amount of the asset ($2,100,000) exceeds the asset's fair value ($1,500,000) reduced by the estimated disposal cost ($12,000).

(e) There is no journal entry for amortization of the patent in 2010.

Explanation: No amortization is taken once an asset is no longer used in operations.

(f)	Patent..	612,000
	Gain from Restoration of Impairment Loss.........	612,000

Explanation: Restoration of the impairment loss is allowed for an asset held for sale. An asset held for disposal can be written up or down in future periods, as long as the write-up does not produce a new carrying value greater than the carrying amount of the asset before an adjustment was made to reflect a decision to dispose of the asset.

(g)   Loss on Impairment is reported in the "other expense and loss" section of the income statement.

ILLUSTRATION 12-3
ACCOUNTING FOR R & D ACTIVITIES (L.O. 9)

To differentiate research and development costs from other similar costs, the FASB issued the following definitions in *SFAS 2:*

> **Research** is planned search or critical investigation aimed at discovery of new knowledge with the hope that such knowledge will be useful in developing a new product or service ... or a new process or technique ... or in bringing about a significant improvement to an existing product or process.

> **Development** is the translation of research findings or other knowledge into a plan or design for a new product or process or for a significant improvement to an existing product or process whether intended for sale or use. It includes the conceptual formulation, design, and testing of product alternatives, construction of prototypes, and operation of pilot plants. It does not include routine or periodic alterations to existing products, production lines, manufacturing processes, and other on-going operations even though those alterations may represent improvements; it does not include market research or market testing activities.

Many costs have characteristics similar to those of research and development costs, for instance, costs of relocation and rearrangement of facilities, start-up costs for a new plant or new retail outlet, marketing research costs, promotion costs of a new product or service, and costs of training new personnel. To distinguish between R & D and those other similar costs, the following schedule (from *SFAS 2*) provides (1) examples of activities that typically would be **included** in research and development, and (2) examples that typically would be **excluded** from research and development.

1. R & D Activities

(a) Laboratory research aimed at discovery of new knowledge.

(b) Searching for applications of new research findings.

(c) Conceptual formulation and design of possible product or process alternatives.

(d) Testing in search for or evaluation of product or process alternatives.

(e) Modification of the design of a product or process.

(f) Design, construction, and testing of preproduction prototypes and models.

(g) Design of tools, jigs, molds, and dies involving new technology.

(h) Design, construction, and operation of a pilot plant not useful for commercial production.

(i) Engineering activity required to advance the design of a product to the manufacturing stage.

2. Activities Not Considered R & D

(a) Engineering follow-through in an early phase of commercial production.

(b) Quality control during commercial production including routine testing.

(c) Trouble-shooting breakdowns during commercial production.

(d) Routine, on-going efforts to refine, enrich, or improve the qualities of an existing product.

(e) Adaptation of an existing capability to a particular requirement or customer's need.

(f) Periodic design changes to existing products.

(g) Routine design of tools, jigs, molds, and dies.

(h) Activity, including design and construction engineering related to the construction, relocation, rearrangement, or startup of facilities or equipment.

(i) Legal work on patent applications, sale, licensing, or litigation.

TIP: R & D activities do not include routine or periodic alterations to existing products, production lines, manufacturing processes, and other ongoing operations, even though these alterations may represent improvements. Routine ongoing efforts to refine, enrich, or improve the qualities of an existing product are not considered R & D activities.

TIP: Disclosure should be made in the financial statements (generally in the notes) of the total R & D costs charged to expense each period for which an income statement is presented.

The costs associated with R & D activities and the accounting treatment accorded them are as follows: (1) **Materials, equipment, and facilities:** Expense the entire costs, unless the items have alternative future uses (in R & D activities or otherwise), then carry materials as inventory (and allocate to R & D expense as consumed) and capitalize equipment and facilities (and depreciate as used). (2) **Personnel:** Salaries, wages, and other related costs of personnel engaged in R & D should be expensed as incurred. (3) **Purchased intangibles:** Expense the entire cost, unless the items have alternative future uses, then capitalize and amortize. (4) **Contract services:** The costs of services performed by others in connection with the reporting company's R & D should be expensed as incurred. (5) **Indirect costs:** A reasonable allocation of indirect costs (except for general and administrative costs, which must be related to be included) are included in R & D costs and expensed. Many costs have characteristics similar to R & D costs. Examples are start-up costs, initial operating losses, and advertising costs. For the most part, these costs are expensed as incurred, similar to the accounting for R & D costs.

EXERCISE 12-5

Purpose: (L.O. 8, 9) This exercise will give you practice in identifying activities that constitute R & D activities.

Listed below are four independent situations involving research and development costs:

1. During 2010 Bebe Co. incurred the following costs:

Research and development services performed by Way Co. for Bebe	$ 325,000
Testing for evaluation of new products	300,000
Laboratory research aimed at discovery of new knowledge	375,000
Research and development services performed by Bebe for Elway Co.	220,000

How much should Bebe report as research and development expense for the year ended December 31, 2010?

2. Holly Corp. incurred the following costs during the year ended December 31, 2010:

Design, construction, & testing of preproduction prototypes & models	$ 220,000
Routine, on-going efforts to refine, enrich, or otherwise improve upon the qualities of an existing product	250,000
Quality control during commercial production including routine testing of products	300,000
Laboratory research aimed at discovery of new knowledge	360,000
Conceptual formulation and design of possible product alternatives	100,000

What is the total amount to be classified and expensed as research and development for 2010?

3. Polanski Company incurred costs in 2010 as follows:

Equipment acquired for use in various R & D projects (current and future)	$ 890,000
Depreciation on the equipment above	135,000
Materials used in R & D	300,000
Compensation costs of personnel in R & D	400,000
Outside consulting fees for R & D work	150,000
Indirect costs appropriately allocated to R & D	260,000

What is the total amount of research and development expense that should be reported in Polanski's 2010 income statement?

4. Liverpool Inc. incurred the following costs during the year ended December 31, 2010:

Laboratory research aimed at discovery of new knowledge	$ 175,000
Routine design of tools, jigs, molds, and dies	60,000
Radical modification to the formulation of a chemical product	125,000
Research and development costs reimbursable under a contract to perform R & D for Johnathon King, Inc.	350,000
Testing for evaluation of new products	275,000

What is the total amount to be classified and expensed as research and development for 2010?

Instructions
Provide the correct answer to each of the four situations.

Solution to Exercise 12-5

1. Research and development services performed by Way Co. for Bebe $ 325,000
    Testing for evaluation of new products   300,000
    Laboratory research aimed at discovery of new knowledge   375,000
        Total R & D expense $ 1,000,000

> **TIP:** R & D costs related to R & D activities conducted for other entities are classified as a receivable (because of the impending reimbursement).

2. Design, construction & testing of preproduction prototypes & models $ 220,000
    Laboratory research aimed at discovery of new knowledge   360,000
    Conceptual formulation & design of possible product alternatives   100,000
        Total R & D expense $ 680,000

3. Depreciation on the equipment acquired for use in
        various R & D projects $ 135,000
    Materials used in R & D   300,000
    Compensation costs of personnel in R & D   400,000
    Outside consulting fees for R & D work   150,000
    Indirect costs appropriately allocated to R & D   260,000
        Total R & D expense $ 1,245,000

> **TIP:** Equipment, facilities, and purchased intangibles that have **alternative future uses** (in other R & D projects or otherwise) are to be **capitalized**; the **related depreciation and amortization are to be classified as R & D**.

4. Laboratory research aimed at discovery of new knowledge $ 175,000
    Radical modification to the formulation of a chemical product   125,000
    Testing for evaluation of new products   275,000
        Total R & D expense $ 575,000

Approach: Read the requirement of each situation before you begin detailed work on the first one. Notice that all four items deal with research and development costs. Therefore, review in your mind the definitions of the words "research" and "development." Recall what you can from the list of activities considered to be R & D. Think of why the items logically appear on the list. It is important to think about these items **before** you dig into the questions because details in the situations may mislead you. To minimize confusion, organize your thoughts and recall what you know about the subject before you begin to process the data at hand.

Explanation: Refer to **Illustration 12-3** for the definitions and examples of research and development activities.

CASE 12-3

Purpose: (L.O. 9) This case is designed to give you practice in differentiating expenditures which are classified as research and development costs and expenditures which are not included with R & D.

Instructions

Various types of expenditures are listed below. Indicate the accounting treatment appropriate for each type of expenditure listed.

Type of Expenditure   **Accounting Treatment**

1.   Construction of long-range research facility for use in current and future projects (three story, 400,000-square-foot building).

2.   Acquisition of R & D equipment for use on current project only.

3.   Acquisition of machinery to be used on current and future R & D projects.

4.   Purchase of materials to be used on current and future R & D projects.

5.   Salaries of research staff designing new laser bone scanner.

6.   Research costs incurred under contract with another corporation and billable to that company monthly.

7.   Material, labor, and overhead costs of prototype laser scanner.

8.   Costs of testing prototype and design modifications.

9.   Legal fees to obtain patent on new laser scanner.

10.   Executive salaries.

11.   Cost of marketing to promote new laser scanner.

12.   Engineering costs incurred to advance the laser scanner to full production stage.

13.   Cost of successfully defending patent on laser scanner.

14.   Commissions to sales staff marketing new laser scanner.

SOLUTION TO CASE 12-3

Type of Expenditure	Accounting Treatment
1. Construction of long-range research facility for use in current and future projects (three story, 400,000-square-foot building).	Capitalize and depreciate as R & D expense.
2. Acquisition of R & D equipment for use on current project only.	Expense immediately as R & D.
3. Acquisition of machinery to be used on current and future R & D projects.	Capitalize and depreciate as R & D expense.
4. Purchase of materials to be used on current and future R & D projects.	Inventory and allocate to R & D projects; expense as consumed.
5. Salaries of research staff designing new laser bone scanner.	Expense immediately as R & D.
6. Research costs incurred under contract with another corporation and billable to that company monthly.	Record as a receivable (reimbursable expenses).
7. Material, labor, and overhead costs of prototype laser scanner.	Expense immediately as R & D.
8. Costs of testing prototype and design modifications.	Expense immediately as R & D.
9. Legal fees to obtain patent on new laser scanner.	Capitalize as patent and amortize to overhead as part of cost of goods manufactured.
10. Executive salaries.	Expense as operating expense (general and administrative).
11. Cost of marketing to promote new laser scanner.	Expense as operating expense (selling).
12. Engineering costs incurred to advance the laser scanner to full production stage.	Expense immediately as R & D.
13. Cost of successfully defending patent on laser scanner.	Capitalize as patent and amortize to overhead as part of cost of goods manufactured.
14. Commissions to sales staff marketing new laser scanner.	Expense as operating expense (selling).

TIP: Refer to **Illustration 12-3** for an explanation of the types of costs associated with R & D activities and the accounting treatment accorded them.

TIP: Refer to **Item 6** above. Sometimes one enterprise conducts R & D activities for other entities under a contractual arrangement. In this case, the contract usually specifies that all direct costs, certain specific indirect costs, plus a profit element, should be reimbursed to the enterprise performing the R & D work. Because reimbursement is expected, such R & D costs should be recorded as a receivable. It is the company for whom the work has been performed that reports these costs as R & D and expenses them as incurred.

ANALYSIS OF MULTIPLE-CHOICE TYPE QUESTIONS

QUESTION

1. (L.O. 2) Innoventions Inc. acquired a patent from Whizkid Inc. on January 1, 2010, in exchange for $7,000 cash and an investment security that had been acquired in 2006. The following facts pertain:

Original cost of investment	$ 14,000
Carrying value of patent on books of Whizkid Inc.	4,500
Fair market value of the investment security on January 1, 2010	23,000

The cost of the patent to be recorded by Innoventions Inc. is:
   a. $7,000.
   b. $11,500.
   c. $21,000.
   d. $30,000.
   e. None of the above.

Approach and Explanation: Recall the guideline for determining the cost of any intangible asset. The cost of an intangible asset includes all costs incurred to acquire the asset. The historical cost principle dictates that cost be measured by the fair market value (i.e., cash equivalent value) of the consideration given or by the fair market value of the consideration received, whichever is the more objectively determinable. Innoventions Inc. gave $7,000 cash plus the investment security with a fair market value of $23,000 at the date of the exchange. The cost of the patent is, therefore, $30,000. (Solution = d.)

QUESTION

2. (L.O. 4) The adjusted trial balance of the Laventhal Corporation as of December 31, 2010 includes the following accounts:

Trademark	$ 30,000
Discount on bonds payable	37,500
Organization costs	12,500
Excess of cost over fair value of identifiable net assets of acquired business	175,000
Advertising costs (to promote goodwill)	20,000

What should be reported as total intangible assets on Laventhal's December 31, 2010 balance sheet?
   a. $205,000
   b. $230,000
   c. $237,500
   d. $275,000

Approach and Explanation: Identify the classification of each item listed. Sum the ones you identify as being intangible assets.

Trademark	$ 30,000
Excess of cost over fair value of identifiable net assets of acquired business	175,000
Total intangible assets	$ 205,000

Discount on bonds payable is to be classified as a contra liability. Organization costs are to be expensed as incurred. Advertising costs incurred are to be reported as an expense on the income statement. The costs to develop, maintain, or restore goodwill are **not** to be capitalized. Only the costs to acquire goodwill with a going business can be recorded as goodwill. The "excess of cost over fair value of net identifiable net assets of acquired business" is a technical term referring to goodwill. (Solution = a.)

QUESTION

3. (L.O. 3, 4) A patent with a remaining legal life of 12 years and an estimated useful life of 8 years was acquired for $288,000 by Bradley Corporation on January 2, 2006. In January 2010, Bradley paid $18,000 in legal fees in a successful defense of the patent. What should Bradley record as patent amortization for 2010?
    a. $24,000
    b. $36,000
    c. $38,250
    d. $40,500

Approach and Explanation: Analyze the Patent account. Use the data given to compute the amounts reflected therein and the resulting amortization for 2010.

Cost at beginning of 2006	$ 288,000
Amortization for 2006-2009	(144,000)*
Book value at beginning of 2010	144,000
Legal fees capitalized	18,000
Revised book value, beginning of 2010	162,000
Remaining years of life	÷ 4
Amortization for 2010	$ 40,500 (Solution = d.)

*Beginning of 2006, patent cost	$ 288,000
Estimated years of service life	÷ 8
Annual amortization for 2006-2009	36,000
Number of years used	4
Total amortization 2006-2009	$ 144,000

QUESTION

4. (L.O. 3, 4) On January 1, 2010, Teeple Corporation acquired a patent for $30,000. Due to the quickly changing technology associated with the patent, Teeple is amortizing the cost of the patent over 5 years. What portion of the patent cost will Temple defer to years subsequent to 2010?
    a. $0
    b. $6,000
    c. $24,000
    d. $30,000

Explanation: $30,000 ÷ 5 yrs. = $6,000 amortization per year.
If $6,000 is amortized, then the amount to defer is computed as follows:

Total patent cost	$ 30,000
Amount amortized in 2010	(6,000)
Amount to defer to subsequent periods	$ 24,000 (Solution = c.)

> **TIP:** Note the importance of reading the question carefully. An intermediate step—the computation of the $6,000 amortization amount for 2010—is one of the distracters. You should read the last sentence of the question stem first to understand the essence of the problem. It is wise to write down the essential computation to keep your focus:
> Total Patent Cost
> - Amount to Amortize in 2010
> = Amount to Defer

QUESTION

5. (L.O. 4) The legal life of a patent is:
    a.   17 years.
    b.   20 years.
    c.   40 years.
    d.   The life of the inventory plus 50 years.

Explanation: A patent offers its holder an exclusive right to use, manufacture, and sell a product or process over a period of 20 years without interference or infringement by others. It is not subject to renewal. (Solution = b.)

QUESTION
6.   (L.O. 4) The cost of permits and licenses are material to the entity for whom you are accounting. The cost of these items should be:
        a.   expensed in the period acquired.
        b.   expensed over the useful life of the items.
        c.   charged against paid-in capital.
        d.   capitalized but not amortized.

Explanation: Licenses and permits offer the holder certain rights. Like all other intangible assets, the cost of these items should be matched with the periods benefited. To comply with the matching principle, the cost of an intangible asset is to be amortized over its useful life. (Solution = b.)

QUESTION
7.   (L.O. 2, 6) The costs of intangible assets which are internally created are typically:
        a.   capitalized but not amortized.
        b.   capitalized and amortized over a long period of time.
        c.   capitalized and amortized over a short period of time.
        d.   expensed as incurred.

Explanation: The following is helpful to keep in mind:

Type of Intangible	Manner Acquired		Amortization
	Purchased	Internally Created	
Limited-life intangibles	Capitalize	Expense, except direct costs	Over useful life
Indefinite-life intangibles	Capitalize	Expense	Do not amortize

If you purchase a patent from an inventor or an owner, the cost of that patent is capitalized. If you develop (internally generate) a product yourself, the research and development costs related to the development of the product or idea that is subsequently patented must be expensed as incurred. However, other costs incurred in connection with securing a patent, as well as attorney's fees and other unrecovered costs of a successful legal suit to protect the patent, can be capitalized as a part of the patent cost. (Solution = d.)

QUESTION
8.   (L.O. 7) As the result of certain changes in circumstances indicating that the carrying amount of plant assets may not be recoverable, Timberlake Company reviewed the assets at the end of 2010 for impairment. The company estimates that it will receive net future cash inflows of $85,000 (undiscounted) as a result of continuing to hold and use these assets. The fair value of the assets at December 31, 2010 is estimated to be $75,000. The assets were acquired two years ago at a cost of $500,000 and have been depreciated using the straight-line method and a five-year service life. The loss from impairment to be reported at the end of 2010 is:
        a. $0.
        b. $215,000.
        c. $225,000.
        d. $300,000.

Explanation: The carrying amount of the asset at the end of 2010 is $300,000 [$500,000 cost less (2 years X $500,000 X 20%)], but the recoverable amount is only $85,000. Thus, the test for recognition of an impairment loss has been met according to *SFAS 144*. The impairment loss is measured by the excess of the carrying amount ($300,000) over the fair value ($75,000). Therefore, Timberlake should recognize a loss of $225,000 ($300,000 - $75,000 = $225,000). (Solution = c.)

QUESTION

9. (L.O. 7) The carrying amount of an intangible is:
    a.   the fair market value of the asset at a balance sheet date.
    b.   the asset's acquisition cost less the total related amortization recorded to date.
    c.   equal to the balance of the related accumulated amortization account.
    d.   the assessed value of the asset for intangible tax purposes.

Approach and Explanation: Write down the definition for the term book value: **book value** is the asset's original cost (acquisition cost) less accumulated amortization. Look for the answer selection that agrees with your definition. (Solution = b.)

QUESTION

10.   (L.O. 7) Windsor Corporation was organized in 2009 and began operations at the beginning of 2010. Prior to the start of operations, the following costs were incurred in 2009:

Attorneys' fees for assistance in obtaining corporate charter and drafting related documents	$ 33,000
Meetings of incorporators	14,000
Improvements to leased office space prior to occupancy	48,000
Fees to promoters to help locate buyers for Windsor's common stock	21,000
	$116,000

What should be the balance of the Organization Expense account based on the above?
    a. $21,000.
    b. $33,000.
    c. $68,000.
    d. $116,000.
    e.   None of the above.

Approach and Explanation: Before reading through the list of costs incurred, define "organization costs" and think of the most common examples. **Organization costs** are costs incurred in the formation of a corporation such as fees to promoters, legal fees, state fees of various sorts, and certain promotional expenditures. They are to be expensed in the period incurred. Windsor should charge the following to Organization Expense:

Attorneys' fees for incorporation	$ 33,000	
Meetings of incorporators	14,000	
Fees to promoters	21,000	
Total organization costs	$ 68,000	(Solution = c.)

TIP: The $48,000 of improvements to leased office space prior to occupancy should be recorded in the Leasehold Improvements account.

QUESTION

11. (L.O. 8) Motts Corporation purchased the following items at the beginning of 2010:

Materials to be used in R & D activities; these materials have alternative future uses and they remain unused at the end of 2010.	$ 50,000
Materials to be used in R & D activities; these materials do not have alternative future uses and $12,000 of them remain unused at the end of 2010.	33,000
Equipment to be used in R & D activities; this equipment was used in one R & D project during 2010 and is expected to be used in other R & D projects to be undertaken over the next 5 years. It has no residual value. Motts normally uses the straight-line depreciation method for equipment.	100,000
Total	$ 183,000

Based on the above information, Motts should report R & D expenses for 2010 of:

a. $183,000.
b. $103,000.
c. $53,000.
d. $21,000.
e. None of the above.

Approach and Explanation: Mentally review the proper accounting treatment for materials and equipment acquired for use in R & D activities. The cost of materials acquired for use in R & D activities should be expensed in the period acquired unless the items have alternative future uses (in R & D projects or otherwise); then they should be carried as inventory and allocated to R & D expense as used. The cost of equipment and facilities acquired for use in R & D activities should be expensed in the period acquired unless the items have alternative future uses (in R & D projects or otherwise); then they should be capitalized and depreciated as used (the resulting depreciation should be classified as R & D expense). Thus, Motts would have the following R & D expense for 2010: (Solution = c.)

Materials acquired, no future alternative use	$ 33,000
Depreciation on equipment used in R & D activities	
($100,000 ÷ 5 years)	20,000
Total R & D expense for 2010	$ 53,000

QUESTION

12. (L.O. 8) In 2010, Barry Sanders Corporation incurred research and development costs as follows:

Equipment	$ 200,000
Personnel	300,000
Indirect costs	100,000
Total	$ 600,000

These costs relate to a product that will be marketed in 2011. It is estimated that these costs will be recouped by December 31, 2013. The equipment has no alternative future use. What is the amount of research and development costs that should be charged to income in 2010?

a. $0
b. $100,000
c. $400,000
d. $600,000

Explanation: All R & D costs are to be expensed in the period incurred. Equipment used in R & D activities that has alternative future use would be capitalized and depreciated. This equipment has no alternative use, so it is expensed immediately. A reasonable allocation of indirect costs should be included in R & D. Costs of personnel engaged in R & D activities are to be expensed in the period incurred. (Solution = d.)

QUESTION

13.   (L.O. 9) The costs of organizing a corporation include legal fees, fees paid to the state of incorporation, fees paid to promoters, and the costs of meetings for organizing the promoters. These costs are said to benefit the corporation for the entity's entire life. These costs should be:
   a.   capitalized and never amortized.
   b.   capitalized and amortized over 40 years.
   c.   capitalized and amortized over 5 years.
   d.   expensed as incurred.

Explanation: Although the accounting profession recognizes that organization costs are incurred with the expectation that future revenues will occur or increased efficiencies will result, the determination of the amount and timing of future benefits is so difficult that a conservative approach is required. All start-up costs, which include organization costs, are to be expensed in the period incurred. The costs of issuing stock (such as the fees paid to underwriters in issuance of stock) are usually treated as a reduction of additional paid-in capital (see **Chapter 15**). (Solution = d.)

QUESTION

14.   (L.O. 9) A development stage enterprise should use the same generally accepted accounting principles that apply to established operating enterprises for:

	Recognition of Revenue	Recognition of Expenses
a.	Yes	Yes
b.	No	No
c.	No	Yes
d.	Yes	No

Explanation: In *SFAS 7* the FASB indicates that the accounting practices and reporting standards should be no different for an enterprise trying to establish a new business than they are for other enterprises. Thus, the "same generally accepted accounting principles that apply to established operating enterprises shall govern the recognition of revenue by a development stage enterprise (DSE) and shall determine whether a cost incurred by a DSE is to be charged to expense when incurred or is to be capitalized or deferred." This means that items constituting preoperating costs should be expensed unless the same costs would be deferred by an established business; the fact that the costs are incurred before the entity has any significant revenue earned is not by itself justification for deferral of such costs. Treating preoperating costs as expenses often results in the reporting of an operating loss in the year of start up of a new entity. (Solution = a.)

QUESTION

15.   (L.O. 10) The total amount of patent cost amortized to date is usually:
   a.   shown in a separate Accumulated Patent Amortization account which is shown contra to the Patent account.
   b.   shown in the current income statement.
   c.   reflected as credits in the Patent account.
   d.   reflected as a contra property, plant and equipment item.

Explanation: In accounting for intangible assets, the amortization of an asset is usually credited directly to the intangible asset account rather than shown separately in a contra asset account. (Solution = c.)

CHAPTER 13

CURRENT LIABILITIES AND CONTINGENCIES

OVERVIEW

Initially, the resources (assets) of a business have to come from entities outside of the particular organization. Two main sources of resources are creditor sources (liabilities) and owners' sources (owners' equity). In this chapter, we begin our in-depth discussion of liabilities.

Due to the nature of some business activities, it is common to find some goods and services being received while payment for these items is made days or weeks later. Therefore, at a specific point in time, such as a balance sheet date, we may find that a business has obligations for merchandise received from suppliers (accounts payable), for money it has borrowed (notes payable), for interest incurred (interest payable), for sales tax charged to customers which has not yet been remitted to the government (sales taxes payable), for salaries and wages (salaries and wages payable), and for other amounts due to government agencies in connection with employee compensation. Such payables are reported as current (short-term) liabilities, because they will fall due within the next 12 months and will require the use of current assets (cash, in these cases) to liquidate them. Accounting for these and other current liabilities is discussed in this chapter.

SUMMARY OF LEARNING OBJECTIVES

1. **Describe the nature, type, and valuation of current liabilities.** Current liabilities are obligations whose liquidation a company reasonably expects to require the use of current assets or the creation of other current liabilities. Theoretically, liabilities should be measured by the present value of the future outlay of cash required to liquidate them. In practice, companies usually record and report current liabilities at their full maturity value. There are several types of current liabilities. The following list details the most common types: (1) accounts payable, (2) notes payable, (3) current maturities of long-term debts, (4) dividends payable, (5) customer advances and deposits, (6) unearned revenue, (7) taxes payable, and (8) employee-related liabilities.

2. **Explain the classification issues of short-term debt expected to be refinanced.** A short-term obligation is excluded from current liabilities if both of the following conditions are met: (1) the company must intend to refinance the obligation on a long-term basis, *and* (2) it must demonstrate an ability to consummate the refinancing.

3. **Identify types of employee-related liabilities.** The employee-related liabilities are: (1) payroll deductions, (2) compensated absences, and (3) bonus agreements.

4. **Identify the criteria used to account for and disclose gain and loss contingencies.** Gain contingencies are not recorded. They are disclosed in the notes only when the probability is high that a gain contingency will become a reality. A company should accrue an estimated loss from a loss contingency by charging expense and recording a liability only if both of the following conditions are met: (1) Information available prior to the issuance of the financial statements indicates that it is probable that a liability has been incurred at the date of the financial statements, and (2) the amount of the loss can be reasonably estimated.

5. **Explain the accounting for different types of loss contingencies.** (1) **Litigation:** The following factors must be considered in determining whether a liability should be recorded with respect to pending or threatened litigation and actual or possible claims and assessments: (a) the time period in which the underlying cause for action occurred; (b) the probability of an unfavorable outcome; and, (c) the ability to make a reasonable estimate of the amount of loss. (2) **Warranties:** If it is probable that customers will make claims under warranties relating to goods or services that have been sold and it can reasonably estimate the costs involved, the company uses the accrual method. Under the accrual basis, it charges warranty costs to operating expense in the year of sale. (3) **Sales promotions:** Premiums, coupon offers, and rebates are made to stimulate sales. Companies should charge their costs to expense in the period of the sale that benefits from the promotion (premium) plan. (4) **Asset retirement obligations**: A company must recognize asset retirement obligations when it has an existing legal obligation related to the retirement of a long-lived asset and it can reasonably estimate the amount.

6. **Indicate how to present and analyze current liabilities and contingencies.** The current liability accounts are commonly presented as the first classification in the liabilities and stockholders' equity section of the balance sheet. Within the current liabilities section, companies may list the accounts in order of maturity, in descending order of amount, or in order of liquidation preference. Detail and supplemental information concerning current liabilities should be sufficient to meet the requirement of full disclosure. If the loss is either probable or estimable but not both, and if there is at least a reasonable possibility that a company may have incurred a liability, it should disclose in the notes both the nature of the contingency and an estimate of the possible loss. Two ratios used to analyze liquidity are the current and acid-test ratios.

TIPS ON CHAPTER TOPICS

TIP: **Current liabilities** are often called **short-term liabilities** or **short-term debt**. **Noncurrent liabilities** are often called **long-term liabilities** or **long-term debt**.

TIP: **Current liabilities** are obligations whose liquidation is reasonably expected to require the use of existing resources properly classifiable as current assets, or the creation of other current liabilities. **Noncurrent liabilities** are obligations which do not meet the criteria to be classified as current.

TIP: An estimated loss from a loss contingency should be accrued by a charge to expense and a credit to a liability if both of the following conditions are met: (1) it is **probable** (likely) that a liability has been incurred at the date of the balance sheet, and (2) the amount of the loss can be **reasonably estimated**. If the loss is either probable or estimable but not both, or if there is at least a **reasonable possibility** that a liability has been incurred, the contingency must be disclosed in the notes (but not accrued). If it is only **remotely possible** (unlikely) that a liability has been incurred, no accrual or note disclosure is required (there are some exceptions to this guideline).

TIP: Self-insurance is not insurance; rather, it is risk assumption. Any company that assumes its own risks puts itself in the position of incurring expenses or losses as they occur. It is **not** generally acceptable to charge expense and report a liability prior to the occurrence of the event even if the amount of loss is reasonably estimable.

EXERCISE 13-1

Purpose: (L.O. 1) This exercise tests your ability to distinguish between current and noncurrent (long-term) liabilities.

Instructions

Indicate how each of the following items would be reported on a balance sheet being prepared at December 31, 2010.

1. Obligation to supplier for merchandise purchased on credit. (Terms 2/10, n/30)
2. Note payable to bank maturing 90 days after balance sheet date.
3. Bonds payable due January 1, 2013.
4. Utilities payable.
5. Interest payable on long-term bonds payable.
6. Income taxes payable.
7. Portion of lessee's lease obligations due in years 2012 through 2016.
8. Revenue received in advance, to be earned over the next six months.
9. Salaries payable.
10. Rent payable.
11. Short-term notes payable.
12. Pension obligations maturing in ten years.
13. Installment loan payment due three months after balance sheet date.
14. Installment loan payments due after one year.
15. Portion of lessee's lease obligations due within a year after the December 31, 2010 balance sheet date.
16. Bank overdraft.
17. Accrued officer bonus.
18. Coupon offers outstanding.
19. Cash dividends declared but not paid.
20. Deferred rent revenue.
21. Stock dividends payable.
22. Bonds payable due June 1, 2011
23. Bonds payable due July 1, 2011 for which a sinking fund will be used to pay off the debt. The sinking fund is classified as a long-term investment.
24. Discount to the bonds payable in item 3 above.
25. Current maturities of long-term debt.
26. Accrued interest on notes payable.
27. Customer deposits.
28. Sales taxes payable.
29. F.I.C.A. withholdings.
30. Contingent liability (reasonable possibility of loss).
31. Contingent liability (probable and estimable).
32. Obligation for warranties.
33. Unearned warranty revenue.
34. Gift certificates outstanding.
35. Loan from stockholder.

Solution to Exercise 13-1

> **TIP:** Apply the definition of a current liability. Analyze each situation and determine if the liability will fall due within a year (or operating cycle) of the balance sheet date and whether it will require the use of current assets or the incurrence of another current liability to be liquidated. If so, it is current; if not, it is long-term. Recall that current assets include cash and assets expected to be converted to cash or sold or consumed within the next year or operating cycle, whichever is longer.

1. Current liability (called Accounts Payable).
2. Current liability.
3. Noncurrent liability.
4. Current liability.
5. Current liability; interest on bonds is usually due semi-annually or annually.
6. Current liability.
7. Noncurrent liability.
8. Current liability.
9. Current liability.
10. Current liability.
11. Current liability.
12. Noncurrent liability.
13. Current liability.
14. Noncurrent liability.
15. Current liability.
16. Current liability (assuming no other bank accounts with positive balances in the same bank).
17. Current liability.
18. Current liability; may also classify a portion as a noncurrent liability.
19. Current liability
20. Current liability or noncurrent liability, depending on when the revenue is expected to be earned.
21. Paid-in capital; it does not meet the definition of a liability. ("Stock dividends payable" is a poor caption for "stock dividend distributable.")
22. Current liability.
23. Noncurrent liability; even though it is coming due within a year, it will not require the use of current assets to be liquidated.
24. Contra noncurrent liability (deducted from the related bonds payable).
25. Current liability.
26. Current liability, generally; in rare cases may be noncurrent.
27. Current liability or noncurrent liability, depending on the time left before they are to be returned or earned.
28. Current liability.
29. Current liability.
30. Note disclosure only.
31. Current liability or noncurrent liability, depending on the date settlement is expected.
32. Current liability and/or noncurrent liability, depending on term of warranty (this account title is used with the expense warranty method).
33. Current liability and/or noncurrent liability, depending on term of warranty (this account title is used with the sales warranty method).
34. Current liability, most likely; could have a portion as a noncurrent liability.
35. Current liability or noncurrent liability, depending on the due date of the loan; loans with related parties are required to be separately disclosed; if this loan is due on demand, the payable must be classified as a current liability.

EXERCISE 13-2

Purpose: (L.O. 1 This exercise will provide an example of the proper accounting for an obligation to an agency of the state government—unremitted sales taxes.

During the month of September, Chelsea's Boutique had cash sales of $702,000 and credit sales of $411,000, both of which include the 6% sales tax that must be remitted to the state by October 15. Sales taxes on September sales were lumped with the sales price and recorded as a credit to the Sales Revenue account.

Instructions
(a)   Prepare the adjusting entry that should be recorded to fairly present the financial statements at September 30.
(b)   Prepare the entry to record the remittance of the sales taxes on October 5 if a 2% discount is allowed for payments received by the State Revenue Department by October 10.

Solution to Exercise 13-2

(a)   9/30   Sales Revenue 63,000
                    Sales Taxes Payable... 63,000
                        Computation:
                        Sales plus sales tax
                            ($702,000 + $411,000) $1,113,000
                        Sales exclusive of tax
                            ($1,113,000 ÷ 1.06)   1,050,000
                        Sales tax $ 63,000

(b)   10/5   Sales Taxes Payable.. 63,000
                    Cash (98% x $63,000)... 61,740
                    Gain on Sales Tax Collections (2% x $63,000)............. 1,260

Explanation: Sales taxes on transfers of tangible personal property and on certain services must be collected from customers and remitted to the proper government authority. A liability is set up to provide for taxes collected from customers but as yet unremitted to the tax authority. The Sales Taxes Payable account should reflect the liability for sales taxes due to the government.

When the sales tax collections credited to the liability account are not equal to the liability as computed by the governmental formula, an adjustment of the liability account may be made by recognizing a gain or a loss on sales tax collections.

EXERCISE 13-3

Purpose: (L.O. 2) This exercise will provide you with two examples of the proper treatment of short-term debt expected to be refinanced.

Situation 1

On December 31, 2009, Mayor Frederick Specialty Foods Company had $1,000,000 of short-term debt in the form of notes payable due February 4, 2010. On January 22, 2010, the company issued 20,000 shares of its common stock for $40 per share, receiving $800,000 proceeds after brokerage fees and other costs of issuance. On February 4, 2010, the proceeds from the stock sale, supplemented by an additional $200,000 cash, are used to liquidate the $1,000,000 debt. The December 31, 2009 balance sheet is issued on February 20, 2010.

Situation 2

Included in Hubbard Corporation's liability account balances on December 31, 2009 were the following:

14% note payable issued October 1, 2009, maturing September 30, 2010	$500,000
16% note payable issued April 1, 2003, payable in six annual installments of $200,000 beginning April 1, 2007	600,000

Hubbard's December 31, 2009 financial statements were issued on March 31, 2010. On January 13, 2010, the entire $600,000 balance of the 16% note was refinanced by issuance of a long-term obligation payable in a lump-sum. In addition, on March 8, 2010, Hubbard consummated a noncancelable agreement with the lender to refinance the 14%, $500,000 note on a long-term basis, with readily determinable terms that have not yet been implemented. Both parties are financially capable of honoring the agreement, and there have been no violations of the agreement's provisions.

Instructions

Situation 1:   Show how the $1,000,000 of short-term debt should be presented on the December 31, 2009 balance sheet, including note disclosure.

Situation 2:   Explain how the liabilities should be classified on the December 31, 2009 balance sheet. How much should be classified as a current liability?

Solution to Exercise 13-3

Situation 1   **Mayor Frederick Specialty Foods Co.**
PARTIAL BALANCE SHEET
December 31, 2009

Current liabilities:
    Notes payable (Note 1) $ 200,000
Long-term debt:
    Notes payable refinanced in February 2010 (Note 1)   800,000

Note 1—Short-term debt refinanced
    As of December 31, 2009, the Company had notes payable totaling $1,000,000 due on February 4, 2010. These notes were refinanced on their due date to the extent of $800,000 received from the issuance of common stock on January 22, 2010. The balance of $200,000 was liquidated using current assets.

OR

Current liabilities:
    Notes payable (Note 1) $ 200,000
Short-term debt expected to be refinanced (Note 1)   800,000
Long-term debt   XXX,XXX
    (Same Note as above)

Situation 2
The entire $600,000 balance of the 16% note is properly excluded from short-term obligations since before the balance sheet was issued, Hubbard refinanced the note by issuance of a long-term obligation. The $500,000, 14% note is properly excluded from short-term obligations due to the fact that, before the balance sheet was issued, Hubbard entered into a financing agreement that clearly permits Hubbard to refinance the short-term obligation on a long-term basis with terms that are readily determinable.

Approach and Explanation: Review the criteria which will require an enterprise to exclude a short-term obligation from current liabilities and apply the criteria to the situation at hand.

In accordance with *SFAS 6*, an enterprise is allowed to exclude a short-term obligation from current liabilities only if both of the following conditions are met:
    1.   It must **intend to refinance** the obligation on a long-term basis, and
    2.   It must **demonstrate an ability** to consummate the refinancing.

Intention to refinance on a long-term basis means the enterprise intends to refinance the short-term obligation so that the use of working capital will not be required during the ensuing fiscal year or operating cycle, if longer. The **ability** to consummate the refinancing must be demonstrated by:
    (a)   **Actually refinancing** the short-term obligation by issuance of a long-term obligation or equity securities after the date of the balance sheet but before it is issued; or
    (b)   Entering into a **financing agreement** that clearly permits the enterprise to refinance the debt on a long-term basis with terms that are readily determinable.

If an actual refinancing occurs, the portion of the short-term obligation to be excluded from current liabilities may not exceed the proceeds from the new obligation or equity securities issued that are to be used to retire the short-term obligation. When a financing agreement is relied upon to demonstrate ability to refinance a short-term obligation on a long-term basis, the amount of short-term debt that can be excluded from current liabilities cannot exceed the amount available for refinancing under the agreement.

> **TIP:** By excluding short-term debt expected to be refinanced from the current liability classification, the company's working capital position and its current ratio are improved.

EXERCISE 13-4

Purpose: (L.O. 3) This exercise will review accounting for compensated absences.

Patricia McKiernan Company began operations on January 2, 2009. It employs 9 individuals who work 8-hour days and are paid hourly. Each employee earns 10 paid vacation days and 6 paid sick days annually. Vacation days may be taken after January 15 of the year following the year in which they are earned. Sick days may be taken as soon as they are earned; unused sick days accumulate but do not vest. Additional information is as follows:

Actual Hourly Wage Rate		Vacation Days Used by Each Employee		Sick Days Used By Each Employee	
2009	**2010**	**2009**	**2010**	**2009**	**2010**
$7.00	$8.00	0	9	4	5

Patricia McKiernan has chosen not to accrue paid sick leave until used, and has chosen to accrue paid vacation time at expected future rates of pay without discounting. The company used the following projected rates to accrue vacation time:

Year in Which Vacation Time Was Earned	Projected Future Pay Rates Used to Accrue Vacation Pay
2009	$7.90
2010	8.60

Instructions
(a)   Prepare journal entries to record transactions related to compensated absences during 2009 and 2010.
(b)   Compute the amounts of any liability for compensated absences that should be reported on the balance sheet at December 31, 2009 and 2010.

Solution to Exercise 13-4

(a)   **2009**

To accrue the expense and liability for vacations:	Wages Expense Vacation Wages Payable	5,688 (1)	5,688
To record sick time paid:	Wages Expense Cash	2,016 (2)	2,016
To record vacation time paid:	No entry.		

2010

To accrue the expense and liability for vacations:	Wages Expense Vacation Wages Payable	6,192 (3)	6,192
To record sick time paid:	Wages Expense Cash	2,880 (4)	2,880
To record vacation time paid:	Wages Expense Vacation Wages Payable Cash	65 5,119 (5)	5,184 (6)

(1)   9 employees x $7.90/hr. x 8 hrs./day x 10 days = $5,688.
(2)   9 employees x $7.00/hr. x 8 hrs./day x 4 days = $2,016.
(3)   9 employees x $8.60/hr. x 8 hrs./day x 10 days = $6,192.
(4)   9 employees x $8.00/hr. x 8 hrs./day x 5 days = $2,880.
(5)   9 employees x $7.90/hr. x 8 hrs./day x 9 days = $5,119.
(6)   9 employees x $8.00/hr. x 8 hrs./day x 9 days = $5,184.

(b)   Accrued liability at year-end:

	2009 Vacation Wages Payable	**2010** Vacation Wages Payable
Jan. 1 balance $ 0		$ 5,688.00
+ accrued	5,688.00	6,192.00
- paid	(0)	(5,119.20)
Dec. 31 balance	$ 5,688.00 (1)	$ 6,760.80 (2)

(1)   9 employees x $7.90/hr. x 8 hrs./day x 10 days   = $ 5,688.00

(2)   9 employees x $7.90/hr. x 8 hrs./ day x 1 day   = $ 568.80
        9 employees x $8.60/hr. x 8 hrs./day x 10 days   =   6,192.00
                                                                                                    $ 6,760.80

> **TIP:**   The expense and related liability for compensated absences should be recognized in the year in which the employees earn the rights to those absences. Vacation and holiday pay must be accrued if it vests or accumulates. Sick pay must be accrued only if it vests.

EXERCISE 13-5

Purpose: (L.O. 3) This exercise will provide an example of recording liabilities associated with payroll taxes.

The payroll of Lionshead Company for July 2010 is as follows:

1. Total payroll was $620,000 of which $120,000 is exempt from F.I.C.A. tax because it represents amounts paid in excess of $102,000 to certain employees.

2. The amount paid to employees in excess of $7,000 was $540,000. The state unemployment tax is 5.7% on the first $7,000 of annual earnings for each employee. Lionshead is allowed a credit of 2.5% by the state for its unemployment experience.

3. The current F.I.C.A. tax is 6.2% on an employee's wages up to $102,000. The Hospital Insurance (Medicare) tax is 1.45% on the employee's total compensation.

4. The federal unemployment tax rate (on the first $7,000 of each employee's earnings) is 0.8% after the state credit.

5. Income tax withheld amounts to $117,000. Union dues of $11,000 was also withheld from employees.

Instructions
Prepare the necessary journal entries to record the salaries paid and the related payroll taxes. Record the employer payroll taxes in a separate entry.

SOLUTION TO EXERCISE 13-5

Wages and Salaries Expense	620,000	
Withholding Taxes Payable		117,000
F.I.C.A. Taxes Payable		39,990
Union Dues Payable		11,000
Cash		452,010

Computations:

$620,000 – 120,000 = $500,000 Subject to F.I.C.A. tax
$500,000 X 6.2% = $31,000 F.I.C.A. taxes—employee portion
$620,000 x 1.45% = $8,990 Medicare taxes—employee portion
$31,000 + $8,990 = $39,990 Social Security taxes—employee portion

$620,000 - $117,000 - $39,990 - $11,000 = $452,010 net cash paid to employees

Payroll Tax Expense	43,190	
Social Security Taxes Payable		39,990
State Unemployment Tax Payable		2,560
Federal Unemployment Tax Payable		640

Computations:

$620,000 - $120,000 = $500,000 Subject to F.I.C.A. tax
$500,000 X 6.2% = $31,000 F.I.C.A. taxes—employer portion
$620,000 X 1.45% = $8,990 Medicare taxes—employer portion
$31,000 + $8,990 = $39,990 Social Security taxes—employer portion
(5.7% - 2.5%) X ($620,000 - $540,000) = $2,560 State Unemployment tax
.8% X ($620,000 - $540,000) = $640 Federal Unemployment tax
$39,990 + $2,560 + $640 = $43,190 Payroll tax expense

ILLUSTRATION 13-1
ACCOUNTING TREATMENT OF LOSS CONTINGENCIES (L.O. 4, 5)

Loss Related to	Usually Accrued	Not Accrued	May Be Accrued*
1. Collectibility of receivables	X		
2. Obligations related to product warranties and product defects	X		
3. Premiums offered to customers	X		
4. Risk of loss or damage of enterprise property by fire, explosion, or other hazards		X	
5. General or unspecified business risks		X	
6. Risk of loss from catastrophes assumed by property and casualty insurance companies including reinsurance companies		X	
7. Threat of expropriation of assets			X
8. Pending or threatened litigation			X
9. Actual or possible claims and assessments**			X
10. Guarantees of indebtedness of others***			X
11. Obligations of commercial banks under "standby letters of credit"***			X
12. Agreements to repurchase receivables (or the related property) that have been sold***			X

*Should be accrued when both criteria are met (probable and reasonably estimable).
**Estimated amounts of losses incurred prior to the balance sheet date but settled subsequently should be accrued as of the balance sheet date.
***Should be disclosed even though possibility of loss may be remote.

EXERCISE 13-6

Purpose: (L.O. 1, 4, 5) This exercise will enable you to practice analyzing situations to determine whether a liability should be reported, and if so, at what amount.

Clare Avery Inc., a publishing company, is preparing its December 31, 2010 financial statements and must determine the proper accounting treatment for each of the following situations:

1. Avery sells subscriptions to several magazines for a two- or three-year period. Cash receipts from subscribers are credited to Unearned Magazine Subscriptions Revenue. This account had a balance of $5,300,000 at December 31, 2010, before adjustment. An analysis of outstanding subscriptions at December 31, 2010 shows that they expire as follows:

During 2011:	$ 800,000
During 2012:	900,000
During 2013:	1,200,000

2. A suit for breach of contract seeking damages of $1,000,000 was filed by an author against Avery on June 1, 2010. The company's legal counsel believes that an unfavorable outcome is probable. A reasonable estimate of the court's award to the plaintiff is in the range between $200,000 and $800,000. The company's legal counsel believes the best estimate of potential damages is $350,000.

3. On January 2, 2010, Avery discontinued collision, fire, and theft coverage on its delivery vehicles and became self-insured for these risks. Actual losses of $40,000 during 2010 were charged to Delivery Expense. The 2009 premium for the discontinued coverage amounted to $75,000, and the controller wants to set up a reserve for self-insurance by a debit to Delivery Expense of $35,000 and a credit to Liability for Self-insurance of $35,000.

4. During December 2010, a competitor company filed suit against Avery for copyright infringement claiming $600,000 in damages. In the opinion of management and company counsel, it is reasonably possible that damages will be awarded to the plaintiff. The best estimate of potential damages is $175,000.

Instructions

For each of the situations above, prepare the journal entry that should be recorded as of December 31, 2010, or explain why an entry should not be recorded. Show supporting computations in good form.

Solution to Exercise 13-6

1. Unearned Magazine Subscription Revenue........................   2,400,000*
        Magazine Subscriptions Revenue............................   2,400,000
            (To adjust the unearned revenue account)

    *Liability account:
Book balance at December 31, 2010	$ 5,300,000
Adjusted balance ($800,000 +	
$900,000 + $1,200,000)	2,900,000
Adjustment required	$ 2,400,000

2. Estimated Loss from Pending Lawsuit................................   350,000
        Estimated Liability from Pending Lawsuit.................   350,000
            (To record estimated minimum damages on
            breach-of-contract litigation)

    This situation involves a contingent liability. Because it is **probable** that a liability has been incurred and the loss is reasonably estimable, the loss should be accrued. When the expected loss amount is in a range, the best estimate within the range is used for the accrual. When no amount within the range is a better estimate than any other amount, the dollar value at the low end is accrued and the dollar amount at the high end of the range is disclosed in the notes.

3. No entry should be made to accrue for an expense because the absence of insurance coverage does not mean that an asset has been impaired or a liability has been incurred as of the balance sheet date. Avery may, however, appropriate retained earnings for self-insurance as long as actual costs or losses are not charged against the appropriation of retained earnings and no part of the appropriation is transferred to income. Appropriation of retained earnings and/or disclosure in the notes to the financial statements are not required, but are recommended.

4. No entry should be made for this loss contingency, because it is not probable that an asset has been impaired or a liability has been incurred as of the balance sheet date. The loss contingency (along with the best estimate of amount) should be disclosed in the notes to financial statements because the likelihood of loss is judged to be reasonably possible.

EXERCISE 13-7

Purpose: (L.O. 5) This exercise will provide an example of accounting for premium claims outstanding.

Shuck Company includes 1 coupon in each box of cereal that it packs and 10 coupons are redeemable for a premium (a toy). In 2010, Shuck Company purchased 9,000 premiums at 90 cents each and sold 100,000 boxes of cereal at $2.00 per box; 40,000 coupons were presented for redemption in 2010. It is estimated that 60% of the coupons will eventually be presented for redemption. This is the first year for this premium offering.

Instructions
Prepare all the entries that would be made relative to sales of cereal and to the premium plan in 2010.

Solution to Exercise 13-7

Inventory of Premiums (9,000 x $.90)..	8,100	
Cash..		8,100
Cash (100,000 x $2.00)	200,000	
Sales		200,000
Premium Expense..	3,600	
Inventory of Premiums [(40,000 ÷ 10) x $.90]		3,600
Premium Expense..	1,800*	
Estimated Liability for Premiums..		1,800

*[(100,000 x 60%) - 40,000] ÷ 10 x $.90 = $1,800

Explanation: The first entry records the purchase of 9,000 toys which will be used as premiums. The second entry records the sales of cereal (100,000 boxes). The third entry records the redemption of 40,000 coupons with customers receiving one premium for every 10 coupons. The cost of the 4,000 toys distributed to these customers is recorded by a debit to expense. The fourth entry is an adjusting entry at the end of the accounting period to accrue the cost of additional premiums included in boxes of cereal sold this period that are likely to be redeemed in future periods. This is an application of the matching principle. The expense of a premium should be recognized in the same period as the related revenue which, in this case, is from the sale of cereal boxes containing the coupons that customers will redeem for a premium.

EXERCISE 13-8

Purpose: (L.O. 5) This exercise will provide an example of the journal entries involved in accounting for a warranty that is included with the sale of a product (warranty is not sold separately). Two methods are examined—the cash basis and the expense warranty method (an accrual method).

Zacko Corporation sells laptop computers under a two-year warranty contract that requires the corporation to replace defective parts and to provide the necessary repair labor. During 2009 the corporation sells for cash 400 computers at a unit price of $2,000. On the basis of past experience, the two-year warranty costs are estimated to be $90 for parts and $100 for labor per unit. (For simplicity, assume that all sales occurred on December 31, 2009, rather than evenly throughout the year.)

Instructions
(a)   Record any necessary journal entries in 2009, applying the cash basis method.
(b)   Record any necessary journal entries in 2009, applying the expense warranty accrual method.
(c)   What liability relative to these transactions would appear on the December 31, 2009 balance sheet and how would it be classified if the cash basis method is applied?
(d)   What liability relative to these transactions would appear on the December 31, 2009 balance sheet and how would it be classified if the expense warranty accrual method is applied?

In 2010 the actual warranty costs to Zacko Corporation were $14,800 for parts and $18,200 for labor.
(e)   Record any necessary journal entries in 2010, applying the cash basis method.
(f)   Record any necessary journal entries in 2010, applying the expense warranty accrual method.
(g)   Under what conditions is it acceptable to use the cash basis method? Explain.

Solution to Exercise 13-8

(a)   Cash (400 x $2,000)... 800,000
              Sales of Computers...   800,000

(b)   Cash (400 x $2,000)... 800,000
              Sales of Computers...   800,000

       Warranty Expense [400 x ($90 + $100)] 76,000
              Estimated Liability Under Warranties   76,000

(c)   No liability would be disclosed under the cash basis method relative to future costs due to warranties on past sales.

(d)   Current Liabilities:
            Estimated Liability Under Warranties $38,000

          Long-term Liabilities:
            Estimated Liability Under Warranties $38,000

(e)   Warranty Expense...   33,000
            Parts Inventory   14,800
            Wages Payable   18,200

(f)   Estimated Liability Under Warranties.......................................   33,000
            Parts Inventory   14,800
            Wages Payable   18,200

(g)   The cash basis is used for income tax purposes. Theoretically, the accrual basis
          (expense warranty method in this case) should be used for financial reporting purposes.
          However, the cash basis is often justifiably used for accounting purposes when warranty
          costs are immaterial or when the warranty period is relatively short.

EXERCISE 13-9

Purpose: (L.O. 6) This exercise will exemplify the journal entries involved in accounting for
               a warranty that is sold separately from the related product. The sales warranty
               accrual method is used for such situations.

The Contessa Company sells scanners for $800 each and offers to each customer a three-year
warranty contract for $90 that requires the company to perform periodic services and to replace
defective parts. During 2009, the company sold 500 scanners and 400 warranty contracts for
cash. It estimates the three-year warranty costs as $30 for parts and $50 for labor and accounts
for warranties on the sales warranty accrual method. Assume all sales occurred on December
31, 2009, and revenue from the sale of the warranties is to be recognized on a straight-line
basis over the life of the contract.

Instructions
(a)   Record any necessary journal entries in 2009.
(b)   What liability relative to these transactions would appear on the December 31, 2009
          balance sheet and how would it be classified?

In 2010, Terence Trent Company incurred actual costs relative to 2009 scanner warranty sales
of $3,800 for parts and $6,000 for labor.
(c)   Record any necessary journal entries in 2010 relative to 2009 scanner warranties.
(d)   What amounts relative to the 2009 scanner warranties would appear on the December
          31, 2010 balance sheet and how would they be classified?

Solution to Exercise 13-9

(a) Cash ($400,000 + $36,000) 436,000
        Sales of Scanners (500 x $800) 400,000
        Unearned Warranty Revenue (400 x $90)...................... 36,000

(b) Current Liabilities:
        Unearned Warranty Revenue $12,000
        (Note: Warranty costs are assumed to be
        incurred equally over the three-year period)

     Long-term Liabilities:
        Unearned Warranty Revenue $24,000

(c) Warranty Expense... 9,800
        Parts Inventory 3,800
        Wages Payable 6,000

     Unearned Warranty Revenue 12,000
        Revenue from Warranties... 12,000

(d) Current Liabilities:
        Unearned Warranty Revenue $12,000

     Long-term Liabilities:
        Unearned Warranty Revenue $12,000

EXERCISE 13-10

Purpose: (L.O. 5) This exercise will review the accounting recognition for an asset retirement obligation.

Silverado Corp. purchased mining equipment with cash on January 1, 2010, at a cost of $3,000,000. Silverado expects to actively extract units from the mine for 5 years at which time it is legally required to perform certain steps to close the mine and remove the mining equipment. It is estimated that it will cost $500,000 to properly dismantle the equipment and close the mine at the end of its useful life. Using an interest rate of 8%, the present value of the asset retirement obligation on January 1, 2010, is $340,290. The estimated residual value of the equipment is zero.

Instructions

(a)   Prepare the journal entries to record the acquisition of the mining equipment and the asset retirement obligation for the mine on January 1, 2010.

(b)   Prepare any journal entries required for the equipment and the asset retirement obligation at December 31, 2010.

(c)   On January 5, 2015, Silverado Corp. pays $481,000 to close the mine and remove the equipment. Prepare the journal entry for the settlement of the asset retirement obligation.

Solution to Exercise 13-10

January 1, 2010

(a)   Mining Equipment... 3,000,000
　　　　　Cash... 　　　　　　3,000,000

　　　Mining Equipment... 340,290
　　　　　Asset Retirement Obligation...................................... 　　　　　　340,290

Explanation: The equipment is recorded at a cost of $3,000,000. In addition, the company must recognize an asset retirement obligation (ARO) when it has an existing legal obligation associated with the retirement of a long-lived asset and when the amount of the liability can be reasonably estimated. The ARO is to be recorded at fair value; fair value can be estimated based on present value techniques.

An asset retirement cost is recorded as part of the related asset because these costs are considered to be a cost of operating the asset and are necessary to prepare the asset for its intended use. The capitalized asset retirement costs should not be recorded in a separate account because there is no future economic benefit that can be associated with these costs alone. Therefore, the specific asset (the mine) should be debited because the future economic benefit comes from the use of this productive asset.

December 31, 2010

(b)   Depreciation Expense.. 668,058
            Accumulated Depreciation 668,058
            ($3,340,290 ÷ 5 = $668,058)

        Interest Expense... 27,223
            Asset Retirement Obligation....................................... 27,223
            ($340,290 x 8% = $27,223)

Explanation: During the life of the asset, the asset cost ($3,000,000) and the asset retirement cost ($340,290) are allocated to expense. In addition, interest must be accrued each period.

TIP: The interest expense for the second year (2011) for the asset retirement obligation would be 8% of the ARO, so 0.08 X ($340,290 + $27,223) = $29,401.

(c)   **January 5, 2015**
        Asset Retirement Obligation 500,000
            Gain on Settlement of ARO... 19,000
            Cash 481,000

By the end of the asset's 5-year service life, the interest accrued on the asset retirement obligation will have brought the balance of the Asset Retirement Obligation account to $500,000. That balance exceeds the actual cost of retiring the asset—hence, a gain results.

ANALYSIS OF MULTIPLE-CHOICE TYPE QUESTIONS

QUESTION
1.   (L.O. 1) A current liability is an obligation that:
    a.   was paid during the current period.
    b.   will be reported as an expense within the year or operating cycle that follows the balance sheet date, whichever is longer.
    c.   will be converted to a long-term liability within the next year.
    d.   is expected to require the use of current assets or the creation of another current liability to liquidate it.

Approach and Explanation: Before you read the answer selections, write down the definition for "current liability." Compare each answer selection with your definition. A **current liability** is an obligation which will come due within one year and whose liquidation is reasonably expected to require the use of existing resources properly classifiable as current assets or the creation of other current liabilities. (Solution = d.)

QUESTION
2.   (L.O. 1) Burt Reynolds Company borrowed money from Loni Anderson Company for nine months by issuing a zero-interest-bearing note payable with a face value of $106,000. The proceeds amounted to $100,000. In recording the issuance of this note, what account should Burt debit for $6,000?
    a.   Interest Payable
    b.   Interest Expense
    c.   Prepaid Interest
    d.   Discount on Note Payable

Approach and Explanation: The excess of the face value of a zero-interest-bearing note payable and the proceeds collected upon its issuance is the cost of borrowing. This cost of borrowing (interest expense) should be recognized over the months the loan is outstanding. Therefore, the total interest ($6,000) is initially debited to a Discount on Note Payable Account. The balance of that account is then amortized (allocated) to interest expense over the life of the note. (Solution = d.)

TIP:	A **zero-interest-bearing note** is often called a **non-interest-bearing-note**.

QUESTION

3. (L.O. 1) Martha's Boutique sells gift certificates. These gift certificates have no expiration date. Data for the current year are as follows:

Gift certificates outstanding, January 1	$ 225,000
Gift certificates sold	750,000
Gift certificates redeemed	660,000
Gross profit expressed as percentage of sales	40%

At December 31, Martha should report unearned revenue of:
a. $90,000.
b. $126,000.
c. $261,000.
d. $315,000.

Approach and Explanation: Draw a T-account for the liability and enter the data given.

Gift Certificates Outstanding

		Beginning Balance	225,000
Redeemed	660,000	Sold	750,000
		Ending Balance	315,000

(Solution = d.)

TIP:	The gross profit percentage is not used in the solution for the balance of unearned revenue. Revenue and unearned revenue are gross amounts, not net amounts.

QUESTION

4. (L.O. 1) A local retailer is required to collect a 6% sales tax for the state's department of revenue and remit in the month that follows the sale. The retailer does not use a separate Sales Taxes Payable account; rather the sales price of products sold and the related sales tax is all credited to Sales Revenue. During the month of March, 2009, credits totaling $25,440 were made to the Sales Revenue account. The amount to be remitted to the state in April for sales taxes collected during the month of March:
a. is $1,526.40.
b. is $1,440.00.
c. is $2,696.64
d. cannot be determined from the data given.

Approach and Explanation: Set up an algebraic expression to describe the relationships between the data given and solve.

$$\text{Sales} + .06 \text{ Sales} = \$25,440$$

$$1.06 \text{ Sales} = \$25,440$$

$$\text{Sales} = \frac{\$25,440}{1.06}$$

$$\text{Sales} = \$24,000$$

$$\$25,440 \text{ Total} - \$24,000 \text{ Sales} = \underline{\$1,440} \text{ Sales Tax} \qquad (\text{Solution} = \text{b.})$$

QUESTION

5.   (L.O. 2) Included in Arnold Howell Company's liability accounts at December 31, 2010 was the following:

12% Note payable issued in 2006 for cash and due in May 2011	$2,000,000

On February 1, 2011 Arnold issued $5,000,000 of five-year bonds with the intention of using part of the bond proceeds to liquidate the $2,000,000 note payable maturing in May. On March 2, 2011, Arnold used $2,000,000 of the bond proceeds to liquidate the note payable. Arnold's December 31, 2010 balance sheet is being issued on March 15, 2011. How much of the $2,000,000 note payable should be classified as a current liability on the balance sheet?

a. $0
b. $800,000
c. $1,000,000
d. $2,000,000

Approach and Explanation: Mentally review the definition of a current liability and the guidelines for reporting short-term debt expected to be refinanced. At the date the balance sheet is issued, we have evidence of the intent and ability to refinance the debt on a long-term basis. That evidence is the post balance sheet issuance of long-term debt securities. The proceeds from the bond issuance exceed the reported amount of the note. Therefore, the entire $2,000,000 note payable should be classified as a long-term liability. (Solution = a.)

QUESTION

6.   (L.O. 3) An employee's net (or take-home) pay is determined by gross earnings minus amounts for income tax withholdings and the employee's:
a.   portion of Social Security taxes, and unemployment taxes.
b.   and employer's portion of Social Security taxes, and unemployment taxes.
c.   portion of Social Security taxes, unemployment taxes, and any voluntary deductions.
d.   portion of Social Security taxes, and any voluntary deductions.

Approach and Explanation: Before you read the answer selections, write down the model for the net (take-home) pay computation. Then find the answer selection that agrees with your model.

      Employee's gross earnings for the current period
-   Federal income tax withholdings
-   Social Security tax withholdings
-   Withholdings for voluntary deductions; such as for charitable contributions, group
     health and life insurance premiums, savings, retirement fund contributions, and
     loan repayments
=   Net (or take-home) pay   (Solution = d.)

> **TIP:**   The employer bears the burden of all unemployment taxes and its share of Social Security, F.I.C.A., and Medicare taxes.

QUESTION

7. (L.O. 4) An example of a contingent liability is:
    a. sales taxes payable.
    b. accrued salaries.
    c. property taxes payable.
    d. a pending lawsuit.

Approach and Explanation: Mentally define contingent liability and think of examples before you read the alternative answer selections. A contingent liability is a situation involving uncertainty as to possible loss or expense that will ultimately be resolved when one or more future events occur or fail to occur. Examples are pending or threatened lawsuits, pending IRS audits, and product warranties. Accrued salaries result in an actual liability. Sales taxes payable and property taxes payable are both actual liabilities if they exist at a balance sheet date. (Solution = d.)

QUESTION

8. (L.O. 4, 5) A contingent loss which is judged to be reasonably possible and estimable should be:

	Accrued	Disclosed
a.	Yes	Yes
b.	Yes	No
c.	No	Yes
d.	No	No

Explanation: A contingent loss that is probable and estimable is to be accrued. A contingent loss that is reasonably possible should be disclosed, but it should not be accrued. A contingent loss that is remotely possible can be ignored (unless it is one of the items on a list of contingencies that must always be disclosed, regardless of the likelihood of loss occurrence, such as guarantees of indebtedness of others). (Solution = c.)

QUESTION

9. (L.O. 4) Mayberry Co. has a loss contingency to accrue. The loss amount can only be reasonably estimated within a range of outcomes. No single amount within the range is a better estimate than any other amount. The amount of loss accrual should be:
    a. zero.
    b. the minimum of the range.
    c. the mean of the range.
    d. the maximum of the range.

Explanation: The FASB calls for the accrual of a loss contingency when it is probable and estimable and states that, when the reasonable estimate of loss is a range and some amount within the range appears at the time to be a better estimate than any other amount within the range, that amount shall be accrued. When no amount within the range is a better estimate then any other amount, however, the minimum amount in the range should be accrued. At first, you may think this does not go along with conservation; however, we are already being conservative by providing the charge to income for the estimated amount. (Solution = b.)

QUESTION

10. (L.O. 5) Scott Corporation began operations at the beginning of 2009. It provides a two-year warranty with the sale of its product. Scott estimates that warranty costs will equal 4% of the selling price the first year after sale and 6% of the selling price the second year after the sale. The following data are available:

	2009	2010
Sales	$400,000	$500,000
Actual warranty expenditures	10,000	38,000

The balance of the warranty liability at December 31, 2010 should be:

a. $12,000.
b. $42,000.
c. $44,000.
d. $50,000.

Approach and Explanation: Draw a T-account and enter the amounts that would be reflected in the account and determine its balance.

Estimated Liability Under Warranties

(2) Expenditures in 2009	10,000	(1) Expense for 2009	40,000
(4) Expenditures in 2010	38,000	(3) Expense for 2010	50,000
		12/31/10 Balance	42,000

(Solution = b.)

(1) $400,000 x (4% + 6%) = $40,000 expense for 2009.
The total warranty cost related to the products sold during 2009 should be recognized in the period of sale (matching principle).
(2)   Given data. Actual expenditures during 2009.
(3) $500,000 x (4% + 6%) = $50,000 expense for 2010.
(4)   Given data. Actual expenditures during 2010.

> **TIP:** Because some items are sold near the end of the year and the warranty is for two years, a portion of the warranty liability should be classified as a current liability (the amount pertaining to the actual expenditures estimated to occur in 2011) and the remainder as a long-term liability.

QUESTION

11. (L.O. 5) Crazy Pete Theme Park is self-insured. Premiums for insurance used to cost $100,000 per year before Crazy Pete discontinued coverage. During 2010, Crazy Pete suffered losses of $39,000 that used to be (but are no longer) covered by insurance. Crazy Pete thinks this was a "light" year and greater losses in future years will offset the lower amount sustained in 2010. In order to avoid volatility in earnings due to being self-insured, Crazy Pete wants to set up a Liability for Self-insurance. A reasonable estimate of losses to be incurred in 2011 is $120,000. The liability to be reported by Crazy Pete at December 31, 2010 due to this situation is:

a. $0.
b. $61,000.
c. $100,000.
d. $120,000.

Approach and Explanation: Even if the amount is estimable, the future losses from self-insurance do not result in liabilities at the December 31, 2010 balance sheet date because the losses in the future will result from future events, not from a past event. It is not generally acceptable to accrue future losses from self-insurance. (Solution = a.)

> **TIP:** Crazy Pete should report $39,000 of losses on its 2010 income statement.

QUESTION

12. (L.O. 5) Powercell, a manufacturer of batteries, offers a cash rebate to buyers of its size D batteries. The rebate offer is good until June 30, 2011. At December 31, 2010, the balance sheet should include an estimated liability for unredeemed rebates in order to comply with the:
    a. Revenue recognition principle.
    b. Expense recognition principle.
    c. Historical cost principle.
    d. Time-period assumption.

Explanation: Premium, coupon, and rebate offers are made to stimulate sales, and their costs should be charged to expense in the period of the sale that benefits from the premium plan. At the end of the accounting period, many of these premium, coupon, and rebate offers may be outstanding and, when presented in subsequent periods, must be redeemed. The number of outstanding premium, coupon, and rebate offers that will be presented for redemption must be estimated in order to reflect the existing current liability and to match expenses with revenues. An adjusting entry is made with a debit to Rebate Expense and a credit to Estimated Liability for Rebates. (Solution = b.)

QUESTION

13. (L.O. 5) The ratio of current assets to current liabilities is called the:
    a. current ratio.
    b. acid-test ratio.
    c. current asset turnover ratio.
    d. current liability turnover ratio.

Explanation: Two major ratios used to measure liquidity of an entity are the (1) current ratio and the (2) acid-test ratio. The current ratio is computed by dividing current assets by current liabilities. The acid-test ratio is computed by dividing quick assets (cash + marketable securities + net receivables) by current liabilities. Marketable securities in this context refer to short-term (temporary) investments. The current ratio is sometimes called the working capital ratio; the acid-test ratio is often called the quick ratio. (Solution = a.)

CHAPTER 14

LONG-TERM LIABILITIES

OVERVIEW

Sources of assets include current liabilities, long-term liabilities, and owners' equity. Liabilities are considered a "temporary" source of assets; whereas, owners' equity is a more "permanent" source of assets. When a company borrows money, it does so with the expectation of using the borrowed funds to acquire assets that can be used to generate more income. The objective is to generate an amount of additional income which exceeds the cost of borrowing the funds (interest).

Long-term debt consists of probable future sacrifices of economic benefits arising from present obligations that are not payable within a year or the operating cycle of the business, whichever is longer. Bonds payable, long-term notes payable, mortgages payable, pension liabilities, and lease obligations are examples of long-term liabilities. This chapter will focus on the first two of these.

Although the subject of accounting for bonds is included in the principles of accounting course, many intermediate students don't remember the details of the procedures and look upon this topic as one of the most difficult they have encountered. Perhaps they have problems with the material because they try to memorize their way through the topic. As a result, it is imperative that you think about the time value of money concepts introduced in Chapter 6 and grasp how they are applied in the computations involved in accounting for long-term debt. When you see the logic and rationale of the accounting procedures, you will find it easier to recall these guidelines years from now.

SUMMARY OF LEARNING OBJECTIVES

1. **Describe the formal procedures associated with issuing long-term debt.** Incurring long-term debt is often a formal procedure. The bylaws of corporations usually require approval by the board of directors and the stockholders before corporations can issue bonds or can make other long-term debt arrangements. Generally, long-term debt has various covenants or restrictions. The covenants and other terms of the agreement between the borrower and the lender are stated in the bond indenture or note agreement.

2. **Identify various types of bond issues.** Various types of bond issues are: (1) *Secured and unsecured bonds.* (2) *Term, serial bonds, and callable bonds.* (3) *Convertible, commodity-backed, and deep-discount bonds.* (4) *Registered and bearer (coupon) bonds.* (5) *Income and revenue bonds.* The variety in the types of bonds results from attempts to attract capital from different investors and risk takers and to satisfy the cash flow needs of the issuers.

3. **Describe the accounting valuation for bonds at the date of issuance.** The investment community values a bond at the present value of its future cash flows, which consist of interest and principal. The rate used to compute the present value of these cash flows is the interest rate that provides an acceptable return on an investment commensurate with the issuer's risk characteristics. The interest rate written in the terms of the bond indenture and ordinarily

appearing on the bond certificate is the stated, coupon, or nominal rate. The issuer of the bonds sets the rate and expresses it as a percentage of the face value (also called the par value, principal amount, or maturity value) of the bonds. If the rate employed by the buyers differs from the stated rate, the present value of the bonds computed by the buyers will differ from the face value of the bonds. The difference between the face value and the present value of the bonds is either a discount or premium.

4.   **Apply the methods of bond discount and premium amortization.** The discount (premium) is amortized and charged (credited) to interest expense over the period of time that the bonds are outstanding. Amortization of a discount increases bond interest expense and amortization of a premium decreases bond interest expense. The profession's preferred procedure for amortization of a discount or premium is the effective interest method. Under the effective interest method, (1) bond interest expense is computed by multiplying the carrying value of the bonds at the beginning of the period by the effective interest rate, and (2) the bond discount or premium amortization is then determined by comparing the bond interest expense with the interest to be paid for the same interest period.

5.   **Describe the accounting procedures for the extinguishment of debt.** At the time of reacquisition, the unamortized premium or discount and any costs of issue applicable to the debt must be amortized up to the reacquisition date. The reacquisition price is the amount paid on extinguishment or redemption before maturity, including any call premium and expense of reacquisition. On any specified date, the net carrying amount of the debt is the amount payable at maturity, adjusted for unamortized premium or discount and issue costs. Any excess of the net carrying amount over the reacquisition price is a gain from extinguishment. The excess of the reacquisition price over the net carrying amount is a loss from extinguishment. Gains and losses on extinguishments are recognized currently in income and are reported in the Other Gains and Losses section of the income statement.

6.   **Explain the accounting procedures for long-term notes payable.** Accounting procedures for notes and bonds are similar. Like a bond, a note is valued at the present value of its future interest and principal cash flows, with any discount or premium being similarly amortized over the life of the note. Whenever the face amount of the note does not reasonably represent the present value of the consideration given or received in the exchange, a company must evaluate the entire arrangement in order to properly record the exchange and the subsequent interest.

7.   **Explain the reporting of off-balance-sheet financing arrangements.** Off-balance-sheet financing is an attempt to borrow funds in such a way to prevent recording obligations. Examples of off-balance-sheet arrangements are (1) non-consolidated subsidiaries, (2) special purpose entities, and (3) operating leases.

8.   **Indicate how to present and analyze long-term debt.** Companies that have large amounts and numerous issues of long-term debt frequently report only one amount in the balance sheet and support this with comments and schedules in the accompanying notes. Any assets pledged as security for the debt should be shown in the assets section of the balance sheet. Long-term debt that matures within one year should be reported as a current liability, unless retirement is to be accomplished with other than current assets or the creation of a new liability other than a current liability. If a company plans to refinance the debt, convert it into stock, or retire it with a bond retirement fund, it should continue to report it as noncurrent, accompanied with a note explaining the method it will use in the debt's liquidation. Disclosure is required of future payments for sinking fund requirements and maturity amounts of long-term debt during each of the next 5 years. Debt to total assets and times interest earned are two ratios that provide information about debt-paying ability and long-run solvency.

*9.   **Describe the accounting for a debt restructuring.** There are two types of debt settlements: (1) transfer or noncash assets, and (2) granting of equity interest. Creditors and debtors record losses and gains on settlements based on fair values. For accounting purposes there are also two types of restructurings with continuation of debt with modified terms: (1) the carrying amount of debt is less than the future cash flows, and (2) the carrying amount of debt exceeds the total future cash flows. Creditors record losses on these restructurings based on the expected future cash flows discounted at the historical effective interest rate. The debtor determines its gain based on undiscounted cash flows.

*This material is covered in Appendix 14A in the text.

TIPS ON CHAPTER TOPICS

TIP: The denomination of a bond is called the **face value**. Synonymous terms are **par value, principal amount, maturity value**, and **face amount**.

TIP: Bond prices are quoted in terms of percentage of par. Thus, a bond with a par value of $4,000 and a price quote of 102 is currently selling for a price of $4,080 (102% of $4,000). A bond with a quote of 100 is selling for its par value.

TIP: The bond contract is called an **indenture**. This term is often confused with the term "debenture." A **debenture** bond is an unsecured bond.

TIP: The interest rate written in the bond indenture and ordinarily appearing on the bond certificate is known as the **stated rate**. Synonymous terms are **coupon rate, nominal rate**, and **contract rate**.

TIP: The rate of interest actually earned by bondholders is called the **effective, yield,** or **market rate**.

TIP: A bond's **issuance price** is determined by the present value of all of the future cash flows promised by the bond indenture. The future cash flows include the face value and interest payments. The bond's present value is determined by using the market rate of interest at the date of issuance. An excess of the issuance price over par is called a **premium**; an excess of par value over the issuance price is called a **discount**.

TIP: In computing the present value of a bond's (1) maturity value and (2) interest payments, the **same** interest rate is used. That rate is the effective interest rate on a per interest period basis. As an example, if a ten-year bond has a stated rate of 10%, pays interest semiannually, and is issued to yield 12%, a 6% rate is used to perform **all** of the present value calculations.

TIP: Bond prices vary inversely with changes in the market rate of interest. This means that as the market rate of interest goes down, bond prices go up; and as the market rate of interest goes up, bond prices go down. It also means that at the date of issuance, if the market rate of interest is below the stated rate, the price will be above par; likewise, if the market rate is above the stated rate, the issuance price will be below par. Hence, **a premium or a discount is an adjustment to interest via an adjustment to price**. The adjustment to interest is recorded by the process of amortizing the premium or discount over the periods the bond is outstanding.

TIP: Interest payments on notes payable are generally made on a monthly or quarterly basis. Interest payments on bonds payable are usually made semiannually. Despite these common practices, interest rates generally are expressed on an annual basis. Therefore, care must be taken that the annual rate be converted to a "rate per period" before other computations are performed.

TIP: The **Discount on Bonds Payable account** is a contra liability account so its balance should be deducted from Bonds Payable on the balance sheet. The **Premium on Bonds Payable account** is an adjunct type valuation account so its balance should be added to the balance of Bonds Payable on the balance sheet. Unamortized Bond Issuance Costs are to be classified as a deferred charge in the "Other Assets" classification on the balance sheet; they should be amortized over the bond's life using the straight-line method.

TIP: The **effective interest method** of amortization is sometimes called the **interest method** or the **present value method** or the **effective method**. When the effective interest method is used, the bond's carrying value will equal its present value (assuming the amortization is up to date). The effective interest method is the only amortization method that qualifies as a generally accepted principle (method). However, when the results of applying the straight-line method of amortization are not materially different than the results of using the effective interest method, the straight-line method may be used without being considered a departure from (i.e., a violation of) GAAP.

TIP: When the accounting period ends on a date other than an interest date, the amortization schedule for a bond or a note payable is unaffected by this fact. That is, the schedule is prepared and computations are made according to the bond periods, ignoring the details of the accounting period. The interest expense amounts shown in the amortization schedule are then apportioned to the appropriate accounting period(s). As an example, if the interest expense for the six months ending April 30, 2011 is $120,000, then $40,000 (2/6) of that amount would go on the income statement for the 2010 calendar year and $80,000 (4/6) of it should be reflected on the income statement for the 2011 calendar year.

TIP: Accounting for loan impairments was discussed in Appendix 7B where loans were held as assets. The principles are the same when dealing with loan impairments where a loan is a liability from the viewpoint of the reporting entity.

ILLUSTRATION 14-1
COMPUTATION AND PROOF OF BOND ISSUANCE PRICE (L.O. 3, 4)

Guemple Company issues a 5-year bond on January 1, 2010 (maturity date is January 1, 2015, with a stated interest rate of 6%. The market rate of interest at the date of issuance is 5%, the par value is $1,000, and interest is due annually on January 1.

The bond is a promise to pay $1,000 on January 1, 2015 and $60 (6% x $1,000) every January 1 beginning January 1, 2011 and ending January 1, 2015. The price of the bond is determined by the present value of all future cash flows related to the bond. The present value of the bond is found by discounting all of the promised payments at the market rate of interest (5%). This process is illustrated by the following timeline and present value calculations:

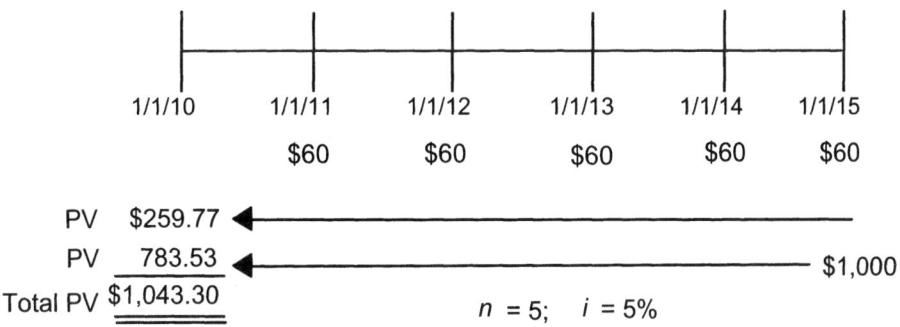

Present value of an ordinary annuity of $60 per period for 5 years at
    5% interest ($60 x 4.32948) $ 259.77
Present value of $1,000 due in 5 periods at 5% interest ($1,000 x .78353).   783.53
Total present value $ 1,043.30

TIP:	The factor of .78353 was derived from the Present Value of 1 table and the factor of 4.32948 was derived from the Present Value of an Ordinary Annuity of 1 table.

Thus, the bond price would be $1,043.30. Theoretically, this is the sum that would be required to be invested now at 5% compounded annually (market rate) to allow for the periodic (annual in this case) withdrawal of $60 (stated amount of interest) at the end of each of 5 years and the withdrawal of $1,000 at the end of 5 years. The following is proof that $1,043.30 is the amount required in this case.

ILLUSTRATION 14-1 (Continued)

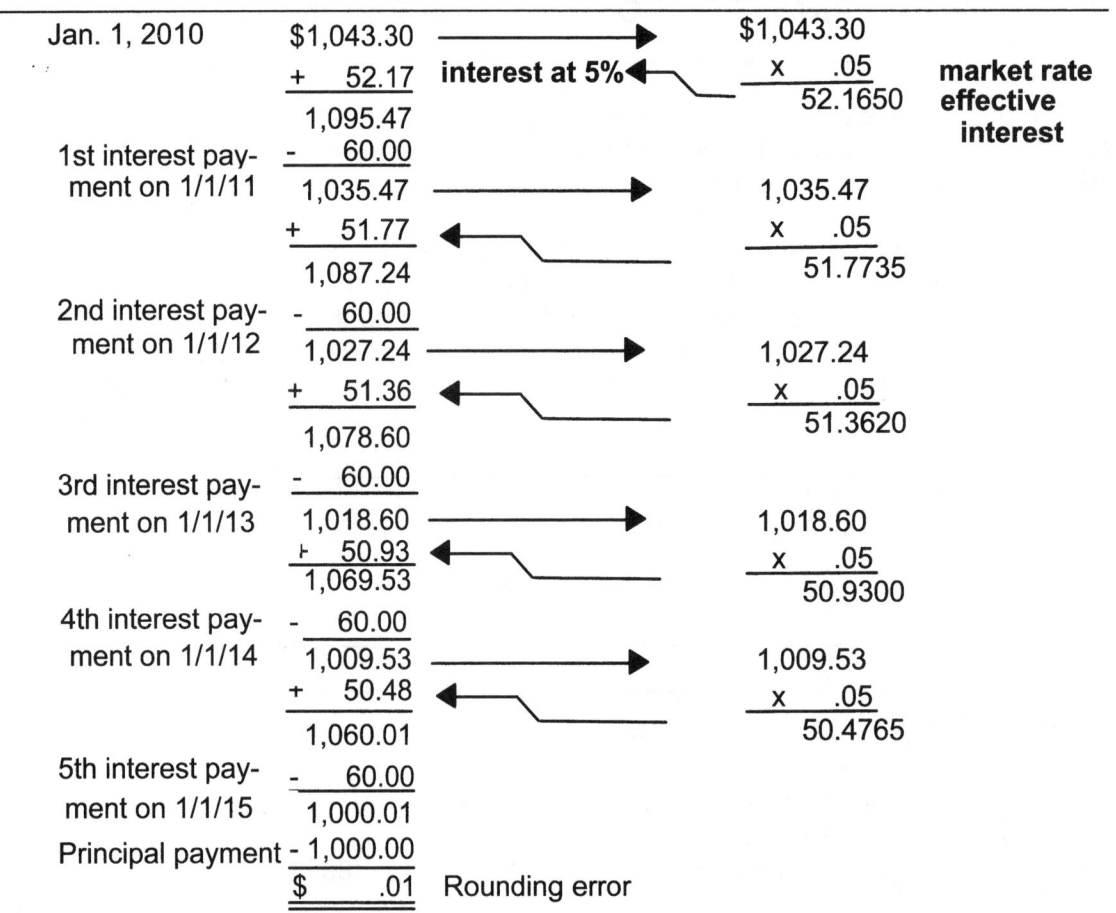

An amortization schedule can be constructed using the computations above. It would appear as follows:

Date	Stated Interest	Effective Interest	Premium Amortization	Carrying Value
1/1/10				$ 1,043.30
1/1/11	$ 60.00	$ 52.17	$ 7.83	1,035.47
1/1/12	60.00	51.77	8.23	1,027.24
1/1/13	60.00	51.36	8.64	1,018.60
1/1/14	60.00	50.93	9.07	1,009.53
1/1/15	60.00	50.47*	9.53	1,000.00
	$300.00	$256.70	$ 43.30	

*The rounding error of $.01 is plugged to interest expense in the last interest period.

ILLUSTRATION 14-2
FORMATS FOR COMMON COMPUTATIONS INVOLVING
BONDS PAYABLE (L.O. 4)

1. Cash Interest Per Period.

    Par value

    x   Stated rate of interest per period

    =   Cash interest per period

    Cash interest is always a constant amount each period.

2. Interest Expense Using Straight-line Amortization Method.

        Cash interest for the period

    +   Discount amortization for the period

    OR - Premium amortization for the period

    =   Interest expense for the period

    Interest expense is a constant amount each period using this method.

3. Amortization Amount Using Straight-line Method.

    Issuance premium or discount ÷ Periods in bonds life = Amortization per period

4. Interest Expense Using Effective Interest Method.

        Carrying value at the beginning of the period

    x   Effective rate of interest per interest period

    =   Interest expense for the interest period

    The carrying value changes each interest period so the interest expense changes each period.

5. Amortization Amount Using Effective Interest Method.

        Interest expense for the interest period

    -   Cash interest for the interest period

    =   Amortization of discount for the interest period

    Interest expense is greater than cash interest for bonds issued at a discount.

    OR

        Cash interest for the interest period

    -   Interest expense for the interest period

    =   Amortization of premium for the interest period

    Cash interest is greater than interest expense for bonds issued at a premium.

6. Carrying Value and Net Carrying Value.

        Par value

    -   Unamortized discount

    OR + Unamortized premium

    =   Carrying value

    -   Unamortized debt issue costs

    =   Net carrying amount

    The process of amortization decreases the unamortized amount of discount or premium; hence the carrying value moves toward the par value.

7. Gain or Loss on Redemption.

        Net carrying amount

    -   Redemption price

    =   Gain if positive, that is, if net carrying value is the greater.

    OR = Loss if negative, that is, if redemption price is the greater.

ILLUSTRATION 14-2 (Continued)

TIP: An **interest payment** promised by a bond is computed by multiplying the bond's par value by its stated interest rate. This amount is often referred to as the **cash interest** or **stated interest**.

TIP: Using the **straight-line method of amortization**, interest expense is determined by either adding the amount of discount amortization to the cash interest or deducting the amount of premium amortization from the cash interest. The periodic amount of amortization is determined by dividing the issuance premium or discount by the number of periods in the bond's life.

TIP: The **life** of a bond is measured by the time between the date of issuance and the date of maturity. The bond's life is shorter than the term of the bond if the bond is issued on a date later than it is dated.

TIP: The **effective interest expense** (interest expense using the effective interest method of amortization) is determined by multiplying the bond's carrying value at the beginning of the period by the effective interest rate. The difference between the interest payment (cash interest) and the effective interest expense for a period is the amount of premium or discount amortization for the period. The amount of amortization for a period causes a reduction in the balance of the unamortized premium or unamortized discount which in turn causes the carrying value to change.

TIP: A bond's **carrying value** (**book value, carrying amount**) is equal to the (1) par value plus any unamortized premium, or (2) par value minus any unamortized discount. When the effective interest method of amortization is used and the amortization is up to date, the bond's carrying value will equal its present value (determined by using the bond's effective interest rate to discount all remaining interest payments and par value). A bond's **net carrying value** is equal to its carrying value minus any related unamortized bond issuance costs.

TIP: The pattern of interest expense using the effective interest method may be compared to the pattern of interest expense using the straight-line method for both a bond issued at a discount and a bond issued at a premium by reference to the graph in **Illustration 14-3**. The relationship between interest expense and cash interest should also be noted. The difference between the cash interest and interest expense for a period is the amount of amortization for the period. The pattern of the periodic amount of amortization is also depicted by the graph.

TIP: If you use the effective interest rate (market rate at the date of a bond's issuance) to compute the (1) present value of the bond at the beginning of a given period, and (2) the present value of the same bond at the end of the given period, the difference between the two present value figures equals the amortization of the bond's premium or discount during that same period. This is true because the effective interest method results in reporting the present value of the liability (using the bond's effective interest rate for the discounting process) at a balance sheet date. That's why the effective interest method is the only method that is GAAP.

EXERCISE 14-1

Purpose: (L.O. 3, 4, 5) This exercise will illustrate (1) the computations and journal entries throughout a bond's life for a bond issued at a discount and (2) the accounting required when bonds are called prior to their maturity date.

Arnold Howell Company issued bonds with the following details:

Face value	$100,000
Stated interest rate	7%
Market interest rate	10%
Maturity date	January 1, 2013
Date of issuance	January 1, 2010
Bond issue costs	$8,000
Call price	102
Interest payments due	Annually on January 1
Method of amortization	Effective interest

Instructions

(a)   Compute the amount of issuance premium or discount.
(b)   Prepare the journal entry for the issuance of bonds.
(c)   Prepare the amortization schedule for these bonds.
(d)   Prepare all of the journal entries (subsequent to the issuance date) for 2010 and 2011 that relate to these bonds. Assume the accounting period coincides with the calendar year.
(e)   Prepare the journal entry to record the retirement of bonds assuming they are called on January 1, 2012.

Solution to Exercise 14-1

(a) $100,000 par x 7% stated rate = $7,000 annual cash interest

Factor for present value of a single sum, i = 10%, n = 3	.75132
Factor for present value of an ordinary annuity, i = 10%, n = 3	2.48685

$100,000 x .75132 =	$ 75,132.00
$7,000 x 2.48685 =	17,407.95
Issuance price	$ 92,539.95

Face value	$ 100,000.00
Issuance price	92,539.95
Discount on bonds payable	$ 7,460.05

(b)

Cash ($92,539.95 - $8,000.00)	84,539.95	
Discount on Bonds Payable	7,460.05	
Unamortized Bond Issue Costs	8,000.00	
Bonds Payable		100,000.00

Approach and Explanation: Always start with the easiest part of a journal entry. The issuance of a bond is **always** recorded by a credit to the Bonds Payable account for the par value of the bonds ($100,000 in this case). Because the issuance price is less than par, a contra type valuation account must be established; it is titled Discount on Bonds Payable and is debited for the issuance discount of $7,460.05. The $8,000 issuance costs are to be amortized over the periods benefited by the loan in order to comply with the matching principle; hence they are initially charged to an asset account. Cash was received for the issuance price less the issuance costs (fees to attorneys, accountants, printers, and underwriters) so debit Cash for the net proceeds of $84,539.95.

> **TIP:** The Unamortized Bond Issue Costs account can be titled Bond Issue Costs. The Discount on Bonds Payable account is sometimes called Unamortized Bond Discount. Regardless of whether the word unamortized appears in the account titles or not, the balances of these accounts at a balance sheet date (after adjustments) represent the unamortized amounts.

(c)

Date	7% Stated Interest	10% Interest Expense	Discount Amortization	Carrying Value
1/1/10				$ 92,539.95
1/1/11	$ 7,000.00	$ 9,254.00	$ 2,254.00	94,793.95
1/1/12	7,000.00	9,479.40	2,479.40	97,273.35
1/1/13	7,000.00	9,726.65[a]	2,726.65	100,000.00
	$ 21,000.00	$ 28,460.05	$ 7,460.05	

[a]Includes rounding error of $.69.

Explanation: Stated interest is determined by multiplying the par value ($100,000) by the contract rate of interest (7%). Interest expense is computed by multiplying the carrying value at the beginning of the interest period by the effective interest rate (10%). The amount of discount amortization for the period is the excess of the interest expense over the stated interest (cash interest) amount. The carrying value at an interest payment date is the carrying value at the beginning of the interest period plus the discount amortization for the period.

> **TIP:** The amount of interest expense of $9,479.40 appearing on the "1/1/12" payment line is the amount of interest expense for the interest period ending on that date. Thus, in this case, $9,479.40 is the interest expense for the twelve months preceding the date 1/1/12, which would be the calendar year of 2011.
>
> **TIP:** Any rounding error should be plugged to (included in) the interest expense amount for the last interest period. Otherwise, there would forever be a small balance left in the Discount on Bonds Payable account long after the bonds were extinguished.
>
> **TIP:** Notice that the total interest expense ($28,460.05) over the three-year period equals the total cash interest ($21,000.00) plus the total issuance discount ($7,460.05). Thus, you can see that the issuance discount represents an additional amount of interest to be recognized over the life of the bonds.

(d)   **December 31, 2010**
      Bond Interest Expense.. 9,254.00
         Interest Payable 7,000.00
         Discount on Bonds Payable 2,254.00

      Bond Issue Expense 2,666.67
         Unamortized Bond Issue Costs............................. 2,666.67
         ($8,000.00 ÷ 3 = $2,666.67)

      January 1, 2011
      Interest Payable 7,000.00
         Cash 7,000.00

      December 31, 2011
      Bond Interest Expense.. 9,479.40
         Interest Payable 7,000.00
         Discount on Bonds Payable 2,479.40

      Bond Issue Expense 2,666.67
         Unamortized Bond Issue Costs............................. 2,666.67

(e)   **January 1, 2012**
      Interest Payable 7,000.00
      Bonds Payable 100,000.00
      Loss on Redemption of Bonds 7,393.31
         Discount on Bonds Payable 2,726.65
         Unamortized Bond Issue Costs............................. 2,666.66
         Cash ($102,000 + $7,000)...................................... 109,000.00

         ($7,460.05 - $2,254.00 - $2,479.40 = $2,726.65 unamortized discount)
         ($8,000.00 - $2,666.67 - $2,666.67 = $2,666.66 unamortized issue costs)
         ($100,000.00 x 102% = $102,000.00 price to retire)
         ($100,000.00 - $2,726.65 = $97,273.35 carrying value)
         ($97,273.35 - $2,666.66 = $94,606.69 net carrying value)
         ($102,000.00 - $94,606.69 = $7,393.31 loss)

> **TIP:** There was a **call premium** (amount in excess of par required) of $2,000.00 in this situation which is included in the loss computation.
>
> **TIP:** Gains or losses on extinguishment of debt are to be classified as Other Gains and Losses on the income statement.
>
> **TIP:** The debit to interest payable (for interest accrued last period) assumes that reversing entries are **not** made. Reversing entries were discussed in **Appendix 3A**.

ILLUSTRATION 14-3
GRAPH TO DEPICT INTEREST PATTERNS FOR BONDS (L.O. 4)

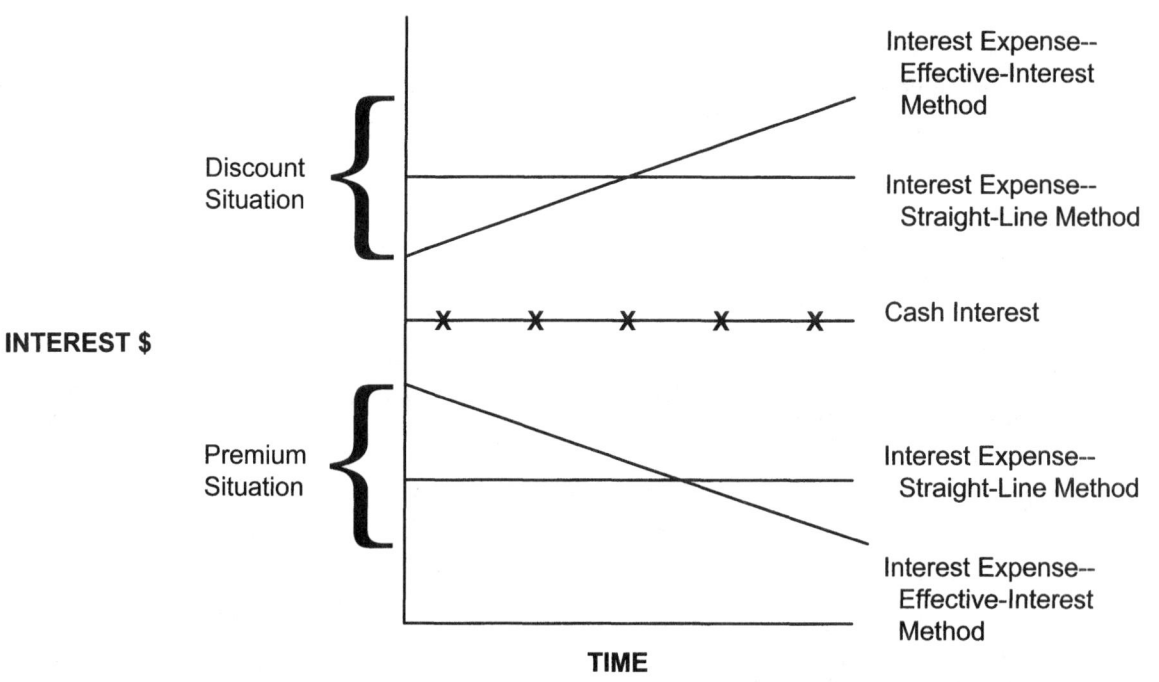

TIP:	Regardless of whether the straight-line method of amortization or the effective interest method of amortization is used, the following will occur:
	1. The amount of cash interest (stated interest) is a constant amount each period.
	2. The bond's carrying amount increases over the bond's life if it is issued at a discount, due to the amortization of the discount.
	3. The bond's carrying amount decreases over the bond's life if it is issued at a premium, due to the amortization of the premium.
TIP:	If the straight-line method of amortization is used, the following relationships will exist:
	1. The amount of amortization is a constant amount each period.
	2. The amount of interest expense is a constant amount each period.
TIP:	If the effective interest method of amortization is used, the following relationships will exist:
	1. The effective interest rate is constant each period.
	2. The interest expense is an increasing amount each period if the bond is issued at a discount (because a constant rate is applied to an increasing carrying amount each period).
	3. The interest expense is a decreasing amount each period if the bond is issued at a premium (because a constant rate is applied to a decreasing carrying amount each period).
	4. The amount of amortization **increases** each period because the difference between the effective interest expense and the cash interest widens each period.

EXERCISE 14-2

Purpose: (L.O. 4) This exercise will serve as an example for both the issuance of bonds between interest payment dates and the use of the straight-line method of amortization.

On May 1, 2010, Peter Pan Tools Corporation issued bonds payable with a face value of $1,400,000 at 104 plus accrued interest. They are registered bonds dated January 1, 2010, bear interest at 9% payable semiannually on January 1 and July 1, and mature January 1, 2020. The company uses the straight-line method of amortization.

Instructions
(a)   Compute the amount of bond interest expense to be reported on Peter Pan's income statement for the year ended December 31, 2010. (Round computations to the nearest dollar.)
(b)   Compute the amount of bond interest payable to be reported on Peter Pan's balance sheet at December 31, 2010.
(c)   Compute the amount of bond interest expense to be reported on Peter Pan's income statement for the year ended December 31, 2011.

Solution to Exercise 14-2

(a)
Interest paid on July 1, 2010 ($1,400,000 x 9% x 6/12)	$ 63,000
Premium amortized on July 1, 2010 ($56,000 x 2/116)	(966)
Accrued interest collected on May 1, 2010 ($1,400,000 x 9% x 4/12)	(42,000)
Interest accrued on December 31, 2010 ($1,400,000 x 9% x 6/12)	63,000
Premium amortized on December 31, 2010 ($56,000 x 6/116)	(2,897)
Total bond interest expense for the year ending December 31, 2010	$ 80,137

Approach and Explanation: Prepare the journal entries to record the issuance of the bonds, the payment of interest and amortization of premium on July 1, 2010, and the year-end adjusting entry. Post the entries to the Interest Expense account and determine its balance at December 31, 2010.

May 1, 2010

Cash	1,498,000[c]	
Bonds Payable		1,400,000
Premium on Bonds Payable		56,000[a]
Bond Interest Expense		42,000[b]
(To record sale of bonds at a premium plus accrued interest)		

[a](104% x $1,400,000) - $1,400,000 = $56,000 issuance premium.
[b]9% x $1,400,000 x 4 months/12 months = $42,000 accrued interest (for January through April 2010).
[c]$1,400,000 face value x 104% = $1,456,000 issuance price.
$1,456,000 issuance price + $42,000 accrued interest = $1,498,000 cash proceeds.

July 1, 2010

Bond Interest Expense ($63,000 - $966)	62,034	
Premium on Bonds Payable ($56,000 x 2/116)...................	966	
Cash ($1,400,000 x 9% x 6/12)...............................		63,000
(To record semiannual payment of interest and amortization of premium for two months)		

> **TIP:** A premium or discount is to be amortized over the period the bonds are outstanding (from the date of issuance to the date of maturity). In this case, May 1, 2010 to January 1, 2020 is 4 months shy of 10 years (which is 116 months).

December 31, 2010

Bond Interest Expense ($63,000 - $2,897)	60,103	
Premium on Bond Payable ($56,000 x 6/116)	2,897	
Bond Interest Payable		63,000
($1,400,000 x 9% x 6/12)		
(To record accrual of interest since last payment date and amortization of premium for 6 months)		

Bond Interest Expense				Bond Interest Payable	
7/1/10	62,034	5/1/10 42,000		12/31/10	63,000
12/31/10	60,103				
Balance				Balance	
12/31/10	80,137			12/31/10	63,000

> **TIP:** Bonds are often issued between interest payment dates. When this occurs, the issuer requires the investor to pay the market price for the bonds plus accrued interest since the last interest date. At the next interest payment date, the corporation will return the accrued interest to the investor by paying the full amount of interest due on outstanding bonds. In the situation at hand, the issuer collects from the investor interest from the date the bonds are dated to the date of issuance (from January 1, 2010 to May 1, 2010 is 4 months). When the next interest date rolls around (July 1, 2010), a full interest payment is made to the investor. Thus, the investor receives the two months' interest earned from May 1, 2010 to June 30, 2010, plus the accrued interest for four months that the investor paid in at the purchase date. Accrued interest at the date bonds are sold by an issuer is handled in this manner to expedite the issuer's payment procedures. At any interest payment date, interest for a full interest period is paid to each bondholder, there is no need to compute the actual time the bond investment was held by a particular bondholder and to prorate the interest because the investor has already paid in any portion of the full interest payment not earned by them during that interest period.

> **TIP:** The journal entry to record the second interest payment on January 1, 2011 would be as follows (assuming reversing entries are not used):
>
> | | | |
> |---|---|---|
> | Bond Interest Payable...................................... | 63,000 | |
> | Cash.. | | 63,000 |
> | (To record a full interest payment) | | |

TIP:	Refer to the journal entry made at the date of issuance (May 1, 2010). Rather than credit Bond Interest Expense for $42,000, you may credit Bond Interest Payable for the accrued interest of $42,000. This procedure will then require a modification to the entry on July 1, 2010. That entry would then include a debit to Bond Interest Payable for $42,000 and a debit to Bond Interest Expense for $20,034 rather than a debit to Bond Interest Expense for $62,034.
TIP:	Refer to the journal entry made at December 31, 2010. You may wish to make two separate entries rather than the one compound entry. The equivalent single entries would be as follows:

December 31, 2010

Bond Interest Expense..	63,000	
Bond Interest Payable..		63,000
(To record accrued interest for the 6 months)		
($1,400,000 x 9% x 6/12 = $63,000)		
Premium on Bonds Payable	2,897	
Bond Interest Expense..		2,897
(To record premium amortization for 6 months)		
($56,000 x 6/116 = $2,897)		

(b)   Accrued interest payable at December 31, 2010:
        $1,400,000 x 9% x 6/12 = $63,000

TIP:	Refer to explanation of part (a) above and balance of T-account for Bond Interest Payable.

(c)

Interest paid on July 1, 2011 ($1,400,000 x 9% x 6/12)	$ 63,000
Premium amortized on July 1, 2011 ($56,000 x 6/116)	(2,897)
Interest accrued on December 31, 2011 ($1,400,000 x 9% x 6/12)	63,000
Premium amortized on December 31, 2011 ($56,000 x 6/116)	(2,897)
Total bond interest expense for the year ending December 31, 2011	$ 120,206

EXERCISE 14-3

Purpose: (L.O. 4) This exercise will illustrate the computation of the bond price when interest is due semiannually. Additionally, it will present the accounting for bonds where the effective interest method of amortization is used and the end of the accounting period does not coincide with the end of an interest period.

P&J Chase Company sells $500,000 of 10% bonds on November 1, 2010. The bonds pay interest on May 1 and November 1 and are to yield 12%. The due date of the bonds is May 1, 2014. The accounting period is the calendar year. No reversing entries are made. Bond premium or discount is to be amortized at interest dates and at year-end.

Instructions

(a)   Compute the price of the bonds at the issuance date.
(b)   Prepare the amortization schedule for this issue.
(c)   Prepare all of the relevant journal entries for this bond issue from the date of issuance through May 2012.

Solution to Exercise 14-3

(a)   Time diagram:

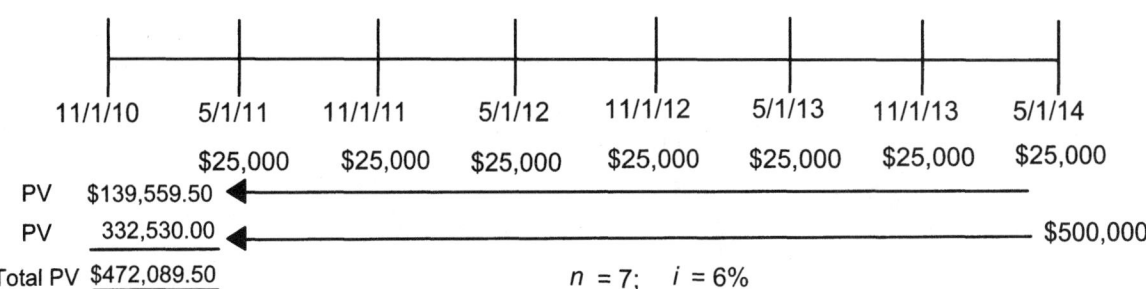

Factor for present value of a single sum, $i = 6\%$, $n = 7$ .66506
Factor for present value of an ordinary annuity, $i = 6\%$, $n = 7$ 5.58238
$500,000 x 5% = $25,000 interest per period
$500,000 x .66506 = $ 332,530.00
$25,000 x 5.58238 =   139,559.50
Issuance price $ 472,089.50

(b)

Date	5% Stated Interest	6% Interest Expense	Discount Amortization	Carrying Value
11/1/10				$ 472,089.50
5/1/11	$ 25,000.00	$ 28,325.37	$ 3,325.37	475,414.87
11/1/11	25,000.00	28,524.89	3,524.89	478,939.76
5/1/12	25,000.00	28,736.39	3,736.39	482,676.15
11/1/12	25,000.00	28,960.57	3,960.57	486,636.72
5/1/13	25,000.00	29,198.20	4,198.20	490,834.92
11/1/13	25,000.00	29,450.10	4,450.10	495,285.02
5/1/14	25,000.00	29,714.98*	4,714.98	500,000.00
	$ 175,000.00	$202,910.50	$ 27,910.50	

*Includes a rounding error of $2.12.

TIP: There are two interest periods per year; therefore, the stated interest rate per interest period is the annual rate (10%) divided by 2, which is 5%.

TIP: If you round all of your computations to the nearest cent, your rounding error will be small. A small (less than $5.00) rounding error provides some comfort that the amortization schedule is largely correct. A large rounding error (more than $10.00) indicates that one or more mistakes are likely included in the computation within the schedule or in the determination of the starting point (issuance price of the debt).

TIP:	The amortization schedule displays amounts according to bond periods. If one interest period overlaps two different accounting periods, the amount of expense and amortization for that interest period must be appropriately allocated to the respective accounting periods.
TIP:	Instead of just memorizing what goes on an amortization schedule, think about the reason the amounts have been included. That will help you to construct a schedule without much effort. In the date column, start with the issuance date, followed by each interest date. The stated interest amount is computed by multiplying the face value of the instrument by the stated rate of interest per interest period. Interest expense is computed by multiplying the carrying value at the beginning of the period (end of the prior line on the amortization schedule) by the market rate of interest per period. The difference between the stated interest and the interest expense for the period is the amount of the amortization for the period. Discount amortization is added to the previous carrying value (or premium amortization is deducted from the previous carrying value) to arrive at the carrying value at the end of the interest period (interest payment date).

(c)

November 1, 2010

Cash	472,089.50	
Discount on Bonds Payable	27,910.50	
Bonds Payable		500,000.00

December 31, 2010

Bond Interest Expense	9,441.79	
Discount on Bonds Payable		1,108.46
Interest Payable		8,333.33

($28,325.37 x 2/6 = $9,441.79)
($3,325.37 x 2/6 = $1,108.46)
($25,000.00 x 2/6 = $8,333.33)

May 1, 2011

Interest Payable	8,333.33	
Bond Interest Expense	18,883.58	
Discount on Bonds Payable		2,216.91
Cash		25,000.00

($28,325.37 - $9,441.79 = $18,883.58)
($3,325.37 - $1,108.46 = $2,216.91)

November 1, 2011

Bond Interest Expense	28,524.89	
Discount on Bonds Payable		3,524.89
Cash		25,000.00

December 31, 2011

Bond Interest Expense	9,578.80	
Discount on Bond Payable		1,245.47
Interest Payable		8,333.33

($28,736.39 x 2/6 = $9,578.80)
($3,736.39 x 2/6 = $1,245.46 + $.01 to balance)
($25,000.00 x 2/6 = $8,333.33)

May 1, 2012

Bond Interest Expense..	19,157.59	
Interest Payable	8,333.33	
Discount on Bonds Payable		2,490.92
Cash...		25,000.00

($28,736.39 - $9,578.80 = $19,157.59)
($3,736.39 - $1,245.47 = $2,490.92)

EXERCISE 14-4

Purpose: (L.O. 3, 4, 8) This exercise will enable you to practice identifying data required to perform computations involving bonds payable and applying the terminology associated with bonds.

On January 1, 2010, Tuna Fishery sold $100,000 (face value) worth of bonds. The bonds are dated January 1, 2010 and will mature on January 1, 2015. Interest is to be paid annually on January 1. Issue costs related to these bonds amounted to $2,000, and these costs are being amortized by the straight-line method. The following amortization schedule was prepared by the accountant for the first 2 years of the life of the bonds:

Date	Stated Interest	Effective Interest	Amortization	Carrying Value of Bonds
1/1/10				$ 104,212.37
1/1/11	$ 7,000.00	$ 6,252.74	$ 747.26	103,465.11
1/1/12	7,000.00	6,207.91	792.09	102,673.02

Instructions

On the basis of the information above, answer the following questions (round your answers to the nearest cent or percent) and explain the reasoning or computations, as appropriate.
(a)   What is the nominal or stated rate of interest for this bond issue?
(b)   What is the effective or market rate of interest for this bond issue?
(c)   Prepare the journal entry to record the sale of the bond issue on January 1, 2010, including the issue costs.
(d)   Prepare the appropriate entry(ies) at December 31, 2012, the end of the accounting year.
(e)   Identify the amount of bond issue costs and the amount of interest expense to be reported on the income statement for the year ended December 31, 2012.
(f)   Show how the account balances related to the bond issue will be presented on the December 31, 2012 balance sheet. Indicate the major classification(s) involved.
(g)   What is the book value of the bonds at December 31, 2012?
(h)   What is the net book value of the bonds at December 31, 2012?
(i)   If the bonds are retired for $100,500 (excluding interest) at January 1, 2013, will the bonds be retired at a gain or a loss? What is the amount of that gain or loss? Where will it be reported on the income statement for the year ending December 31, 2013?

Solution to Exercise 14-4

(a)   Stated interest = Stated rate of interest x Par
$7,000 = Stated rate of interest x $100,000
$7,000 ÷ $100,000 = Stated rate of interest
7% = Stated rate of interest

(b)   Effective interest = Market rate x Carrying value at beginning of period
$6,252.74 = Market rate x $104,212.37
$6,252.74 ÷ $104,212.37 = Market rate
6% = Market rate

(c)   Cash.. 102,212.37
       Unamortized Bond Issue Costs..................................... 2,000.00
          Bonds Payable 100,000.00
          Premium on Bonds Payable.............................   4,212.37

(d)   Bond Interest Expense... 6,160.38
       Premium on Bonds Payable....................................... 839.62
          Interest Payable 7,000.00
          ($102,673.02 x 6% = $6,160.38)

       Bond Issue Expense 400
          Unamortized Bond Issue Costs........................   400

(e)   Bond issue expense[1] $400
       Bond interest expense[2] $6,160.38
       [1]$2,000   5 years = $400
       [2]$102,673.02 X 6% = $6,160.38

(f)   **Other assets**
          Unamortized bond issue costs $ 800
       Current liabilities
          Interest payable $7,000
       Long-term liabilities
          Bonds payable, 7%, due 1/1/15 $ 100,000.00
          Unamortized premium[1]   1,833.40
                                                       $ 101,833.40

       [1]$4,212.37 - $747.26 - $792.09 - $839.62 = $1,833.40

(g) $101,833.40 [See solution for part (f).]
       Book value is another name for carrying value or carrying amount.

       The amount, $101,833.40, can also be computed by:
          Carrying value at 1/1/12 per schedule $ 102,673.02
          Amortization for 2012 [part (d)]   (839.62)
          Carrying value at 12/31/12 $ 101,833.40

(h)

Bonds payable balance	$ 100,000.00
Premium on bonds payable balance	1,833.40
Book value at 12/31/12	101,833.40
Unamortized bond issue costs	(800.00)*
Net book value at 12/31/12	$ 101,033.40

*[$2,000 - 3($400) = $800]

(i)   Gain. A gain will result because the retirement price is less than the net carrying value at the date of retirement.

Net carrying value at 1/1/13 [part (g)]	$ 101,033.40
Retirement price	100,500.00
Gain on retirement of debt	$ 533.40

This gain from retirement of debt should be classified in the Other Gains and Losses section on the income statement.

EXERCISE 14-5

Purpose: (L.O. 3) This exercise will illustrate how to account for the redemption of bonds by cash payment prior to maturity.

The balance sheet for Waisman Corporation reports the following information on December 31, 2009:

Long-term liabilities

9% Bonds payable, due December 31, 2013	$ 1,000,000	
Less: Discount on bonds payable	60,000	
		$ 940,000

Interest is payable annually on December 31. The straight-line method of amortization is used. Interest rates have declined in the market place since the above mentioned bonds were issued. Waisman decides to borrow money from another source at a lower interest rate to lower its annual interest charges. Therefore, on July 1, 2010, Waisman redeems all of the old outstanding bonds at 102 (recall that bond prices vary inversely with changes in the market rate of interest).

Instructions

Prepare the journal entry(ies) to record the redemption of these bonds on July 1, 2010.

Solution to Exercise 14-5

Bond Interest Expense...	45,000	
Cash		45,000
(To record the payment of accrued interest at July 1, 2010)		
($1,000,000 x 9% x 6/12 = $45,000)		

Bond Interest Expense...	7,500	
Discount on Bonds Payable...		7,500
(To record the amortization of discount for six months)		
[($60,000 ÷ 4) x 6/12]		

Bonds Payable..	1,000,000	
Loss on Bond Redemption..	72,500[3]	
Discount on Bonds Payable...		52,500[2]
Cash		1,020,000[1]
(To record the redemption of the bonds payable at 102)		

[1]$1,000,000 face value x 1.02 = $1,020,000 redemption price.
[2]$60,000 - $7,500 = $52,500 balance at July 1, 2010.
[3]$1,020,000 redemption price - $947,500 carrying value = $72,500 loss on redemption.

Approach and Explanation: Break the required entries into three simple parts— payment of accrued interest, update of discount amortization, and extinguishment of the liability. The bond holder is entitled to interest for the months between the last interest payment date and the redemption date, which is six months in this case. The amortization of the discount must be updated to arrive at the carrying value of the debt at the redemption date. In this case, six months of amortization must be recorded. The straight-line amortization method is being used so the $60,000 balance in the discount account at December 31, 2010 applies evenly to the remaining four years of the bond's term. The amortization for six months would, therefore, be one-half of the $15,000 annual amount.

For the entry to record the redemption, do the following: (1) Begin with the easiest part of the journal entry. Credit Cash to record the payment of the redemption price which is 102% of the face value of the bonds. (2) Remove the carrying value of the bonds from the accounts by debiting Bonds Payable for the face value of the bonds and crediting Discount on Bonds Payable for the balance of the related unamortized discount ($60,000 balance at December 31, 2009 less the $7,500 amortization for the first six months of 2010 = $52,500). (3) Record the difference between the redemption (retirement) price and the carrying value of the bonds as a gain or loss on redemption. An excess of carrying value over redemption price results in a gain. In the case at hand, the redemption price ($1,020,000) exceeds the carrying value of the bonds ($1,000,000 - $52,500 = $947,500). Since it cost $1,020,000 to eliminate a debt that appears on the books at only $947,500, a loss results.

EXERCISE 14-6

Purpose: (L.O. 6, 8) This exercise will illustrate the accounting for the issuance of a note payable to acquire land when the note bears an interest rate that is unreasonably low in relation to the market rate of interest.

On December 31, 2009, Jason Weiss, Inc. purchased land by giving $40,000 in cash and a 3% interest-bearing note with a face value of $500,000. There was no established exchange price for the land, nor a ready market for the note. The land had an assessed value of $320,000 for purposes of taxation by the county. The note is due December 31, 2013. Interest is payable each December 31. Jason's incremental borrowing rate is 10%.

Instructions
(a)   Draw a time line for the note and determine the amount to record as the cost of the land.
(b)   Prepare the amortization schedule for the note payable.
(c)   Determine the amount to report as interest expense on the income statement for the fiscal year ending March 31, 2011.
(d)   Determine the amount to report as interest paid on the statement of cash flows for the fiscal year ending March 31, 2011.
(e)   Determine the amounts to appear (with respect to the above information) on the balance sheet at March 31, 2011, and indicate the proper classification for each item.

Solution to Exercise 14-6

(a)   Time line:

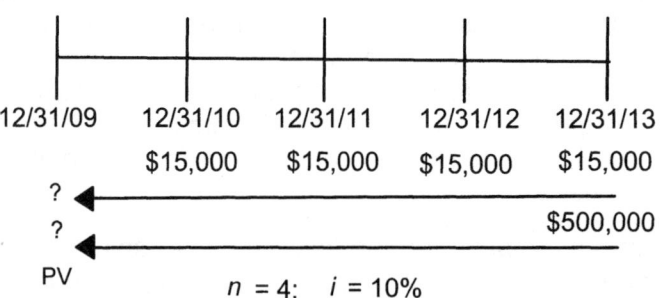

12/31/09 Land	429,052.90	
Discount on Note Payable	110,947.10	
Note Payable		500,000.00
Cash		40,000.00

   The market rate of interest is used to compute the present value of the note which is then used to establish the exchange price for the land. The cash down payment of $40,000.00 plus the present value of the note of $389,052.90 equals the $429,052.90 cost of the land. The market rate of interest should be the rate the borrower normally would have to pay to borrow money for similar activities.

Computation of the present value of the note:

Maturity value		$500,000.00
Present value of $500,000 due in 4 years at 10% ($500,000 x .68301)	$341,505.00	
Present value of $15,000 payable annually for 4 years at 10% ($15,000 x 3.16986)	47,547.90	
Present value of the note and interest		389,052.90
Discount on note receivable		$110,947.10

(b)

Amortization Schedule for Note Payable

Date	3% Stated Interest	10% Effective Interest	Amortization of Discount	PV Balance
12/31/09				$ 389,052.90
12/31/10	$15,000.00[a]	$ 38,905.29[b]	$ 23,905.29[c]	412,958.19[d]
12/31/11	15,000.00	41,295.82	26,295.82	439,254.01
12/31/12	15,000.00	43,925.40	28,925.40	468,179.41
12/31/13	15,000.00	46,820.59[e]	31,820.59	500,000.00
Totals	$60,000.00	$170,947.10	$110,947.10	

[a]$500,000.00 face value x 3% stated interest rate = $15,000.00 stated interest
[b]$389,052.90 present value x 10% effective interest rate = $38,905.29 effective interest.
[c]$38,905.29 effective interest - $15,000.00 stated interest = $23,905.29 discount amortization.
[d]$389,052.90 PV balance 12/31/09 + $23,905.29 discount amortization for 12 months = $412,958.19 PV balance 12/31/10.
[e]Includes rounding difference of $2.65.

Explanation: When a note is given in exchange for property, goods, or services in a bargained transaction entered into at arms length, the stated interest rate is assumed to be fair and is thus used to compute interest revenue unless:
1.   No interest rate is stated, or
2.   The stated interest rate is unreasonable, or
3.   The face amount of the note is materially different from the current cash sales price for the same or similar items or from the current market value of the debt instrument.

In these circumstances, the present value of the note is measured by the fair value of the property, goods, or services. If the fair value of the property, goods, or services is not readily determinable, the market value of the note is used to establish the present value of the note. If the note has no ready market, the present value of the note is approximated by discounting all of the related future cash payments (for interest and principal) on the note at the market rate of interest. This rate is referred to as an imputed rate and should be equal to the borrower's incremental borrowing rate (that is, the rate of interest the maker of the note would currently have to pay if it borrowed money from another source for this same purpose). Jason Weiss, Inc. issued a note in exchange for land. No information was given about the fair value of the services or the market value of the note. Thus, the debtor company's incremental borrowing rate of 10% was used to impute interest and determine the note's present value.

(c)   Interest from April 1, 2007 thru December 31, 2010:

$38,905.29 x 9/12	$29,178.97
Interest from January 1, 2008 thru March 31, 2011:	
$41,295.82 x 3/12	10,323.96
Interest for the fiscal year ending March 31, 2011:	$39,502.93

TIP: The amount of interest shown on the 12/31/10 line in the amortization schedule is the amount of interest that pertains to the interest period that is just ending on that date (12/31/10 in this case). When interest is payable annually, an interest period is twelve months in length. When interest is payable semi-annually, each interest period is six months long.

TIP: When the end of an accounting period does not coincide with an interest payment date, interest must be apportioned to the proper periods. For example, we will use the amortization schedule above and assume that the accounting period ends on March 31, 2010. The effective interest of $38,905.29 for the calendar year ending December 31, 2010 must be apportioned between two fiscal years: the one ending March 31, 2010 and the one ending March 31, 2011. 3/12 X $38,905.29 = $9,726.32 would be allocated to the fiscal year ending March 31, 2010 and 9/12 X $38,905.29 = $29,178.97 would be allocated to the fiscal year ending March 31, 2011. The twelve months ending March 31, 2011 would include the 9/12 X $38,905.29 plus three months of the $41,295.82 interest amount shown on the 12/31/11 payment line.

Entering the interest amounts from the amortization schedule into the proper places on a time line should greatly help your comprehension of these computations. The following pictoral will aid you in following the logic of the computations.

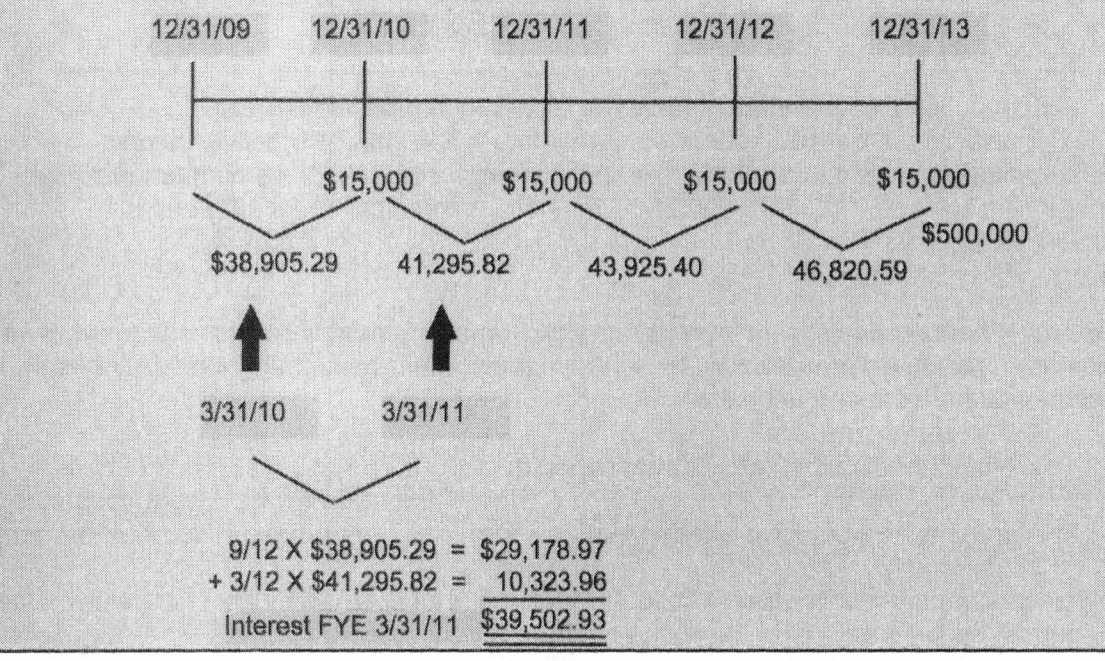

(d)   A payment of cash of $15,000 was made for interest on December 31, 2010. Thus, a cash outflow of $15,000 would be reflected in the operating activity section of the statement of cash flows for the fiscal year ending March 31, 2011.

(e)
Balance Sheet
March 31, 2011

Property, Plant & Equipment		Current Liabilities	
Land	$429,052.90	Interest Payable	$3,750.00[a]
		Long-term Liabilities	
		Note Payable	$500,000.00
		Less: Discount on	
		Note	80,467.85[b]
			$419,532.15

[a]3/12 x $15,000 = $3,750.00
[b]3/12 x $26,295.82 = 6,573.96 amortization of discount for 01/01/11 - 03/31/11

$110,947.10	Balance of Discount on Note Payable on 12/31/09
(23,905.29)	Amortization for 01/01/10 thru 12/31/10
(6,573.96)	Amortization for 01/01/11 thru 3/31/11
$ 80,467.85	Balance of Discount on Note Payable on 03/31/11

EXERCISE 14-7

Purpose: (L.O. 6) This exercise will illustrate the accounting entries for a long-term note payable.

The Weiss Corporation issued a $400,000, 10%, 10-year mortgage note on December 31, 2009. The terms provide for semiannual installment payments of $32,097.03 on June 30 and December 31. The note along with $80,000 cash was given in exchange for a new building. The accounting period is the calendar year.

Instructions
Prepare the journal entries to record:
(a) The acquisition of the building and inception of the mortgage loan payable.
(b) The first mortgage payment on June 30, 2010.
(c) The second mortgage payment on December 31, 2010.

SOLUTION TO EXERCISE 14-7

December 31, 2009

(a) Building... 480,000.00

  Cash... 80,000.00

  Mortgage Note Payable..................................... 400,000.00

June 30, 2010

(b) Interest Expense... 20,000.00*

  Mortgage Note Payable....................................... 12,097.03**

  Cash.. 32,097.03

*Principal balance at December 31, 2009		$400,000.00
Semiannual interest rate	X	.05
Interest expense for first 6 months		$ 20,000.00

**First payment	$32,097.03
Interest portion of first payment	(20,000.00)
Reduction in principal - first installment payment	$12,097.03

December 31, 2010

(c) Interest Expense... 19,395.15*

  Mortgage Note Payable....................................... 12,701.88**

  Cash.. 32,097.03

*Principal balance at December 31, 2009	$400,000.00
Reduction in principal - first installment payment	(12,097.03)
Principal balance at June 30, 2010	387,902.97
Semiannual interest rate	.05
Interest expense for second 6 months	$ 19,395.15

**Second payment	$32,097.03
Interest portion of second payment	(19,395.15)
Reduction in principal - second installment payment	$12,701.88

Explanation to part (a): The cost of the building is determined by the fair market value of the consideration given which is the $80,000 cash plus the $400,000 present value of the note payable.

Explanation to parts (b) and (c): The mortgage note payable is recorded initially at its face value ($400,000), which is often referred to as the note's beginning principal, and each installment payment reduces the outstanding principal amount. The installment payments are an equal amount each interest period; however, the portion of the payment going to cover interest charges and the portion going to reduce the outstanding principal varies each period. In this exercise, the installment payments are due semiannually; thus, the length of an interest period is six months and the annual interest rate (10%) must be expressed on a semiannual basis (5%) to perform the interest computation. Interest is a function of outstanding balance, interest rate, and time. Thus, the interest sustained for the first six months is determined by the note's initial carrying value (the face value of $400,000), the annual rate of 10%, and a six-month time period. The interest sustained for the second six months cannot be determined until the outstanding principal balance is updated for the portion of the first installment payment that is to be applied to the principal balance. The updated principal balance (carrying value) is used to compute the interest charges for the second interest period. Although the exercise does not require a complete payment schedule (often called an amortization schedule) for this note, one is presented below for your observation and study. Notice that as subsequent installment payments are made, a decreasing portion of each payment goes to cover interest and an increasing portion is applied to the principal balance. The reason for this is the fact that interest is computed by a constant interest rate (5% each interest period) multiplied by a decreasing principal balance (carrying value).

> **TIP:** The stated rate of interest (10% in this case) is assumed to be equal to the market rate of interest; therefore, the present value of the note at its inception is the same as the face value ($400,000) and there is no discount or premium related to this mortgage note payable.
>
> **TIP:** A mortgage note will usually require the borrower to make monthly payments, and interest is then compounded monthly. In this exercise, semiannual payments are assumed (thus interest is compounded twice a year) in order to simplify the amortiza-tion schedule but yet allow you an opportunity to view a situation involving the compounding of interest more than once a year.

Mortgage Installment Payment Schedule

Semiannual Interest Period	(A) Cash Payment	(B) Interest Expense (D) X 5%	(C) Reduction of Principal (A) - (B)	(D) Principal Balance (D) - (C)
12/31/09				$400,000.00
6/30/10	$ 32,097.03	$ 20,000.00	$ 12,097.03	387,902.97
12/31/10	32,097.03	19,395.15	12,701.88	375,201.09
6/30/11	32,097.03	18,760.05	13,336.98	361,864.11
12/31/11	32,097.03	18,093.21	14,003.82	347,860.29
6/30/12	32,097.03	17,393.01	14,704.02	333,156.27
12/31/12	32,097.03	16,657.81	15,439.22	317.717.05
6/30/13	32,097.03	15,885.85	16,211.18	301,505.87
12/31/13	32,097.03	15,075.29	17,021.74	284,484.13
6/30/14	32,097.03	14,224.21	17,872.82	266,611.31
12/31/14	32,097.03	13,330.57	18,766.46	247,844.85
6/30/15	32,097.03	12,392.24	19,704.79	228,140.06
12/31/15	32,097.03	11,407.00	20,690.03	207,450.03
6/30/16	32,097.03	10,372.50	21,724.53	185,725.50
12/31/16	32,097.03	9,286.28	22,810.75	162,914.75
6/30/17	32,097.03	8,145.74	23,951.29	138,963.46
12/31/17	32,097.03	6,948.17	25,148.86	113,814.60
6/30/18	32,097.03	5,690.73	26,406.30	87,408.30
12/31/18	32,097.93	4,370.42	27,726.61	59,681.69
6/30/19	32,097.03	2,984.08	29,112.95	30,568.74
12/31/19	32,097.03	1,528.29[a]	30,568.74	0.00
Totals	$641,940.60	$241,940.60	$400,000.00	

[a]Includes rounding difference of 15¢.

> **TIP:** Notice that the total interest to be incurred over the ten-year period is $241,940.60 on the loan of $400,000.00. The pattern of interest charges is one of a decreasing amount each interest period because interest is a function of present value balance, constant rate, and time.

EXERCISE 14-8

Purpose: (L.O. 6, 8) This exercise will illustrate how an installment note payable affects the financial statements.

The use of a mortgage note is a common vehicle to finance the acquisition of long-lived tangible assets. A mortgage note usually requires the borrower to repay the loan by equal periodic payments over the life of the loan. Each payment goes to cover the interest accrued during the time segment since the previous payment and to reduce the principal balance.

Instructions

Using the amortization schedule from **Exercise 14-7**, answer the following questions:

(a) How much interest expense would be reported on the income statement for the year ending December 31, 2010?

(b) How would the two payments during the year 2010 of $32,097.05 each be reflected in the statement of cash flows for the year ending December 31, 2010?

(c) How would the balance of $375,201.09 at December 31, 2010 be reported on a balance sheet as of that date?

SOLUTION TO EXERCISE 14-8

(a)

$20,000.00	Interest expense 1/01/10 - 6/30/10
19,395.15	Interest expense 7/01/10 - 12/31/10
$39,395.15	Total interest expense for the year ending 12/31/10

(b) The amounts paid during year 2010 for interest ($20,000.00 + $19,395.15 = **$39,395.15**) should be reported as a cash outflow due to operating activities. The amounts paid during year 2010 for principal reduction ($12,097.03 + 12,701.88 = **$24,798.91**) would be reported as payments on debt which are classified as cash outflows from financing activities on a statement of cash flows for the year ended December 31, 2010.

(c) The balance of the Mortgage Note Payable account is reported as a liability in the balance sheet. The portion of the installment payments scheduled to be due and paid within the next year (that is, the year that follows the balance sheet date) that represents the reduction of the principal balance is to be reported in the current liability section of the balance sheet; the remaining unpaid principal balance is classified in the long-term liability section.

$ 13,336.98	Amount due June 30, 2011
14,003.82	Amount due December 31, 2011
$ 27,340.80	Current liability as of December 31, 2010
$347,860.29	Long-term liability as of December 31, 2010

TIP: If Weiss Corporation (**Exercise 14-7**) had its accounting period end on March 31, 2011 rather than December 31, 2010, the answers to parts "a"., "b"., and "c". of **Exercise 14-8** would be as follows:

a.
$10,000.00	$20,000.00 X 3/6 = Interest expense 3/31/10 to 6/30/10
19,395.15	$19,395.15 X 6/6 = Interest expense 7/01/10 to 12/31/10
9,380.03	$18,760.05 X 3/6 = Interest expense 01/01/11 to 03/31/11
$38,775.18	Total interest expense for the year ending 03/31/11

b. The payments on 6/30/10 and 12/31/10 fall in the year ending March 31, 2011. Therefore, this answer would be the same as in **Exercise 14-8**:

$20,000 + $19,395.15 = $39,395.15 cash outflow due to operating activities (interest paid)

$12,097.03 + $12,701.88 = $24,789.91 cash outflow due to financing activity (payment on debt)

c. For the balance sheet:

$ 13,336.98	Amount due June 30, 2011
14,003.82	Amount due December 31, 2011
$ 27,340.80	Current liability as of March 31, 2010
$347,860.29	Long-term liability as of March 31, 2010

Notice that answers "b" and "c" above are the same as answers "b" and "c" in the **Solution to Exercise 14-8**. This is because the cash payments are made at a point in time and a principal reduction applies at a point in time when a cash payment is made. Fractions (such as 3/12 and 9/12) are applied to interest amounts (which are for a period of time) to apportion interest to the appropriate accounting periods. However, fractions are **never** applied to principal reduction figures.

*ILLUSTRATION 14-4
SUMMARY OF ACCOUNTING FOR IMPAIRMENT AND
TROUBLED DEBT RESTRUCTURINGS (L.O. 9)

Event	Accounting Procedure
1. Impairment	**Creditor:** Loss based upon difference between present value of future cash flows discounted at historical effective interest rate and carrying amount of note. Recognize interest revenue (or bad debt expense reduction) based upon new carrying amount and original effective rate. **Debtor:** No recognition.
2. Restructuring—Settlement of Debt a. Transfer of noncash assets.	**Creditor:** Recognize ordinary loss on restructure. **Debtor:** Recognize gain on restructure and recognize gain or loss on asset transfer.
b. Granting of equity interest.	**Creditor:** Recognize loss on restructure. **Debtor:** Recognize gain on restructure.
3. Restructurings—Continuation of Debt with Modified Terms a. Carrying amount of debt is less than future cash flows (no gain for debtor).	**Creditor:** Recognize ordinary loss based upon present value of restructured cash flows. Use the historical effective rate of the loan to compute this present value amount. Recognize interest revenue based upon new recorded value and original effective rate. **Debtor:** Recognize no gain on restructure. Determine new effective interest rate to be used in recording interest expense.
b. Carrying amount of debt is greater than total future cash flows (gain for debtor)	**Creditor:** Recognize loss based upon present value of restructured cash flows. Recognize interest revenue based upon new recorded value and original effective rate. **Debtor:** Recognize gain on restructure and reduce carrying amount to the sum of the undiscounted cash flows. Recognize no interest expense over the remaining life of the debt.

TIP: When there is a restructuring that involves the continuation of debt with modification of terms, the computations made by the creditor to assess impairment are based on discounted future cash flows (at the original effective interest rate). However, the debtor's gain is calculated based upon undiscounted amounts. As a consequence, the gain recorded by the debtor will not equal the loss recorded by the creditor under many circumstances.

TIP: When there is a restructuring that involves a settlement of debt by transfer of noncash assets, the debtor has the following gain-loss computations:
  (1) The excess of the carrying amount of the debt over the fair market value of the assets is recorded as a gain on restructuring; this gain is reported as an other item on the income statement.
  (2) The difference between the fair market value of the assets and their recorded value (book value) is recorded as a gain or loss on disposition of assets; this gain or loss is reported in the other gains or other losses section of a multiple-step income statement.
      (a) If the fair market value of the assets exceeds their book value, a gain results.
      (b) If the book value of the assets exceeds their fair market value, a loss results.

*EXERCISE 14-9

Purpose: (L.O. 9) This exercise will illustrate the accounting for a transfer of noncash assets to settle a debt obligation in a troubled debt situation.

Boston Co. owes $194,400 to San Diego Trust Co. The debt is a 10-year, 8% note. Because Boston Co. is in financial trouble, San Diego agrees to accept some property and cancel the entire debt. The property has a cost of $150,000, accumulated depreciation of $80,000, and a fair market value of $110,000.

Instructions
(a)   Prepare the journal entry on Boston's books for the debt restructure.
(b)   Prepare the journal entry on San Diego's books for the debt restructure.

Solution to Exercise 14-9

(a)   **BOSTON'S ENTRY:**

Notes Payable	194,400	
Accumulated Depreciation	80,000	
Property		150,000
Gain on Property Disposition		
(Not extraordinary)		40,000*
Gain on Restructuring of Debt (Extraordinary)		84,400**

*$110,000 - ($150,000 - $80,000) = $40,000
**$194,400 - $110,000 = $84,400

Approach and Explanation: (1) Begin with the easiest part of the journal entry. Remove the debt amount by a debit to Notes Payable for $194,400. (2) Remove the carrying value of the property by a debit to Accumulated Depreciation for $80,000 and a credit to Property for the $150,000 cost. (3) Compute and record the gain from settlement ($84,400 credit) and, (4) compute and record the gain from disposition of assets ($40,000). (5) Double check the entry to make sure it balances.

The debtor is required to determine the excess of the carrying amount of the payable ($194,400) over the fair value of the assets transferred ($110,000) and report that difference as an extraordinary gain ($84,400). The difference between the fair value of those assets and their carrying amounts is to be recognized as a gain or loss on disposition of assets. In this case, the fair value of $110,000 exceeds the carrying amount of $70,000; therefore, an gain of $40,000 is to be recognized.

(b)   **SAN DIEGO'S ENTRY:**

Property	110,000	
Allowance for Doubtful Accounts	84,400	
(or Loss on Restructuring)		
Notes Receivable		194,400

Approach and Explanation: (1) Remove the carrying amount of the receivable from the accounts by a credit to Notes Receivable for $194,400. (2) Record the acquisition of the property by a debit to Property for its fair value of $110,000. (3) Record the loss on settlement of $84,400 by a debit to Allowance for Doubtful Accounts or to a loss account. (4) Double check the entry to make sure it balances.

The creditor is required to determine the excess of the carrying amount of the receivable over the fair value of the assets being transferred to the creditor and record it as a charge against the Allowance for Doubtful Accounts account or to a loss account (such a loss is not to be classified as an extraordinary item).

*EXERCISE 14-10

Purpose: (L.O. 9) This exercise will illustrate the accounting for a troubled debt restructuring involving a modification of terms of an existing debt arrangement.

Omega Corp. owes $165,000 to San Diego Trust Co. The debt is a 10-year, 10% note due December 31, 2009. Because Omega Corp. is in financial trouble, San Diego agrees to extend the maturity date to December 31, 2011, reduce the principal to $150,000, and reduce the interest rate to 4%, payable annually on December 31. This restructuring takes place on December 31, 2009.

Instructions
(a)   Prepare the journal entries on Omega's books on December 31, 2009, 2010, and 2011.
(b)   Prepare the journal entries on San Diego's books on December 31, 2009, 2010, and 2011.
Round all computations to the nearest dollar.

Solution to Exercise 14-10

(a)   **OMEGA'S ENTRIES:**
December 31, 2009
Notes Payable..3,000		
Gain on Restructuring (Extraordinary).....................		3,000

December 31, 2010
Notes Payable..6,000		
Cash (4% x $150,000)...		6,000

December 31, 2011
Notes Payable.. 156,000		
Cash [$150,000 + (4% x $150,000)].........................		156,000

Explanation: The situation described is a troubled debt restructuring involving continuation of debt with modified terms. Because in this situation the carrying amount of the debt ($165,000) at the time of restructure exceeds the undiscounted total future cash flows [$150,000 + ($150,000 x 4% x 2) = $162,000], the debtor will adjust the debt's carrying amount for the difference and recognize a gain ($3,000). Also, from the debtor's viewpoint, all future cash payments will go to reduce the principal; no interest expense will be recognized in the future in connection with this loan.

(b)   **SAN DIEGO'S ENTRIES:**
December 31, 2009
Allowance for Doubtful Accounts		
(or Bad Debt Expense)..	30,619	
Notes Receivable		30,619

Explanation: The creditor in this case is required to calculate the loss based upon the expected future cash flows **discounted** at the historical effective rate on the loan. This write-down of the receivable will allow interest revenue to be reported in future years based on the historical effective rate (10%).

Pre-restructure carrying amount..............................		$165,000
Present value of restructured cash flows:		
Present value of $150,000 due in 2 years		
at 10% ($150,000 x .82645)..........................	$123,968	
Present value of $6,000 interest payable		
annually for 2 years at 10%		
($6,000 x 1.73554)	<u>10,413</u>	<u>134,381</u>
Creditor's ordinary loss on restructure.....................		<u>$ 30,619</u>

The loss would be recorded by a debit to Bad Debt Expense if no allowance was previously recorded.
December 31, 2010
Cash	6,000	
Notes Receivable	7,438	
Interest Revenue		13,438*

    *A new amortization schedule would appear as follows:

Date	Cash Interest	10% Effective Interest	Increase in Carrying Value	Carrying Value of Note
12/31/09				$ 134,381
12/31/10	$ 6,000[a]	$ 13,438[b]	$ 7,438[c]	141,819
12/31/11	6,000	14,181	8,181	150,000

[a]$150,000 x 4% = $6,000.
[b]$134,381 x 10% = $13,438.
[c]$13,438 - $6,000 = $7,438.

December 31, 2011

Cash..	6,000	
Notes Receivable...	8,181	
Interest Revenue...		14,181**

**Refer to the amortization schedule above.

Cash..	150,000	
Notes Receivable		150,000

ANALYSIS OF MULTIPLE-CHOICE TYPE QUESTIONS

QUESTION
1. (L.O. 2) Bonds for which the owners' names are **not** registered with the issuing corporation are called:
   a. bearer bonds.
   b. term bonds.
   c. debenture bonds.
   d. secured bonds.

Approach and Explanation: Briefly define each answer selection. Choose the one that is described in the question's stem. **Bearer** (or **coupon**) **bonds** are bonds for which the name of the owner is not registered with the issuer; bondholders are required to send in coupons to receive interest payments and the bonds may be transferred directly to another party. **Registered bonds** are bonds registered in the name of the owner. **Term bonds** are bonds that mature (become due for payment) at a single specified future date. **Debenture bonds** are unsecured bonds. **Secured bonds** are bonds having specific assets pledged as collateral by the issuer. (Solution = a.)

QUESTION
2. (L.O. 3) The periodic amortization of a premium on bonds payable will:
   a. cause the carrying value of the bonds to increase each period.
   b. cause the carrying value of the bonds to decrease each period.
   c. have no effect on the carrying value of the bonds.
   d. cause the carrying value always to be less than the par value of the bonds.

Approach and Explanation: Think about the process of amortizing a premium on bonds payable and how it affects the carrying value of the bonds. The Premium on Bonds Payable account has a normal credit balance. A premium is an adjustment to interest via an adjustment to price. Therefore, the entry to amortize the premium involves a debit to Premium on Bonds Payable and a credit to Bond Interest Expense. The amortization process reduces the balance of the unamortized premium. The carrying value of a bond issued at a premium is calculated by adding the premium balance to the face value of the bond. Thus, the carrying value of bonds payable issued at a premium will decrease each period until the maturity date (at which time the carrying value will equal the face value). (Solution = b.)

QUESTION
3. (L.O.3) A large department store issues bonds with a maturity date that is 20 years after the issuance date. If the bonds are issued at a discount, this indicates that at the date of issuance, the:
   a. nominal rate of interest and the stated rate of interest coincide.
   b. nominal rate of interest exceeds the yield rate.
   c. yield rate of interest exceeds the coupon rate.
   d. stated rate of interest exceeds the effective rate.

Approach and Explanation: Before reading the answer selections, write down the relationship that causes a bond to be issued at a discount: market rate of interest exceeds the stated rate of interest. Then list the synonymous terms for market rate and for stated rate: (1) market rate, effective rate, and yield rate; (2) stated rate, coupon rate, nominal rate, and contract rate. Selection "a" is incorrect because the nominal rate and the stated rate are just different names for the same thing. Selections "b" and "d" are incorrect because an excess of nominal rate (stated rate) over the yield rate (effective rate) will result in a premium, not a discount. Selection "c" is correct because when the yield rate (market rate) exceeds the coupon rate (stated rate), an issuance discount will result. (Solution = c.)

QUESTION
4. (L.O. 3) The amount of cash to be paid for interest on bonds payable for any given year is calculated by multiplying the:
   a. face value of the stated interest rate.
   b. face value by the market interest rate at the date of issuance.
   c. carrying value at the beginning of the year by the market interest rate in existence at the date of issuance.
   d. carrying value at the beginning of the year by the stated interest rate.

Explanation: The amount of cash interest to be paid is the amount promised by the bond contract (indenture) which is the contractual (stated) interest rate multiplied by the face value of the bond. (Solution = a.)

QUESTION
5. (L.O. 4) The amortization of a discount on bonds payable results in reporting an amount of interest expense for the period which:
   a. exceeds the amount of cash interest for the period.
   b. equals the amount of cash interest for the period.
   c. is less than the amount of cash interest for the period.
   d. bears no predictable relationship to the amount of cash interest for the period.

Approach and Explanation: Think about the process of amortizing a discount on bonds payable and how it affects interest expense. The Discount of Bonds Payable has a normal debit balance. Thus, to amortize it, you credit Discount on Bonds Payable and debit Bond Interest Expense. A debit to the expense account increases its balance. Thus, interest expense is comprised of the amount to be paid in cash for interest for the period plus the amount of discount amortization for the period. Another way of viewing this situation is as follows: a discount is an additional amount of interest to be paid at maturity but is recognized (charged to expense) over the periods benefited (which would be the periods the bonds are to be outstanding). (Solution = a.)

QUESTION

6. (L.O. 4) If bonds are initially sold at a discount and the straight-line method of amortization is used, interest expense in the earlier years of the bond's life will:
    a. be less than the amount of interest actually paid.
    b. be less than it will be in the latter years of the bond's life.
    c. be the same as what it would have been had the effective interest method of amortization been used.
    d. exceed what it would have been had the effective interest method of amortization been used.

Approach and Explanation: Quickly sketch the graph that shows the patterns of and relationships between interest paid, interest expense using the straight-line method, and interest expense using the effective interest method. The graph appears in **Illustration 14-3**. Treat each of the possible answer selections as a True-False question. Look at the graph after reading each of the answer selections to determine if it is a correct answer.

Selection "a" is False because interest expense for a bond issued at a discount will be greater than interest actually paid throughout the bond's entire life, regardless of the amortization method used. Selection "b" is False because interest expense is a constant amount each period when the straight-line method is used; hence interest expense will be the same amount in the latter years as it is in the earlier years. Selection "c" is False because in the earlier years of life for a bond issued at a discount, interest expense computed using the straight-line method is greater than interest expense computed using the effective interest method. Selection "d" is True. The interest expense will increase over a bond's life when the bond is issued at a discount and the effective interest method of amortization is used. In the earlier years of life, that expense amount is less than interest expense using the straight-line method; and, in the latter years of life, that expense amount is more than interest expense computed using the straight-line method. (Solution = d.)

QUESTION

7. (L.O. 4) At the beginning of 2010, the Alston Corporation issued 10% bonds with a face value of $400,000. These bonds mature in five years, and interest is paid semiannually on June 30 and December 31. The bonds were sold for $370,560 to yield 12%. Alston uses a calendar-year reporting period. Using the preferable method of amortization, what amount of interest expense should be reported for 2010? (Round your answer to the nearest dollar.)
    a. $44,333
    b. $44,467
    c. $44,601
    d. $45,888

Approach and Explanation: Write down the formula for computing interest using the effective method of amortization. Use the data in the question to work through the formula.

	Carrying value at the beginning of the period	$ 370,560.00
x	Effective rate of interest per interest period	6%
=	Interest expense for the first interest period	22,233.60
-	Cash interest for the interest period	20,000.00*
=	Amortization of discount for the first interest period	2,233.60
+	Carrying value at the beginning of the first period	370,560.00
=	Carrying value at the beginning of the second period	372,793.60
x	Effective rate of interest per interest period	6%
=	Interest expense for the second interest period	22,367.62
+	Interest expense for the first interest period	22,233.60
=	Interest expense for the calendar year of 2010	$ 44,601.22

*$400,000 x (10% ÷ 2) = $20,000   (Solution = c.)

TIP: The interest must be computed on a per interest period basis. In this question, the interest period is six months. The interest for 2010 is comprised of the interest for the bond's first two interest periods.

QUESTION

8. (L.O. 5) At December 31, 2010 the following balances existed on the books of the Malloy Corporation:

Bonds Payable	$ 500,000
Discount on Bonds Payable	40,000
Interest Payable	12,500
Unamortized Bonds Issue Costs	30,000

If the bonds are retired on January 1, 2011, at 102, what will Malloy report as a loss on redemption?

a. $92,500
b. $80,000
c. $67,500
d. $50,000

Approach and Explanation: Write down the format for the computation of the gain or loss on redemption and plug in the amounts from this question.

	Par value	$ 500,000
-	Unamortized discount	40,000
=	Carrying amount	460,000
-	Unamortized debt issue costs	30,000
=	Net carrying amount	430,000
-	Redemption price	510,000*
=	Gain (Loss) on redemption	$ (80,000)

*$500,000 x 102% = $510,000.

(Solution = b.)

QUESTION

9. (L.O. 5) "In-substance defeasance" is a term used to refer to an arrangement whereby:
    a. a company gets another company to cover its payments due on long-term debt.
    b. a governmental unit issues debt instruments to corporations.
    c. a company provides for the future repayment of a long-term debt by placing purchased securities in an irrevocable trust.
    d. a company legally extinguishes debt before its due date.

Explanation: In-substance defeasance is an arrangement whereby a company provides for the future repayment of one or more of its long-term debt issues by placing purchased securities in an irrevocable trust, the principal and interest of which are pledged to pay off the principal and interest of its own debt securities as they mature. The company, however, is not legally released from being the primary obligor under the debt that is still outstanding. (Solution = c.)

QUESTION

10. (L.O. 6) Bandy Rentals borrowed money from a local savings and loan to build new mini-warehouses. Bandy gave a 20-year mortgage note in the amount of $100,000 with a stated rate of 10.75%. The lender charged 4 points to close the financing. Based on this information:
    a. Bandy should debit Interest Expense in recording the points at the date the money is borrowed.
    b. Bandy's effective interest rate is now less than the 10.75% stated rate.
    c. Bandy should record the Mortgage Note Payable for only $96,000 since only $96,000 cash was received.
    d. Bandy should amortize the points to interest expense over the life of the loan.

Explanation: Bandy will receive $96,000 cash but will have to repay $100,000 plus interest at 10.75% on the $100,000. Thus, the points raise the effective interest rate above the stated rate and should be accounted for as interest expense over the life of the loan. (Solution = d.)

QUESTION

11.   (L.O. 6) A corporation borrowed money from a bank to build a building. The long-term note signed by the corporation is secured by a mortgage that pledges title to the building as security for the loan. The corporation is to pay the bank $80,000 each year for 10 years to repay the loan. Which of the following relationships can you expect to apply to the situation?

   a.   The balance of mortgage payable at a given balance sheet date will be reported as a long-term liability.
   b.   The balance of mortgage payable will remain a constant amount over the 10-year period.
   c.   The amount of interest expense will decrease each period the loan is outstanding, while the portion of the annual payment applied to the loan principal will increase each period.
   d.   The amount of interest expense will remain constant over the 10-year period.

Explanation: Mortgage notes payable are recorded initially at face value, and entries are required subsequently for each installment payment. Each payment consists of (1) interest on the unpaid principal balance of the loan, and (2) a reduction of loan principal. Because a portion of each payment is applied to the principal, the principal balance decreases each period. Interest for a period of time is computed by multiplying the stated (contract) rate of interest by the principal balance outstanding at the beginning of the period. Thus, the amount of each payment required to cover interest decreases while the portion of the payment applied to the loan principal balance will increase each period. (Solution = c.)

QUESTION

12.   (L.O. 8) The debt to total assets ratio measures the:

   a.   relationship between interest expense and income.
   b.   portion of assets financed through creditor sources.
   c.   portion of debt used to acquire assets.
   d.   relationship between debt and interest expense.

Approach and Explanation: Write down the computation for the debt to total assets ratio and think about is components and their relationship. The debt to total assets ratio is computed by dividing total debt by total assets. This ratio measures the percentage of the total assets provided by creditors. The higher the percentage of debt to total assets, the greater the risk that the company may be unable to meet its maturing obligations. (Solution = b.)

QUESTION

13.   (L.O. 8) The times interest earned ratio provides an indication of the:

   a.   company's ability to meet interest payments as they become due.
   b.   relationship between current liabilities and current assets.
   c.   percentage of assets financed by debt.
   d.   relationship between debt and interest expense.

Approach and Explanation: Write down the computation for the interest earned ratio and think about the relationship of the components of the ratio. The interest earned ratio is computed by dividing interest before income taxes and interest expense by interest expense. This ratio provides an indication of the relationship between income (before taxes and interest expense have deducted) and the amount of interest expense for the period. It is an indication of the company's ability to meet interest payments as they become due. (Solution = a.)

QUESTION

14. (L.O. 9) A debtor in a troubled debt restructuring has debt that is settled by a transfer of land with a fair value that is less than the carrying amount of the debt but is more than the book value of the land. Should a gain or loss on restructuring of debt be recognized? Should a gain or loss on the disposition of assets be recognized?

	Gain or Loss on Restructuring of Debt	Gain or Loss on Disposition of Assets
a.	Gain	Gain
b.	Gain	Loss
c.	Loss	Loss
d.	Loss	Gain

Approach and Explanation: Assign amounts to the (1) carrying amount of the debt, (2) carrying amount of the loan, and (3) fair value of the land. Be sure your assigned amounts maintain the relationships stated in the question. Then use a journal entry approach to solve. For instance: Fair value of land, $100,000; carrying amount of debt, $127,000; and book value of land, $65,000. For the journal entry, debit the debt account(s) for $127,000; credit Land for $65,000; credit Gain on Disposition of Assets for $35,000 (an excess of the fair value over the book value indicates that a gain has been experienced on the old asset). The rest of the entry is due to a gain or loss on restructuring of debt. A credit for $27,000 is needed for the entry to balance; hence, there is a gain on settlement. If you are able to settle a debt by giving an asset with a value that is less than the carrying amount of the debt, you have an advantageous settlement of debt; hence a gain on restructuring of debt should be recognized.

Debt..	127,000	
Land		65,000
Gain on Disposition of Assets..		35,000
Gain on Restructuring of Debt		27,000

(Solution = a.)

Problem Solving Survival Guide
VOLUME II: CHAPTERS 15-24

INTERMEDIATE ACCOUNTING
Thirteenth Edition

Marilyn F. Hunt, M.A., C.P.A.

Donald E. Kieso, Ph.D., C.P.A.
KPMG Peat Marwick Emeritus Professor of Accounting
Northern Illinois University
DeKalb, Illinois

Jerry J. Weygandt, Ph.D., C.P.A.
Arthur Andersen Alumni Professor of Accounting
University of Wisconsin
Madison, Wisconsin

Terry D. Warfield, Ph.D.
Associate Professor
Director, Andersen Center for Financial Reporting and Control
University of Wisconsin
Madison, Wisconsin

WILEY
JOHN WILEY & SONS, INC.

Cover Photo: Jon Arnold Images/SuperStock, Inc.

To order books or for customer service call 1-800-CALL-WILEY (225-5945).

ISBN-13 9780470380581

Printed in the United States of America

10 9 8 7 6 5 4 3 2 1

Printed and bound by BindRite Inc.

CHAPTER 15

STOCKHOLDERS' EQUITY

OVERVIEW

A major source of assets of an entity is owners' equity. Owners' equity of a corporation is called **stockholders' equity** or **shareholders' equity** because the owners of the business hold shares of stock as evidence of their ownership claims. Stockholders' equity typically has two major classifications for reporting purposes: **contributed capital (paid-in capital)** and **retained earnings**. Contributed capital includes the subclassifications of **capital stock** and **additional paid-in capital**.

This chapter discusses the issuance of stock and the reacquisition of shares. When shares are reacquired and held in the treasury, two alternative generally accepted accounting methods are available for use: the cost method and the par value method. The cost method is the more popular method.

The term **earnings** refers to net income for a period. The term **retained earnings** refers to accumulated earnings. That is, retained earnings is the total of all amounts reported as net income since the inception of the corporation less the sum of any amounts reported as net losses and dividends declared since the inception of the corporation. Thus, distributions of corporate profits to stockholders reduce retained earnings. A corporation may distribute cash, noncash assets, or additional shares of the corporation's own stock to its owners in the form of dividends. A distribution of assets may represent a distribution of income or a return of invested capital. A distribution of a corporation's own stock results in capitalizing retained earnings. Corporate distributions are also discussed in this chapter.

SUMMARY OF LEARNING OBJECTIVES

1. **Discuss the characteristics of the corporate form of organization.** Among the specific characteristics of the corporate form that affect accounting are: (1) influence of state corporate law; (2) use of the capital stock or share system; and (3) development of a variety of ownership interests. In the absence of restrictive provisions, each share of stock carries the right to share proportionately in (1) profits and losses; (2) management (the right to vote for directors); (3) corporate assets upon liquidation; (4) any new issues of stock of the same class (called the preemptive right).

2. **Identify the key components of stockholders' equity.** Stockholders' or owners' equity is classified into two categories: contributed capital and earned capital. **Contributed capital (paid-in capital)** describes the total amount paid in on capital stock. Put another way, it is the amount that stockholders advance to the corporation for use in the business. Contributed capital includes items such as the par value of all outstanding capital stock and premiums less any discounts on issuance. **Earned capital (retained earnings)** is the capital that develops if the business operates profitably; it consists of all undistributed income that remains invested in the company.

3. **Explain the accounting procedures for issuing shares of stock.** The accounting considerations involved in the issuance of different types of stock are: (1) **Par value stock:** Accounts required to be kept are (a) preferred stock or common stock; (b) paid-in capital in

excess of par or additional paid-in capital; and, (c) discount on stock. (2) **No-par stock:** No-par stock with a stated value requires the same accounts to be kept as a par value stock. No-par stock with no stated value requires only a capital stock account (preferred stock or common stock). (3) **Stock issued in combination with other securities (lump sum sales):** The two methods of allocation available are (a) the proportional method; and, (b) the incremental method. (4) **Stock issued in noncash transactions:** When stock is issued for services or property other than cash, the property or services should be recorded at either the fair market value of the stock issued or the fair market value of the noncash consideration received, whichever is more clearly determinable.

4.   **Explain the accounting for treasury stock.** The cost method is generally used in accounting for treasury stock. This method derives its name from the fact that the Treasury Stock account is maintained at the cost of the shares purchased. Under the cost method, a company debits the Treasury Stock account for the cost of the shares acquired and credits it for this same cost upon reissuance. The price received for the stock when originally issued does **not** affect the entries to record the acquisition and reissuance of the treasury stock.

5.   **Explain the accounting for and reporting of preferred stock.** Preferred stock is a special class of shares that possesses certain preferences or features not possessed by the common stock. The features that are most often associated with preferred stock issues are: (1) preference as to dividends, (2) preference as to assets in the event of liquidation, (3) convertible into common stock, (4) callable at the option of the corporation, and (5) nonvoting. At issuance, the accounting for preferred stock is similar to that for common stock. When convertible preferred stock is converted into common stock, a company uses the book value method. It debits Preferred Stock along with any related additional paid-in capital account, and credits Common Stock and an additional paid-in capital account (if an excess exists).

6.   **Describe the policies used in distributing dividends.** The state incorporation laws normally provide information concerning the legal restrictions related to the payment of dividends. Corporations rarely pay dividends in an amount equal to the legal limit. This is due, in part, to the fact that assets represented by undistributed earnings are used to finance future operations of the business. If a company is considering declaring a dividend, it must ask two preliminary questions: (1) Is the condition of the corporation such that the dividend is **legally permissible**? (2) Is the condition of the corporation such that a dividend is **economically sound**?

7.   **Identify the various forms of dividend distributions.** Dividends are of the following types: (1) cash dividends, (2) property dividends (3) liquidating dividends (dividends based on capital other than retained earnings), (4) stock dividends (the issuance by a corporation of its own stock to its stockholders on a pro rata basis, but without receiving consideration).

8.   **Explain the accounting for small and large stock dividends, and for stock splits.** Generally accepted accounting principles require that the accounting for small stock dividends (less than 20 or 25%) be based on the fair market value of the stock issued. When declaring a small stock dividend, a company debits Retained Earnings for the fair market value of the stock to be distributed. The entry includes a credit to Common Stock Dividend Distributable for the par value times the number of dividend shares, with any excess credited to Paid-in Capital in Excess of Par. Between the declaration date and the date of issuance, common stock dividend distributable is reported as a capital stock item in the stockholders' equity section of the balance sheet. If the number of shares to be issued in the dividend exceeds 20 or 25% of the shares outstanding (large stock dividend), Retained Earnings is debited only for the par value of the dividend shares, and no additional paid-in capital is recorded.

A stock dividend is a capitalization of retained earnings that results in a reduction in retained earnings and a corresponding increase in certain contributed capital accounts. The par value per share and total stockholders' equity remain unchanged with a stock dividend. All stockholders retain their same proportionate share of ownership in the corporation. A stock split results in an increase or decrease in the number of shares outstanding, with a corresponding proportional decrease or increase in the par or stated value per share. No accounting entry is required for a stock split. Similar to a stock dividend, the dollar amount of total stockholders' equity remains unchanged. A stock split is usually intended to improve the marketability of the shares by causing a reduction in the market price of the stock being split.

9.   **Indicate how to present and analyze stockholders' equity.** The stockholders' equity section of a balance sheet includes capital stock, additional paid-in capital, and retained earnings. A company may also present additional items such as treasury stock and accumulated other comprehensive income. Companies often provide a statement of stockholders' equity. Common ratios that use stockholders equity amounts include: rate of return on common stock equity, payout ratio, and book value per share.

*10.   **Explain the different types of preferred stock dividends and their effect on book value per share.**   The dividend preferences of preferred stock affect the dividends paid to stockholders Preferred stock can be (1) cumulative or noncumulative, and (2) fully participating, partially participating, or nonparticipating. If preferred dividends are in arrears, if the preferred stock is participating, or if preferred stock has a redemption or liquidation value higher than its carrying amount, retained earnings must be allocated between preferred and common stockholders in computing book value per share.

   *This material is covered in Appendix 15A in the text.

TIPS ON CHAPTER TOPICS

TIP: **Stockholders' equity** is often referred to as **capital**. In accounting for stockholders' equity, the emphasis is on the source of capital. **Retained earnings** is sometimes called **earned capital** because it is the portion of stockholders' equity which has been generated by the entity's operations. **Paid-in capital** is often called **contributed capital** or **invested capital** because it arises from owner contributions. Contributed capital includes capital stock accounts and additional paid-in capital accounts.

TIP: **Paid-in capital** is often called **contributed capital**. **Additional paid-in capital** is often called **additional contributed capital** or **paid-in capital in excess of par**. Although **capital surplus** is a term sometimes used for additional paid-in capital, it is not recommended terminology.

TIP: Make sure you understand the components of **total paid-in capital**, which include the capital stock accounts **plus** additional paid-in capital accounts. **Capital stock** accounts include Common Stock, Preferred Stock, and Stock Dividends Distributable.

TIP: Additional paid-in capital can arise from many situations which include the following: the issuance of capital stock at a price above par, some treasury stock transactions, the retirement of stock, the declaration of an ordinary (small) stock dividend, and the conversion of bonds to stock.

TIP: **Premium** on capital stock is defined as an excess of issuance price over par for newly issued stock. In recording the issuance, this excess is often credited to an account called Premium on Capital Stock or Paid-in Capital in Excess of Par. Regardless of the account title, the premium amount is usually reported on the balance sheet by the caption Additional Paid-in Capital.

TIP: As you progress through this chapter, pay particular attention to the effect of the various transactions on total paid-in capital, retained earnings, and total stockholders' equity.

TIP: There is a tremendous amount of terminology relating to capital stock. You should have a clear understanding of all of the terms mentioned in this chapter before going on to subsequent chapters.

TIP: **Stockholders** are often called **shareholders.**

TIP: The **market value** of a share of stock at a given point in time is the value at which the stock can be bought or sold.

TIP: **Dividends in arrears** are **not** to be reported as a liability. Dividends become a liability when they are declared. By definition, dividends in arrears are dividends on cumulative preferred stock which have been passed (not declared). Dividends in arrears should be disclosed, however, in the notes to the financial statements.

TIP: A corporation acquires resources (assets) from new owners by issuing stock; the issuance is recorded on the company's books by an increase in assets and an increase in owners' equity. When that initial owner later sells his (her) stock through the stock market, there is **no** journal entry to be made on the corporation's books; only the stockholders' name is changed in the corporation's records. The assets, liabilities, and owners' equity of the corporation are **not** affected by the purchase (or sale) of stock by investors in the stock market.

TIP: A preferred stock's preference as to dividends is usually expressed as a percentage of the par or stated value; sometimes, the preference is expressed in terms of dollars.

TIP: Retained earnings represents a source of corporate assets. The balance of the Retained Earnings account at any point in time reflects the total unspecified assets which have been obtained through profitable operations of the reporting entity. The balance of the Retained Earnings account has **no** direct relationship to the amount of cash held by the entity; a corporation can have a large balance in the Cash account and a small balance in Retained Earnings or a small balance in Cash and a large balance in Retained Earnings.

TIP: Dividends are **not** an expense; they do not meet the definition of expense. Dividends are a distribution of income, not a determinant of income. In recording the declaration of any dividend (except for a liquidating dividend), the accountant may use a temporary account called Dividends Declared, rather than debiting the Retained Earnings account directly. At the end of the period, in the closing process, the balance of the Dividends Declared account is closed directly to the Retained Earnings account.

EXERCISE 15-1

Purpose: (L.O. 3) This exercise will highlight the relationship between authorized, issued, outstanding, and subscribed shares.

The following data are available regarding the common stock of the Daffy Corporation at December 31, 2010:

Authorized shares	200,000
Unissued shares	60,000
Treasury shares	12,000

Instructions
Compute the number of outstanding shares.

Solution to Exercise 15-1

Authorized shares	200,000
Unissued shares	(60,000)
Issued shares	140,000
Treasury shares	(12,000)
Outstanding shares	128,000

Approach and Explanation: Write down the formula for determining the number of outstanding shares:

$$\text{Issued Shares} - \text{Treasury Shares} = \text{Outstanding Shares}$$

Fill in the data given. Authorized shares are either issued or unissued. Issued shares are either outstanding shares or treasury shares. The number issued can readily be computed in this situation. Treasury shares are issued shares but are not outstanding (in the hands of shareholders).

CASE 15-1

Purpose: (L.O. 4) This case will review the proper accounting procedures for the issuance of no par stock.

Problems may be encountered in accounting for transactions involving the stockholders' equity section of the balance sheet.

Instructions
(a)   Describe how to account for the issuance for cash of common stock with no par value at a price in excess of the stated value of the common stock.
(b)   Describe how to account for the costs of the issuance of stock.

(AICPA Adapted)

Solution to Case 15-1

(a)   The issuance for cash of common stock with no par value at a price in excess of the stated value of the common stock is accounted for as follows:

- Cash is debited for the proceeds from the issuance of the common stock.

- Common Stock is credited for the stated value of the common stock.

- An additional paid-in capital account is credited for the excess of the proceeds from the issuance of the common stock over its stated value.

TIP: A no-par stock with a stated value is accounted for in a manner similar to stock with a par value; that is, the stated value is recorded in the capital stock account and an excess of the issuance price over stated value is recorded in an additional paid-in capital account. The entire proceeds from the issuance of a no-par stock with no stated value is recorded in the capital stock account.

(b)   The costs of issuing stock are accounted for as follows:

- Direct costs incurred to sell stock such as underwriting costs and commissions, accountants' fees, attorneys' fees, filing fees, printing costs, taxes, and costs to advertise the issue should be reported as a reduction of the amounts paid in. Issue costs are therefore charged (debited) to Paid-in Capital in Excess of Par (additional paid-in capital) because they are unrelated to corporate operations. In effect, issue costs are a cost of financing and should be viewed as a reduction of the proceeds received from the sale of the stock.

- Management salaries and other indirect costs related to the issuance of stock should be expensed as incurred because it is difficult to establish a relationship between these costs and the proceeds received upon sale. In addition, a corporation will annually incur costs for maintaining the stockholders' records and handling ownership transfers. These recurring costs, primarily registrar and transfer agent's fees, are normally charged to expense in the period in which they are incurred.

EXERCISE 15-2

Purpose: (L.O. 4) This exercise will illustrate how to record selected transactions related to the issuance of capital stock.

On February 1, 2010, Bimini Bay Corporation received authorization to issue 400,000 shares of $10 par value common stock and 100,000 shares of $50 par value preferred stock. The following transactions occurred during 2010:

Feb. 24   Issued 100,000 shares of common stock for cash at a price of $18 per share.

Feb. 28   Issued 50,000 shares of common stock in exchange for a group of modular warehouses.

Mar. 5   Sold 20,000 shares of Bimini Bay preferred stock at $51 each.

Mar. 23   Sold a package of shares for $1,340,000. The package consisted of 20,000 shares of Bimini Bay common stock and 20,000 shares of Bimini Bay preferred stock. The market value of the preferred was $51 per share, and the market value of the common was $18 per share at this date.

Nov. 4   Issued 20,000 shares of common stock at $24 per share.

Nov. 14   Sold a package of shares for $1,510,000. The package consisted of 20,000 shares of Bimini Bay common stock and 20,000 shares of Bimini Bay preferred stock. The market value of the common stock was $24 at this date; however, no recent quote on the preferred stock could be found.

Instructions
Prepare the journal entries to record the transactions listed above.

Solution to Exercise 15-2

February 24
Cash (100,000 x $18)	1,800,000	
Common Stock (100,000 x $10)		1,000,000
Paid-in Capital in Excess of Par—Common		
(100,000 x $8)..		800,000

February 28
Warehouses (50,000 x $18)...	900,000	
Common Stock (50,000 x $10)		500,000
Paid-in Capital in Excess of Par—Common		
(50,000 x $8)..		400,000

March 5

Cash (20,000 x $51)	1,020,000	
Preferred Stock (20,000 x $50)		1,000,000
Paid-in Capital in Excess of Par—Preferred		
(20,000 x $1)		20,000

March 23

Cash.	1,340,000	
Discount on Preferred Stock ($1,000,000 - $990,434)	9,566	
Preferred Stock (20,000 x $50)		1,000,000
Common Stock (20,000 x $10)		200,000
Paid-in Capital in Excess of Par—Common		
($349,566 - $200,000)...		149,566

Computations:

20,000 x $18	=	$ 360,000	fair value of common
20,000 x $51	=	1,020,000	fair value of preferred
		$ 1,380,000	total fair value

$$\frac{\$360,000}{\$1,380,000} \times \$1,340,000 = \underline{\$349,566} \text{ allocated to common}$$

$$\frac{\$1,020,000}{\$1,380,000} \times \$1,340,000 = \underline{\$990,434} \text{ allocated to preferred}$$

November 4

Cash (20,000 x $24)	480,000	
Common Stock (20,000 x $10)		200,000
Paid-in Capital in Excess of Par—Common		
(20,000 x $14)...		280,000

November 14

Cash	1,510,000	
Preferred Stock (20,000 x $50).......................................		1,000,000
Paid-in Capital in Excess of Par—Preferred		
($1,030,000* - $1,000,000).......................................		30,000
Common Stock (20,000 x $10)		200,000
Paid-in Capital in Excess of Par—Common		
(20,000 x $14)...		280,000

*20,000 x $24 = $480,000 market value of common
  $1,510,000 - $480,000 = $1,030,000 allocated to preferred

Explanation:

Feb. 24   The **issuance of stock in exchange for cash** is recorded by crediting stockholder equity accounts for the amount of the cash consideration received ($1,800,000). The par value ($10) per share is entered into the related capital stock account, and the excess of the issuance price over par value per share ($8) is recorded in the related additional paid-in capital account. When more than one class of stock is authorized, any additional paid-in capital amounts are properly identified to indicate the related class of stock.

Feb. 28   The **issuance of stock in exchange for noncash assets** requires an application of the historical cost principle. The asset and the stock are to be recorded at the fair value of the consideration given (the stock) or the fair value of the consideration received (warehouses), whichever is the more clearly determinable. Because some shares of common were issued only four days earlier at $18 per share, the February 24 transaction provides good evidence of the fair value (cash equivalent value) of the stock issued on February 28. No mention of the fair value of the warehouses is made.

Mar. 5   In recording the **issuance of preferred shares for cash**, the par value of the preferred shares issued is placed in a capital stock account for that class of stock. The amount received in excess of par is an element of additional paid-in capital; the account title clearly indicates the related class of stock. The account title "Premium on ... Stock" is sometimes used to record the excess of issuance price over par.

Mar. 23   When **shares of two classes of stock are sold for one lump sum** and the fair value of each class of security is known, the lump sum received is allocated between the two classes of securities on a proportional basis; that is, based on the relative fair values of the securities involved. Thus, a ratio is developed for each security, and that ratio is equal to the total fair value of the particular shares in question divided by the total fair value of all of the shares in the transaction. Therefore, 26.087% ($360,000 ÷ $1,380,000) of the proceeds are allocated to stockholder equity accounts attributable to common stock, and 73.913% ($1,020,000 ÷ $1,380,000) of the proceeds are allocated to the issuance price of the preferred stock. Because the proceeds attributable to the preferred stock ($990,434) are less than the par value of the preferred shares being sold ($50 x 20,000 shares), the preferred shares are being issued at a total discount of $9,566. The Discount on Preferred Stock account is a negative component of additional paid-in capital.

Nov. 4   The **issuance of stock for cash** increases assets and total stockholders' equity by the issuance proceeds. The par value of the issued shares is recorded in a capital stock account, regardless of the issuance price. An additional paid-in capital account is debited or credited (whichever is appropriate) for the difference between the total proceeds and the total par value of the shares.

Nov. 14   In a situation where **more than one class of securities are issued in a lump sum issuance**, and the market value of all classes of securities is **not** determinable, the incremental method may be used. The market value of the securities is used as a basis for those classes that are known (market value for common stock, in this case) and the remainder of the lump sum is allocated to the class for which the market value is **not** known (preferred stock, in this case).

ILLUSTRATION 15-1
COST METHOD OF ACCOUNTING FOR TREASURY STOCK (L.O. 4)

When treasury stock is purchased:
1. Cash is credited for the cost of the treasury shares acquired.
2. Treasury Stock is debited for the cost of the treasury shares acquired.

When treasury stock is sold:
1. Cash is debited for the selling price of the treasury shares sold.
2. Treasury Stock is credited for the cost of the treasury shares sold.
3. The selling (reissuance) price of the treasury shares is compared with the cost of those shares:
a. An excess of selling price over cost is credited to Paid-in Capital from Treasury Stock.
b. An excess of cost over selling price is debited to any additional paid-in capital account related to previous treasury stock transactions or retirements of stock in the same class. When the balances in Paid-in Capital from Treasury Stock and Paid-in Capital from Retirements are exhausted, Retained Earnings is debited for the remainder.

TIP:	Memorize the definition of treasury stock: **Treasury stock** is a corporation's own stock that has been issued, fully paid, and subsequently reacquired, but not cancelled. Thus, treasury shares are issued shares but are not outstanding shares. Treasury stock is **not** an asset; rather it is a contraction of owners' equity.
TIP:	Regardless of the method used to account for treasury stock, the **purchase** of treasury stock will cause owners' equity to **decrease** by the cost of the shares acquired; the **sale** of treasury stock will cause owners' equity to **increase** by the selling price of the shares sold. Although the net impact is the same under both methods, the choice of method will affect the individual stockholders' equity accounts involved in recording the transaction.
TIP:	When the **cost method** is used to account for treasury stock, the Treasury Stock account is classified contra to the sum of all of the other stockholders' equity accounts, and its balance is the cost of the treasury shares held. When the **par value method** is used to account for treasury stock transactions, the Treasury Stock account is classified contra to the related capital stock account (such as Common Stock), and its balance is the par value of the treasury shares held.
TIP:	The par value method of accounting for treasury stock views treasury stock as if it were temporarily retired and records the acquisition the same way a retirement is recorded except that the par value of the stock is charged to Treasury Stock rather than to the capital stock account used in recording the original issuance.

ILLUSTRATION 15-2
JOURNAL ENTRIES FOR RECORDING
TREASURY STOCK TRANSACTIONS USING THE COST METHOD (L.O. 4)

Assume that the following transactions occur in chronological order and that there are no prior balances in any additional paid-in capital accounts.

1. 1,000 shares of $10 par stock are sold for $13 per share.

Cash	13,000	
Common Stock		10,000
Paid-in Capital in Excess of Par		3,000

2. 100 treasury shares are acquired for $11 each.

Treasury Stock	1,100	
Cash	1,100	

3. 10 treasury shares are sold at $14 each.

Cash	140	
Treasury Stock		110
Paid-in Capital from Treasury Stock		30

4. 10 treasury shares are sold at $6 each.

Cash	60	
Paid-in Capital from Treasury Stock	30	
Retained Earnings	20	
Treasury Stock		110

5. All 80 remaining treasury shares are retired.

Common Stock	800	
Paid-in Capital in Excess of Par	240	
Treasury Stock		880
Paid-in Capital from Retirement of Common Stock		160

TIP: The accounts and amounts used to record the original issuance of shares are used to record the retirement of the same shares.

TIP: When the **cost method** is used to account for treasury stock transactions, a "gain on the sale of treasury stock" is an expression used to indicate that treasury stock was sold for a price in excess of the treasury stock's cost; a "loss on the sale of treasury stock" refers to treasury stock which is sold for a price that is less than the cost of the treasury shares. For example, transaction #3 above results in a "gain" of $3 ($14 - $11) per share and transaction #4 results in a "loss" of $5 ($11 - $6) per share.

ILLUSTRATION 15-2 (Continued)

TIP:	When a corporation engages in treasury stock transactions, a gain or loss is **never** reported on the income statement because a corporation cannot have an accounting gain or loss when dealing with the owners of the business in their capacity of being owners of the business. The purchase and sale of treasury stock are capital transactions; there is no element of income in a capital transaction.
TIP:	Treasury stock transactions can sometimes **reduce** retained earnings but can **never increase** retained earnings.
TIP:	Regardless of the method used to account for treasury stock, most state corporate laws require that retained earnings be restricted in the amount of the cost of treasury stock acquired. Restricted retained earnings are unavailable for dividend declaration.
TIP:	Most companies use the cost method to account for treasury stock transactions, rather than the par value method.
TIP:	When reporting treasury stock on the balance sheet using the cost method, the caption "Treasury stock" is shown along with the amount of the cost of the treasury shares being deducted from the subtotal of paid-in capital plus retained earnings to arrive at total stockholders' equity. When reporting treasury stock on the balance sheet using the par value method, the caption "Treasury stock" is shown along with the par amount of the treasury shares being deducted from the Capital Stock account. Thus, the Treasury Stock account is referred to as a contra stockholders' equity account using the cost method; with the par value method, the Treasury Stock account is classified as a contra capital stock account (which may be more broadly referred to as a contra stockholders' equity account).

EXERCISE 15-3

Purpose: (L.O. 4, 9) This exercise will illustrate how the components of stockholders' equity should be reported in the balance sheet.

Bobbit Corporation's charter authorizes 200,000 shares of $20 par value common stock, and 50,000 shares of 6% cumulative and nonparticipating preferred stock, par value $100 per share.

The corporation engaged in the following stock transactions between the date of incorporation and December 31, 2010:
(1)   Issued 40,000 shares of common stock for $1,920,000.
(2)   Issued 10,000 shares of preferred stock in exchange for machinery valued at $1,120,000.
(3)   Purchased 1,000 shares of common stock at $46 per share for the treasury. The cost method was used to record the transaction.
(4)   Sold 500 shares of treasury stock for $51 per share.

At December 31, 2010, Bobbit's retained earnings balance was $2,200,000. State law requires that the amount of retained earnings available for dividends be restricted by an amount equal to the cost of treasury shares held.

Instructions

Prepare the stockholders' equity section of the balance sheet in good form.

Solution to Exercise 15-3

Bobbit Corporation
PARTIAL BALANCE SHEET
December 31, 2010

Stockholders' equity		
Preferred stock, $100 par; 6% cumulative and nonparticipating; 50,000 shares authorized; 10,000 shares issued and outstanding		$1,000,000
Common stock, $20 par; 200,000 shares authorized, 40,000 shares issued, 39,500 shares outstanding		800,000
Additional paid-in capital:		
From preferred stock	$ 120,000	
From common stock	1,120,000	
From treasury stock	2,500	1,242,500
Total paid-in capital		3,042,500
Retained earnings (restricted in the amount of $23,000 cost of treasury stock held)		2,200,000
Total paid-in capital and retained earnings		5,242,500
Less: Cost of 500 treasury common shares		23,000
Total stockholders' equity		$ 5,219,500

Approach: Reconstruct the journal entries for the transactions and post those entries to T-accounts. Use the resulting balances in the accounts to prepare the stockholders' equity section of the balance sheet at December 31, 2010.

Explanation:

(1)	Cash	1,920,000	
	Common Stock (40,000 x $20)		800,000
	Paid-in Capital in Excess of Par—Common		
	($1,920,000 - $800,000)...		1,120,000
(2)	Machinery..	1,120,000	
	Preferred Stock (10,000 x $100)...................................		1,000,000
	Paid-in Capital in Excess of Par—Preferred		
	($1,120,000 - $1,000,000)..		120,000
(3)	Treasury Stock—Common (1,000 x $46).........................	46,000	
	Cash	46,000	

(4)	Cash (500 x $51)..	25,500	
	Treasury Stock—Common (500 x $46)..............................		23,000
	Paid-in Capital from Treasury Stock		
	($25,500 - $23,000)..		2,500

A restriction on retained earnings can be reported by parenthetical note in the retained earnings caption on the balance sheet or by a note to the financial statements. A restriction on retained earnings does **not** affect the total balance of retained earnings; it merely makes a portion of retained earnings unavailable to serve as the basis of a dividend declaration.

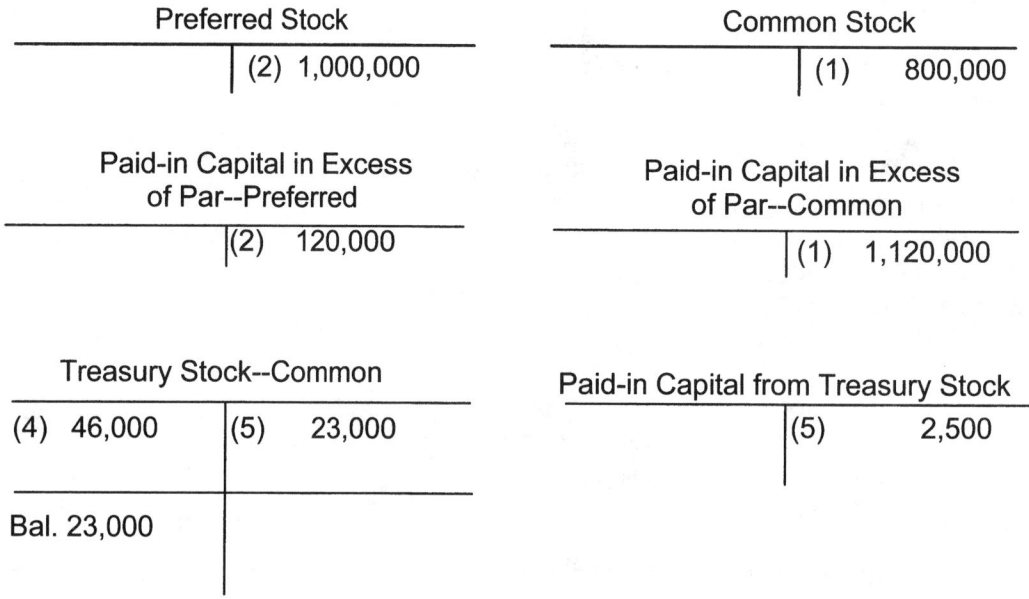

Preferred Stock		Common Stock	
	(2) 1,000,000		(1) 800,000

Paid-in Capital in Excess of Par--Preferred		Paid-in Capital in Excess of Par--Common	
	(2) 120,000		(1) 1,120,000

Treasury Stock--Common		Paid-in Capital from Treasury Stock	
(4) 46,000	(5) 23,000		(5) 2,500
Bal. 23,000			

TIP: The **par value** of a stock is an arbitrary value assigned to a share of stock at the time of incorporation and is printed on the stock certificate. Par value usually has **no** direct relationship to the stock's issuance price or to its market value at any date subsequent to the issuance date.   The **par value** of a stock has legal significance because it establishes the amount of **legal capital**, which is an amount of owners' equity that must be maintained by the corporation for the protection of creditors.

TIP: When a corporation issues more than one class of capital stock, each additional paid-in capital account should specify the class of stock to which it relates. Although a separate account may be maintained in the general ledger for each source of additional paid-in capital, the balances of all additional paid-in capital accounts are typically summed and reported by a single amount on the balance sheet by the caption Additional Paid-in Capital.

TIP: When stock is issued in a noncash exchange, the historical cost principle is used to determine the issuance price. Thus, the exchange price is the fair value (cash equivalent) of the consideration given or the fair value of the consideration received, whichever is the more objectively determinable.

CASE 15-2

Purpose: (L.O. 2, 3) This case examines the major classifications within the stockholders' equity section of the balance sheet.

Stockholders' equity is an important element of a corporation's balance sheet.

Instructions
Identify and discuss the general categories of stockholders' equity (capital) for a corporation. Enumerate specific sources included in each general category.   (AICPA Adapted)

Solution to Case 15-2

The general categories of a corporation's stockholders' equity are:
- Paid-in capital or contributed capital (capital stock **plus** additional paid-in capital).
- Retained earnings.
- Accumulated Other Comprehensive Income

Contributed capital represents the amounts paid in for all classes of shares of stock and the amounts capitalized by order of the corporation's board of directors. Included in contributed capital is legal capital, which is usually the aggregate par value or stated value of the shares issued. Legal capital is usually not subject to withdrawal; it is intended to protect corporate creditors. Contributed capital also includes other amounts in addition to the legal capital. These amounts are generally referred to as additional paid-in capital and include the following:

- Premiums on capital stock issued (excess of issuance price over par or stated value).
- Excess of proceeds from reissuing treasury stock over its cost when using the cost method of accounting for treasury stock.
- Assessments on stockholders.
- Conversion of convertible bonds or preferred stock to common stock. (See Chapter 16).
- Declaration of small (ordinary) stock dividend.
- Reacquisition and retirement of outstanding shares at an amount below their original issuance price.

TIP: Additional paid-in capital is a classification of accounts (like current assets is another classification). Therefore, there is no one account titled "additional paid-in capital"; rather, there are numerous individual accounts within that classification (such as Paid-in Capital in Excess of Par (or Premium on Common Stock), Paid-in Capital in Excess of Stated Value, and Paid-in Capital from Treasury Stock).

Retained earnings are the accumulated net earnings of a corporation in excess of any net losses from operations and dividends (cash or stock). Total retained earnings should also include prior-period adjustments as direct increases or decreases and may include certain restrictions on retained earnings, making a portion of the balance unavailable to serve as a basis for dividends. These restrictions may arise as a result of a restriction in a bond indenture or other formal agreement or they may be created at the discretion of the board of directors.

Accumulated Other Comprehensive Income reflects the sum of items reported to date as Other Comprehensive Income on the income statement.

Items reflected as credits (increases) in this sum include:
(1)   unrealized holding gains on available-for-sale securities held as an investment.
(2)   accumulated foreign currency translation gain adjustments.

Items reflected as debits (decreases) in this sum include:
(1)   unrealized holding losses on available-for-sale securities held as an investment.
(2)   accumulated foreign currency translation loss adjustments.
(3)   excess of additional pension liability over unrecognized prior service cost.
(4)   guarantees of employee stock option plan (ESOP) debt.
(5)   unearned or deferred compensation related to employee stock award plans.
(6)   amounts owed to a company by employees for loans to buy company stock.

EXERCISE 15-4

Purpose: (L.O. 6, 10) This exercise will illustrate the use of the cost method of accounting for treasury stock transactions under a variety of price relationships.

LaToya Corporation reported the following stockholder equity items at December 31, 2009:

Common Stock, $10 par	$ 350,000
Paid-in Capital in Excess of Par	70,000
Retained Earnings	710,000
Total Stockholders' Equity	$ 1,130,000

During 2010, LaToya had the following treasury stock transactions:
1.   Purchased 1,000 shares at $15 per share.
2.   Purchased 1,000 shares at $13 per share.
3.   Sold 1,000 shares at $11 per share.
4.   Sold 1,000 shares at $14 per share.
5.   Purchased and immediately retired 1,000 shares at $16 per share.

Instructions
Prepare the journal entries for the treasury stock transactions listed above assuming the cost method is used. Apply a FIFO approach in determining the cost of treasury shares sold.

Solution to Exercise 15-4
Cost Method

1.	Treasury Stock (1,000 x $15)...	15,000	
	Cash...		15,000
2.	Treasury Stock (1,000 x $13)...	13,000	
	Cash...		13,000
3.	Cash (1,000 x $11)..	11,000	
	Retained Earnings...	4,000	
	Treasury Stock (1,000 x $15)...............................		15,000

4. Cash (1,000 x $14).. 14,000
    Treasury Stock (1,000 x $13).............................   13,000
    Paid-in Capital from Treasury Stock.....................   1,000

5. Common Stock (1,000 x $10) 10,000
    Paid-in Capital in Excess of Par (1,000 x $2)................ 2,000*
    Paid-in Capital from Treasury Stock............................. 1,000
    Retained Earnings.. 3,000
        Cash (1,000 x $16)...   16,000

    *$350,000 Common Stock balance ÷ $10 par = 35,000 shares issued
     $70,000 PIC in Excess of Par balance ÷ 35,000 shares = $2 original
        issuance premium per share

Approach and Explanation: Follow the guidelines listed in **Illustration 15-1** and the examples in **Illustration 15-2**. An explanation for each entry above is as follows:

1. Treasury Stock is debited for the cost of the treasury shares acquired.

2. Treasury Stock is debited for the cost of the treasury shares acquired.

3. Cash is debited for the selling price of the treasury shares sold. Treasury Stock is credited for the cost of the treasury shares sold. The excess of the cost over the selling price of the treasury shares is to be charged to Paid-in Capital from Treasury Stock or Paid-in Capital from Retirements to the extent that these accounts have balances that came from previous transactions involving stock of the same class. In this scenario, there is no balance in either of these accounts so the entire excess is charged to Retained Earnings.

4. Cash is debited for the selling price of the treasury shares sold. Treasury Stock is credited for the cost of the treasury shares sold. The excess of the selling price over the cost of the treasury shares is to be credited to Paid-in Capital from Treasury Stock.

5. A retirement of stock is to be handled in a manner similar to the par value method of handling the purchase of treasury stock except that the capital stock account will be debited rather than Treasury Stock. Thus, the amounts recorded for the original issuance of the stock are removed from the accounts (debit Common Stock for $10 per share and debit Paid-in Capital in Excess of Par for $2 per share). The excess of the retirement price ($16 per share) over the original issuance price ($12 per share) is charged to additional paid-in capital arising from previous reissuances or retirements of treasury stock of the same class before reducing Retained Earnings. Because Paid-in Capital from Treasury Stock ($1,000) is insufficient to absorb the $4,000 excess in this situation, the remainder ($3,000) is charged to Retained Earnings.

ILLUSTRATION 15-3
DETERMINING HOW TO RECORD A DISTRIBUTION OF STOCK (L.O. 7, 8)

When a corporation distributes additional shares of its own stock to its existing stockholders for no consideration, the accountant must record the distribution as one of the following, whichever is appropriate: (1) a small stock dividend, (2) a large stock dividend, or (3) a stock split. The following flowchart will provide guidance in determining the proper treatment.

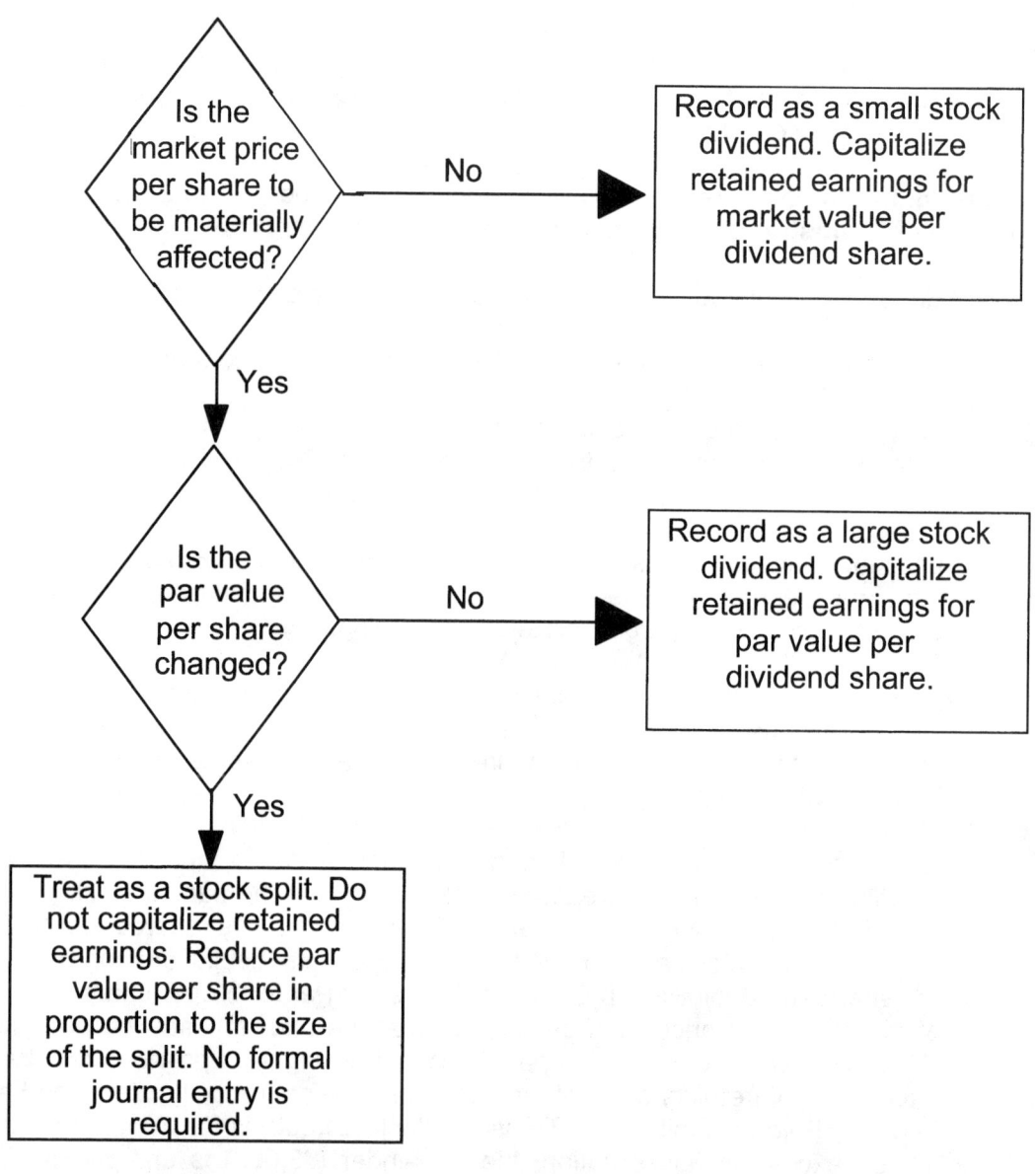

ILLUSTRATION 15-4
JOURNAL ENTRIES FOR RECORDING DIVIDENDS AND SPLITS (L.O. 7, 8)

Cash Dividend

Data The board of directors declares a cash dividend of $100,000.

Date of Declaration	Retained Earnings (or Cash Dividends Declared).......	100,000	
	Dividends Payable...		100,000
Date of Payment	Dividends Payable...	100,000	
	Cash		100,000

TIP: There are three dates associated with the declaration of any dividend: (1) the declaration date, (2) the date of record, and (3) the date of payment (or distribution). A journal entry is required at the date of declaration and at the date of payment. There is no journal entry at the date of record.

TIP: The declaration of a cash dividend reduces working capital; the payment of a previously declared (and unrecorded) cash dividend has no effect on working capital. Unless otherwise indicated, Dividends Payable will require a cash payment to settle the obligation.

Property Dividend

Data Dave Jones Corporation declares a property dividend on March 1 to be distributed to stockholders on April 15. The property is an investment in shares of Bonnie Corporation and has a carrying value of $11,000. The market value of the Bonnie shares is $14,000 on March 1 and $14,900 on April 15.

Date of Declaration	Investments in Securities..	3,000	
	Gain on Appreciation of Securities		3,000
	Retained Earnings (or Property Dividends Declared)..	14,000	
	Property Dividends Payable		14,000
Date of Payment	Property Dividends Payable	14,000	
	Investments in Securities..................................		14,000

TIP: Any change in the fair value of the property between the date of declaration and the date of payment of the dividend is ignored.

TIP: A property dividend (dividend payable in assets of the corporation other than cash) is an example of a nonreciprocal transfer of nonmonetary assets. A nonreciprocal transfer is a transaction in which value is going only in one direction (one party gives but does not receive value; the other party receives but does not give value). This differs from an exchange transaction in which each of two parties both gives and receives value. Generally accepted accounting principles requires that a nonreciprocal transfer of nonmonetary assets be recorded at the fair value of the assets transferred. Thus, any difference between the transferred asset's fair value and its carrying amount is to be recognized as a gain or a loss.

ILLUSTRATION 15-4 (Continued)

Liquidating Dividend

Data   Harker Corporation declares a liquidating dividend of $4,000.

Date of	Additional Paid-in Capital*...	4,000
Declaration	Dividends Payable..	4,000

    *One of a number of additional paid-in capital accounts may be used, depending on the relevant state law, such as Paid-in Capital in Excess of Par or Paid-in Capital from Treasury Stock.

Date of	Dividends Payable..	4,000
Payment	Cash	4,000

> **TIP:** A **liquidating dividend** is a distribution to stockholders from invested capital. Thus, a liquidating dividend results in a reduction of paid-in capital (usually additional paid-in capital) and does not affect retained earnings. A stockholder's investment in the corporation is reduced, but maybe not eliminated, by this type of dividend. If a dividend is only **partially liquidating**, both paid-in capital and retained earnings are reduced.

Small Stock Dividend

Data   D & E Henry Corporation has 100,000 shares of $10 par common stock outstanding on March 1, 2010. On March 2, the board of directors declares a 10% stock dividend distributable on April 4 to stockholders of record on March 16. The market price per share of common is $24 on March 2, $23 on March 16, and $25 on April 4.

Date of	Retained Earnings (or Stock Dividend Declared)........	240,000
Declaration	Common Stock Dividend Distributable	100,000
	Paid-in Capital in Excess of Par.................................	140,000
	(10% x 100,000 = 10,000 shares)	
	(10,000 shares x $24 = $240,000)	
	(10,000 shares x $10 par = $100,000)	
	($240,000 - $100,000 = $140,000)	

Date of	Common Stock Dividend Distributable........................	100,000
Distribution	Common Stock...	100,000

> **TIP:** If a balance sheet is prepared between the date of declaration and the date of distribution, the Common Stock Distributable account is classified in the Paid-in Capital section of stockholders' equity.

> **TIP:** Although a stock dividend results in a reduction in retained earnings, it also causes an increase in paid-in capital by the same amount. There is **no change in total stockholders' equity** when a stock dividend is declared or distributed.

ILLUSTRATION 15-4 (Continued)

> **TIP:** The term **capitalization of retained earnings** refers to the process of transferring an amount from retained earnings to paid-in capital. Stock dividends result in the capitalization of retained earnings. Thus, stock dividends are declared as a means of informing stockholders that assets arising from past income will be retained in the business rather than distributed as dividends to the stockholders.
>
> **TIP:** The amount of retained earnings to be capitalized for a stock dividend depends on whether or not the issuance of the dividend shares is expected to have a material effect on the market price per share of stock. If a material effect is **not** expected, the market price at the date of declaration is used; if a material effect is expected, the par value is used. Generally, when the number of shares in the dividend are equal to 20% or less of the number of shares currently outstanding, the dividend is called a **small or ordinary stock dividend**, and no material effect on market price per share is expected. When the number of shares in the dividend are equal to 25% or more of the number of shares currently outstanding, the dividend is called a **large stock dividend** or a **stock split-up effected in the form of a dividend**, and a material effect will likely occur.
>
> **TIP:** The account title, Stock Dividend Payable, is a poor title for Stock Dividend Distributable. The word "payable" implies it is a liability; however, it is not a liability because there is no associated debt that must later be paid by the use of cash or other assets or services. Stock Dividend Distributable is a capital stock account and, there fore, is to be reported as an element of paid-in capital. This account only has a balance for the short period of time between the date of declaration and the date of distribution of the dividend.

Large Stock Dividend

Data JJH Corporation has 100,000 shares of $10 par common stock outstanding on March 1, 2010. On March 2, the board of directors declares a 40% stock split-up effected in the form of a dividend. The par value per share is unchanged. The dividend shares are to be distributed on April 3 to stockholders of record on March 15. The market price per share of common stock is $24 on March 2, $15 on March 15, and $16 on April 3.

Date of Declaration

Retained Earnings (or Stock Dividend Declared)........	400,000	
Common Stock Dividend Distributable		400,000
(40% x 100,000 = 40,000 shares)		
(40,000 x $10 par = $400,000)		

Date of Record

No entry.

Date of Distribution

Common Stock Dividend Distributable	400,000	
Common Stock		400,000

ILLUSTRATION 15-4 (Continued)

Stock Split

Data Howell Cove Corporation has 100,000 shares of $10.00 par common stock outstanding on March 1, 2010. On March 2, the board of directors declares a 4-for-1 stock split. The par value per share is to be reduced to $2.50. The split is to be effective April 2 for shareholders of record on March 13.

Date of Declaration No entry.

Date of Record No entry.

Date of Distribution No entry. Par value per share is reduced from $10.00 to $2.50. The number of shares outstanding is increased proportionally from 100,000 to 400,000. The balance of Common Stock remains at $1,000,000 (400,000 x $2.50).

TIP: A stock split does not involve any transfer of retained earnings to paid-in capital; rather, the par value per share is changed in proportion to the multiple of issued shares.

EXERCISE 15-5

Purpose: (L.O. 7, 8) This exercise will review the effects of various types of distributions to stockholders.

Instructions

For each transaction listed across the top of the following matrix, indicate the effect on each of the items listed down the left side of the matrix. Use "INC" to indicate an increase, "DEC" to indicate a decrease, and "NE" for no effect.

TRANSACTION

ITEM	Declaration of a cash dividend	Payment of a previously recorded cash dividend	Declaration & payment of a property dividend	Declaration & payment of a liquidating dividend	Declaration & distribution of a small stock dividend	Declaration & distribution of a large stock dividend	Stock Split
Working capital							
Assets							
Total capital stock							
Total additional paid-in capital							
Retained earnings							
Total stock-holders' equity							
Par value per share							
Total number of shares outstanding							

Solution to Exercise 15-5

TRANSACTION

ITEM	Declaration of a cash dividend	Payment of a previously recorded cash dividend	Declaration & payment of a property dividend	Declaration & payment of a liquidating dividend	Declaration & distribution of a small stock dividend	Declaration & distribution of a large stock dividend	Stock Split
Working capital	DEC	NE	DEC	DEC	NE	NE	NE
Assets	NE	DEC	DEC	DEC	NE	NE	NE
Total capital stock	NE	NE	NE	NE	INC	INC	NE
Total additional paid-in capital	NE	NE	NE	DEC	INC	NE	NE
Retained earnings	DEC	NE	DEC	NE	DEC	DEC	NE
Total stockholders' equity	DEC	NE	DEC	DEC	NE	NE	NE
Par value per share	NE	NE	NE	NE	NE	NE	DEC
Total number of shares outstanding	NE	NE	NE	NE	INC	INC	INC

Approach: Write down the journal entry(ies) associated with each situation. (Refer to Illustration 15-4 to check your entries.) Take the account in each entry and examine their individual effects on each of the items listed.

EXERCISE 15-6

Purpose: (L.O. 9) This exercise will illustrate the preparation of a statement of stockholders' equity and the related stockholders' equity section of the balance sheet.

On January 1, 2010, Huseman Corporation had the following stockholders' equity balances:

Common Stock ($1 stated value, 800,000 shares authorized)		$ 300,000
Paid-in Capital in Excess of Stated Value	710,000	
Retained Earnings	390,000	
Accumulated Other Comprehensive Income	30,000	
Treasury Stock (3,000 shares)(cost method)	6,000	

During 2010, the following occurred:
- Issued 50,000 shares of common stock at $3 per share.
- Declared a $70,000 cash dividend.
- Purchased 1,000 shares of treasury stock at $2 per share.
- Declared and distributed a 5% stock dividend when the market value was $3 per share.
- Earned net income for the year of $200,000
- Reported an unrealized holding loss on available-for-sale securities, net of tax, $8,000.

Instructions
(a)   Prepare a statement of stockholders' equity for the year ending December 31, 2010.
(b)   Prepare the stockholders' equity section of the balance sheet as of December 31, 2010.

Solution to Exercise 15-6
(a)

Huseman Corporation
STATEMENT OF STOCKHOLDERS' EQUITY
For the Year Ended December 31, 2010

	Total	Compre-hensive Income	Retained Earnings	Accumulated Other Com-prehensive Income	Common Stock ($1 Stated Value)	Paid-in Capital in Excess of Stated Value	Treasury Stock
Balance January 1	$1,424,000		$390,000	$30,000	$300,000	$710,000	$(6,000)
Issued 50,000 shares of common stock at $3	150,000				50,000	100,000	
Declared a $70,000 cash dividend	(70,000)		(70,000)				
Purchased 1,000 shares for treasury at $2	(2,000)						(2,000)
Declared & distributed a 5% stock dividend			(51,900)		17,300	34,600	
Net income for year	200,000	$200,000	200,000				
Other Comprehensive Income	(8,000)	(8,000)		(8,000)			
Balance, December 31	$1,694,000	$192,000	$468,100	$22,000	$367,300	$844,600	$(8,000)

TIP: Notice how the columns on this statement foot (add down) and crossfoot (add across). Also notice that in the cross footing process, to avoid double counting,

> we ignore the amounts in the Comprehensive Income column because those amounts are already included in the Accumulated Other Comprehensive Income column or in the Retained Earnings column.

Explanation: A corporation is to disclose **all** changes that took place in **all** stockholder equity items during the reporting period. A convenient and effective way of meeting that requirement is to present a **statement of stockholders' equity** (sometimes called a stockholders' equity statement). When this statement is presented, it replaces the statement of retained earnings because it contains all the information that a statement of retained earnings would contain plus data regarding changes in other components of stockholders' equity.

The computations for the 5% stock dividend are as follows:
350,000 shares issued - 4,000 treasury shares = 346,000 shares outstanding.
346,000 shares outstanding x 5% = 17,300 dividend shares.
17,300 shares x $3 market value = $51,900 decrease in Retained Earnings.
17,300 shares x $1 stated value = $17,300 increase in Common Stock.
17,300 shares x ($3 - $1) = $34,600 increase in additional paid-in capital.

> **TIP:** Refer to **Illustration 4-4** of this *Problem Solving Survival Guide* for a more comprehensive discussion of the reporting of other comprehensive income for a period of time and the resulting accumulated other comprehensive income amount. When a company has reported components of other comprehensive income, an item called Accumulated Other Comprehensive Income (or Loss) is to be reported as a separate component of stockholders' equity. It may be a positive or negative element of stockholders' equity.

(b)

Huseman Corporation
BALANCE SHEET (Partial)
As of December 31, 2010

Stockholders' Equity
    Paid-in capital
        Common stock ($1 stated value, 800,000 shares
        authorized, 367,300 shares issued, 363,300

shares outstanding	$ 367,300
Paid-in capital in excess of stated value	844,600
Total paid-in capital	1,211,900
Retained earnings	468,100
Total paid-in capital and retained earnings	1,680,000
Accumulated other comprehensive income	22,000
Treasury stock, 4,000 shares, at cost	(8,000)
Total stockholders' equity	$1,694,000

ILLUSTRATION 15-5
RATIOS FOR ANALYSIS OF STOCKHOLDERS' EQUITY (L.O. 9)

The following three ratios use stockholders' equity amounts to evaluate a company's profitability and long-term solvency.

1. **Rate of return on common stock equity.** This widely used ratio measures profitability from the common stockholders' viewpoint. This ratio shows how many dollars of net income were earned for each dollar invested by the owners. The ratio is computed as follows:

$$\text{Rate of return on common stock equity} = \frac{\text{Net income - preferred dividends}}{\text{Average common stockholders' equity}^a}$$

aThe par value of preferred stock is deducted from total stockholders' equity to arrive at the amount of common stock equity used in this ratio.

TIP: When the rate of return on common stock equity is greater than the rate of return on total assets, the company is said to be "trading on the equity at a gain" or "favorably trading on the equity." **"Trading on the equity"** describes the practice of using borrowed money at fixed interest rates or issuing preferred stock with constant dividend rates in hopes of using the assets obtained (by use of the money from the borrowing or issuance of preferred stock) in such a way that the rate of return on the assets exceeds the rate of interest or dividends. If this can be done, the capital obtained from bondholders or preferred stockholders earns enough to pay interest or dividends and to leave a margin for the common stockholders. When this condition exists, trading on the equity is profitable. However, if the cost of debt exceeds the return on total assets, the return on common stockholders' equity will be less than the return on total assets; hence, the entity will be **unfavorably trading on the equity.**

2. **Payout ratio.** The payout ratio is the relationship of cash dividends to net income; it is a measure of profitability. The ratio is computed for common stockholders as follows:

$$\text{Payout ratio} = \frac{\text{Cash dividends}}{\text{Net income less preferred dividends}}$$

TIP: Some investors look for a stock that has a payout ratio sufficiently high to provide a good yield on the stock; other investors view the potential appreciation in the market value of the stock as more important than the prospect of high dividends.

TIP: Another closely watched ratio is the **dividend yield** which is computed by dividing the cash dividend per share by the market price of the stock. This ratio affords investors of some idea of the rate of return that will be received in cash dividends from their investment.

3. **Book value per share.** The book value or **equity value per share** of stock is a much-used basis for evaluating the net worth of a corporation. Book value per share of stock is the amount each share would receive **if** the company were liquidated on the basis of amounts reported on the balance sheet. The ratio loses much of its relevance if the valuations on the balance sheet do not approximate fair market value of the assets. Assuming no preferred stock is outstanding, the ratio is as follows:

$$\text{Book value per share} = \frac{\text{Common stockholders' equity}}{\text{Outstanding shares}}$$

TIP: Refer to **Exercise 15-9** for an example of how to handle the computation of book value per share when both preferred stock and common stock are outstanding.

EXERCISE 15-7

Purpose: (L.O. 9) This exercise will give you an example of how to compute the return on common stock equity.

	Dec. 31 2009	Dec. 31 2010
Preferred stock, 8%, par $100, noncumulative	$250,000	$250,000
Common stock	600,000	800,000
Retained earnings	150,000	370,000
Dividends paid on preferred stock for the year	20,000	20,000
Net income for the year	120,000	240,000

Instructions
Compute Bradley's return on common stockholders' equity (rounded to the nearest percentage) for 2010.

Solution to Exercise 15-7

$$\frac{\text{Return on common}}{\text{stockholders' equity}} = \frac{\text{Net income - Preferred dividends}}{\text{Average common stockholders' equity}}$$

$$\frac{\$240,000 \ - \ \$20,000}{1/2 \ (\$750,000^1 \ + \ \$1,170,000^2)} = \frac{\$220,000}{\$960,000} = \underline{23\%}$$

[1]Beginning total stockholders' equity ($250,000 + $600,000 + $150,000) - par value of preferred stock ($250,000) = $750,000 beginning common stockholders' equity.

[2]Ending total stockholders' equity ($250,000 + $800,000 + $370,000) - par value of preferred stock ($250,000) = $1,170,000 ending common stockholders' equity.

Explanation: A widely used ratio that measures profitability from the common stockholders' viewpoint is **return on common stockholders' equity.** This ratio shows how many dollars of net income were earned for each dollar invested by the owners. It is computed by dividing net income applicable to common stockholders (net income - preferred dividends) by average common stockholders' equity.

ILLUSTRATION 15-6
STEPS IN ALLOCATING DIVIDENDS TO
PREFERRED AND COMMON STOCKHOLDERS (L.O. 10)

Step 1: Assign arrearage to preferred, if any.

If there are any dividends in arrears, the amount of arrearage is first allocated to the preferred stockholders. The remaining amount of dividends to be allocated is computed. (If the amount declared is not enough to cover the arrearage, all dividends declared go to preferred holders, the remaining arrearage is computed for disclosure, and the rest of the steps are not performed.)

Step 2: Assign current period preference to preferred.

The amount of the preferred stockholders' current year preference is computed and that amount is allocated to the preferred stockholders. The remaining amount of dividends to be allocated is computed. (If the dividends declared are not enough to cover the preferred's current year preference, all of the dividends declared are allocated to the preferred stock-holders, the remaining arrearage is computed for disclosure, and the rest of the steps are not performed.)

Step 3: Assign common an equal percentage dividend.

An amount of dividends to common stockholders to "match" the "percentage-on-par" dividend given to preferred (for current year preference only) is computed. If the remaining amount of dividends is sufficient to cover this "matching process," the amount of "matching" is allocated to common and the remaining amount of dividends is the amount in which both preferred and common will "participate." (If the amount declared is not enough to "match" the preferred, whatever is available after the preferred get their portion as calculated in steps "1" and "2" is allocated to common.)

Step 4: Assign the participation amount to preferred and common.

If the preferred stock is nonparticipating, any remaining dividends are assigned to the common stockholders. If the preferred stock is participating, the amount of dividends available for "participation" is allocated between preferred and common based on an "equal percentage on par basis." That percentage is determined by dividing the amount of dividends available for participation by the sum of the aggregate par value of the preferred and the aggregate par value of the common.

Step 5: Total the amounts allocated and compute per share amounts.

The amounts from the previous steps are added for each class. The total amount allocated to preferred stockholders and to common stockholders is often expressed on a per share basis. To calculate the amount per share, divide the total dividends allocated to the class by the number of outstanding shares in that class.

*EXERCISE 15-8

Purpose: (L.O. 10) This exercise will illustrate the allocation of dividends when a corporation has both preferred stock and common stock outstanding.

Charlie B. Daly Corporation has the following stock outstanding without any changes for years 2009, 2010, and 2011.

50,000 shares of $10 par, 4% preferred	$ 500,000
200,000 shares of $5 par common	1,000,000
	$ 1,500,000

Dividends are declared as follows:
2009	$15,000
2010	$50,000
2011	$72,000

Instructions

Compute the amount of dividends (total and per share) to be allocated to the preferred stockholders and the common stockholders for each of the three years under each of the **independent** assumptions below:
(a)   The preferred stock is noncumulative and nonparticipating.
(b)   The preferred stock is cumulative and nonparticipating.
(c)   The preferred stock is cumulative and participating.

Solution to Exercise 15-8

Approach: Compute the preferred's current year preference (50,000 shares x $10 par x 4% = $20,000) and the amount to "match" the common holders (200,000 shares x $5 par x 4% = $40,000). Then use the steps listed in **Illustration 15-6** to solve.

(a)

		Preferred	Common	Total
2009:	Total to distribute			$15,000
	Step 1:			
	Step 2: Less than preference	$15,000		$15,000
	Step 3:			
	Step 4:			
	Step 5:	$15,000	$ -0-	$15,000
	÷ by	50,000	200,000	
	=	$ .30	$ .00	
2010:	Total to distribute			$50,000
	Step 1:			
	Step 2: 4% x $500,000	$20,000		$20,000
	Step 3: Remainder		$30,000	30,000
	Step 4:			
	Step 5:	$20,000	$30,000	$50,000
	÷ by	50,000	200,000	
	=	$ .40	$ .15	
2011:	Total to distribute			$72,000
	Step 1:			
	Step 2: 4% x $500,000	$20,000		$20,000
	Step 3: 4% x $1,000,000		$40,000	40,000
	Step 4: Remainder		12,000	12,000
	Step 5:	$20,000	$52,000	$72,000
	÷ by	50,000	200,000	
	=	$ .40	$ .26	

(b)

		Preferred	Common	Total
2009:	Total to distribute			$15,000
	Step 1:			
	Step 2: Less than preference	$15,000		$15,000
	Step 3:			
	Step 4:			
	Step 5:	$15,000	$ -0-	$15,000
	÷ by	50,000	200,000	
	=	$ .30	$ .00	
2010:	Total to distribute			$50,000
	Step 1: $20,000 - $15,000	$ 5,000		$ 5,000
	Step 2: 4% x $500,000	20,000		20,000
	Step 3: Remainder		$25,000	25,000
	Step 4:			
	Step 5:	$25,000	$25,000	$50,000
	÷ by	50,000	200,000	
	=	$ .50	$ .125	

		Prefered	Common	Total
2011	Total to distribute			$72,000
	Step 1:			
	Step 2: 4% x $500,000	$20,000		$20,000
	Step 3: 4% x $1,000,000		$40,000	40,000
	Step 4: Remainder		12,000	12,000
	Step 5:	$20,000	$52,000	$72,000
	÷ by	50,000	200,000	
	=	$ 40	$ 26	

(c)

		Preferred	Common	Total
2009:	Total to distribute			$15,000
	Step 1:			
	Step 2: Less than preference	$15,000		$15,000
	Step 3:			
	Step 4:			
	Step 5:	$15,000	$ -0-	$15,000
	÷ by	50,000	200,000	
	=	$ .30	$ .00	
2010:	Total to distribute			$50,000
	Step 1: $20,000 - $15,000	$ 5,000		$ 5,000
	Step 2: 4% x $500,000	20,000		20,000
	Step 3: Remainder		$25,000	25,000
	Step 4:			
	Step 5:	$25,000	$25,000	$50,000
	÷ by	50,000	200,000	
	=	$ .50	$ .125	

> **TIP:** Notice that in performing step 3, the remaining dividends ($25,000) are not sufficient in amount to allocate a "matching" dividend to the common stockholders (4% x $1,000,000 > $25,000).

		Preferred	Common	Total
2011:	Total to distribute			$72,000
	Step 1:			
		$20,000		$20,000
	Step 2: 4% x $500,000		$40,000	40,000
	Step 3: 4% x $1,000,000	4,000	8,000	12,000
	Step 4: To participate at .8%*	$24,000	$48,000	$72,000
	Step 5:			
	÷ by	50,000	200,000	
	=	$ .48	$ .24	

$$*\frac{\text{Amount to participate}}{\text{Total par}} = \frac{\$12,000}{\$1,500,000} = .008 \text{ or } .8\%$$

.008 x $500,000 = $4,000 allocated to preferred
.008 x $1,000,000 = $8,0000 allocated to common

> **TIP:** Notice that in 2011 under assumption (c) that the common stockholders receive a total dividend that is equal—percentage wise on par—to the dividend received by the preferred stockholders ($.48 ÷ $10 = 4.8%; $.24 ÷ $5 = 4.8%). This happens when the three following conditions are met:
> (1) The preferred stock is fully participating.
> (2) There are enough dividends declared to reach the point where both classes "participate."
> (3) There are no dividends in arrears.

*EXERCISE 15-9

Purpose: (L.O. 10) This exercise will illustrate the computation of book value per share when more than one class of stock is outstanding.

The stockholders' equity section of a recent balance sheet is presented below:

AL GORE CORPORATION
Partial Balance Sheet
December 31, 2010

Stockholders' equity		
Paid-in capital		
Capital stock		
6% preferred stock, $100 par value, cumulative call price		
$105, 50,000 shares authorized, 10,000 shares		
issued and outstanding		$1,000,000
Common stock, $20 par, 200,000 shares authorized		
41,500 shares issued, 40,000 shares outstanding		830,000
Total capital stock		1,830,000
Additional paid-in capital		
In excess of par value—preferred stock	$ 120,000	
In excess of par value—common stock	1,165,000	
From treasury stock—common	2,500	
Total additional paid-in capital		1,287,500
Total paid-in capital		3,117,500
Retained earnings		2,200,000
Total paid-in capital and retained earnings		5,317,500
Less: Treasury stock—common (1,500 shares)		69,000
Total stockholders' equity		$5,248,500

Instructions
Assuming the preferred stockholders have annually received dividends equal to their current year preference in all prior years except 2009 and 2010:
(a) Determine the book value per share of preferred stock.
(b) Determine the book value per share of common stock.

Solution to Exercise 15-9

(a) The book value per share of preferred stock is $117 which is computed as follows:

Call price per preferred share	$105
Dividends in arrears per preferred share	
($100 par x 6% preference per year x 2 years)	12
Book value per preferred share	$117

(b)

Total stockholders' equity		$5,248,500
Less: Total preferred stock equity:		
Call price ($105 x 10,000 shares)	$1,050,000	
Dividends in arrears ($100 X 6% X 2 X 10,000 shares)	120,000	1,170,000
Common stock equity		$4,078,500
Shares of common stock outstanding		40,000
Book value per share of common stock ($4,078,500 ÷ 40,000)		$101.9625

> **TIP:** Notice that **none** of the paid-in capital in excess of par value arising from the issuance of preferred stock at a price above par ($120,000) is directly allocated to preferred stock in the book value per share of preferred stock computation.
>
> **TIP:** If only one class of stock is outstanding, the book value of common is computed simply by dividing total stockholders' equity by the total number of shares outstanding.

Approach: To compute the book value per share of common stock when there is preferred stock also outstanding, use the following steps:

Step 1: **Compute the total book value of preferred stock** by multiplying the book value per share of preferred stock by the number of preferred shares outstanding. The book value per share of preferred is one of the following (listed) in order of preference):

a. Liquidation value of preferred plus dividends in arrears.
b. Call or redemption price of preferred plus dividends in arrears.
c. Par value of preferred plus dividends in arrears.

Step 2: **Compute the total book value of common stock** by deducting the total book value of preferred stock from total stockholders' equity.

Step 3: **Compute the book value per share of common stock** by dividing the total book value of common stock by the number of common stock shares outstanding.

ANALYSIS OF MULTIPLE-CHOICE TYPE QUESTIONS

QUESTION
1.   (L.O. 5) Which of the following rights does a preferred stockholder normally possess?
     a.   right to vote
     b.   right to receive a dividend before a common shareholder
     c.   preemptive right
     d.   right to participate in management

Explanation: A preferred stockholder usually has a preference over common stockholders as to dividends and as to distribution of assets upon liquidation. A preferred stockholder normally has to forego other rights because of the preference described above. The rights the preferred stockholder normally forgoes are the right to participate in management (right to vote on operational and financial decisions) and the preemptive right. A common stockholder normally has the right to vote and the preemptive right (right to maintain the same percentage ownership when additional shares of common stock are issued). (Solution = b.)

QUESTION
2.   (L.O. 3) The Tom Powell Corporation has 10,000 shares of $10 par common stock authorized. The following transactions took place during 2010, the first year of the corporation's existence:
     •   Sold 1,000 shares of common stock for $18 per share.
     •   Issued 1,000 shares of common stock in exchange for a patent valued at $20,000.
     •   Reported net income of $7,000.
     At the end of Tom Powell's first year, total paid-in capital amounted to:
     a. $8,000.
     b. $18,000.
     c. $20,000.
     d. $28,000.
     e.   none of the above.

Approach and Explanation: (1) Write down the components of paid-in capital: (a) balances of capital stock accounts, and (b) balances of additional paid-in capital accounts. (2) Reconstruct the journal entries for the transactions listed and post those entries to T-accounts. (3) Compute the balances of the relevant accounts. (4) Sum the relevant account balances.

```
Cash ............................................................................ 18,000
     Common Stock......................................................           10,000
     Paid-in Capital in Excess of Par.............................            8,000

Patent        20,000
     Common Stock......................................................           10,000
     Paid-in Capital in Excess of Par.............................           10,000

Income Summary ......................................................  7,000
     Retained Earnings................................................            7,000
```

Common Stock		Paid-in Capital in Excess of Par	
		10,000			8,000
		10,000			10,000
	Bal.	20,000		Bal.	18,000

Common stock $ 20,000
Additional paid-in capital   18,000
Total paid-in capital $ 38,000   (Solution = e.)

QUESTION

3. (L.O. 3) Which of the following represents the total number of shares that a corporation may issue under the terms of its charter?
a. authorized shares
b. issued shares
c. unissued shares
d. outstanding shares
e. treasury shares

Approach and Explanation: Explain the meaning of each of the terms used as answer selections. Choose the one that matches the stem of the question. Issued shares (ones the corporation has issued to date) **plus** unissued shares (shares that have not been issued yet but may be issued in the future in accordance with the terms of the charter) **equals** total authorized (approved) shares. Outstanding shares are the issued shares which are now in the hands of the public. Treasury shares are issued shares which are not outstanding at the present time. (Solution = a.)

QUESTION

4. (L.O. 3) If common stock with a par value is issued by a closely-held corporation for noncash assets, the amount to be recorded as paid-in capital related to this transaction is determined by the:
a. fair market value of the noncash assets received.
b. par value of the stock issued.
c. legal value of the stock issued.
d. book value of the noncash assets on the seller's books.

Approach and Explanation: Recall that any time assets are acquired, the historical cost principle is applied; that is, the assets are to be recorded at historical cost. Cost is measured by the fair market value (cash equivalent value) of the consideration given or the fair market value of the consideration received, whichever is the more objectively determinable. Assuming equipment with a fair value of $70,000 is received in exchange for stock of a closely-held corporation with a par value of $20,000, the journal entry to record the transaction would be as follows:

Equipment 70,000
    Common Stock...   20,000
    Paid-in Capital in Excess of Par Value....................................   50,000

Notice that two paid-in capital accounts (one capital stock account and one additional paid-in capital account) are affected. The increase in total paid-in capital is $70,000. (Solution = a.)

QUESTION

5. (L.O. 4) Treasury shares are:
a. shares held as an investment by the treasurer of the corporation.
b. shares held as an investment of the corporation.
c. issued and outstanding shares.
d. unissued shares.
e. issued but not outstanding shares.

Approach and Explanation: Write down the definition of treasury stock. Treasury stock is a corporation's own stock that has been issued, fully paid for, and reacquired by the corporation but **not** retired (cancelled). Treasury shares are shares that have been issued previously (so are not unissued) but are not outstanding now, as they have been subsequently reacquired by the company. Treasury shares refer to a company's own shares so they cannot be an investment. A company cannot own itself. The acquisition of treasury stock represents a contraction of capital (owners' equity) rather than the acquisition of an asset. (Solution = e.)

TIP: If and when treasury shares are formally retired, they revert back to an unissued status.

QUESTION

6. (L.O. 4) Assume the cost method is used to account for treasury stock. A "gain" on the sale of treasury stock should be classified as an:
   a. extraordinary item on the income statement.
   b. element of other income on the income statement.
   c. increase in additional paid-in capital.
   d. increase in retained earnings.

Explanation: When the cost method is used, a "gain" on the sale of treasury stock refers to the disposition of treasury stock at a price in excess of cost. This excess is recorded as a credit to Paid-in Capital from Treasury Stock. Selections "a" and "b" are incorrect because treasury stock transactions are capital transactions and capital transactions do not give rise to components of income determination. Answer selection "d" is incorrect because, regardless of the method used, treasury stock transactions can sometimes reduce retained earnings but may **never** increase retained earnings. (Solution = c.)

QUESTION

7. (L.O. 3, 4) Wheeler Corporation started business in 2000 by issuing 100,000 shares of $10 par common stock for $24 each. In 2006, 10,000 of these shares were purchased for $35 per share by Wheeler Corporation and held as treasury stock. (The cost method is used to account for treasury stock.) On April 15, 2010, these 10,000 shares were exchanged for a piece of land adjacent to some property currently owned by Wheeler. The property had an assessed value of $270,000 on the rolls of the county's property tax assessor. Wheeler's stock is actively traded and had a market price of $40 on April 15, 2010. The amount of paid-in capital from treasury stock transactions resulting from the above events would be:
   a. $50,000.
   b. $130,000.
   c. $160,000.
   d. $300,000.

Approach and Explanation: Prepare and analyze journal entries to record the purchase and "sale" of the treasury shares.

Treasury Stock	350,000	
Cash		350,000
(Purchase of 10,000 shares for treasury at $35 each)		
Land	400,000	
Treasury Stock..		350,000
Paid-in Capital from Treasury Stock		50,000

The issuance (and reissuance) of stock is always recorded at the fair value of the consideration given (the stock) or the fair value of the consideration received (the land), whichever is the more objectively determinable. The stock is actively traded in this case so the $40 current market price of a share of stock (the consideration given) is more objectively determinable than the fair value of the land received in exchange. Using the $400,000 ($40 x 10,000 shares) as the "selling price" of the treasury stock, that exceeds the cost of the treasury shares ($35 x 10,000 shares = $350,000) by $50,000. Hence, the paid-in capital from treasury stock transactions is $50,000 from the data given. (Solution = a.)

QUESTION

8. (L.O. 4) Refer to **Question 7** above. What effect did the exchange of treasury stock for land on April 15, 2010 have on total stockholders' equity?
   a. Increase of $50,000.
   b. Increase of $60,000.
   c. Increase of $300,000.
   d. Increase of $400,000.

Approach and Explanation: Analyze the journal entry to record the exchange of treasury stock for land. That entry is shown in the **Explanation for Question 7** above. The credit to Treasury Stock for $350,000 increases stockholders' equity by $350,000 because of the reduction of the contra equity account Treasury Stock. The credit to Paid-in Capital from Treasury Stock increases additional paid-in capital by $50,000 and thus increases total paid-in capital. Thus, assets increase by $400,000 and stockholders' equity increases by $400,000 which is the selling price of the treasury shares. The purchase of treasury stock typically decreases assets and stockholders' equity by the cost of the treasury shares, and the sale of treasury stock typically increases assets and shareholders' equity by the selling price of the treasury shares. (Solution = e.)

QUESTION
9.   (L.O. 5) Preferred stock which can be returned to the corporation and exchanged for common stock at the option of the shareholder is referred to as:
a.   cumulative preferred stock.
b.   convertible preferred stock.
c.   participating preferred stock.
d.   callable preferred stock.

Approach and Explanation: Holders of **convertible preferred stock** may, at their option, exchange their preferred shares for common stock at a predetermined ratio. Holders of **cumulative preferred stock** are entitled to receive dividends in arrears before any dividends can be paid to common stockholders; dividends in arrears refers to a passed dividend. Thus, dividends not paid in any year on cumulative preferred must be made up in a later year before any profits can be distributed to common stockholders. Holders of **participating preferred stock** share ratably with common stockholders in any dividend distributions beyond the preferred stock's annual preference. With **callable preferred stock**, the issuing corporation can call or redeem at its option the outstanding preferred shares at specified future dates and at stipulated prices. (Solution = b.)

QUESTION
10.   (L.O. 5) According to a proposed accounting standard, redeemable preferred stock should be:
a.   included with common stock.
b.   included with nonredeemable preferred stock.
c.   excluded from the stockholders' equity heading.
d.   included as a contra item in stockholders' equity.

Approach and Explanation: Redeemable preferred stock is preferred stock that has a mandatory redemption date or a redemption feature that is outside the control of the issuer. In these cases, the company has given to the holder a right to receive future cash flows of the company, and many believe this obligation should be reported as debt rather than equity. Under current accounting standards, most companies report redeemable preferred stock between debt and equity classifications. Under a proposed accounting standard, companies will be required by the FASB to report redeemable preferred stock as debt. (Solution = c.)

QUESTION
11.   (L.O. 7) The date that determines who is to be considered a stockholder for the purpose of receiving a dividend is the:
a.   declaration date.
b.   record date.
c.   payment date.
d.   distribution date.

Explanation: The date the board of directors formally declares (authorizes) a dividend and announces it to stockholders is called the **declaration date.** The **record date** marks the time when ownership of the outstanding shares is determined for dividend purposes from the stockholders' records maintained by the corporation. On the **payment date,** the dividend checks are mailed to the stockholders. (Solution = b.)

QUESTION

12.   (L.O. 7) The declaration and payment of cash dividends by a corporation will result in a(an):
a.   increase in Cash and an increase in Retained Earnings.
b.   increase in Cash and a decrease in Retained Earnings.
c.   decrease in Cash and an increase in Retained Earnings.
d.   decrease in Cash and a decrease in Retained Earnings.

Approach and Explanation: Prepare the journal entries required to record the declaration and payment of a cash dividend. Separately analyze each debit and credit to determine the effect on the balance of Cash and on the Retained Earnings account. Assuming cash dividends of $10,000 are declared, the entries and analysis are as follows:

At the date of declaration:			Effect
Retained Earnings	10,000		Decrease in Retained Earnings
Dividends Payable		10,000	Increase in current liabilities

At the date of payment:			Effect
Dividends Payable	10,000		Decrease in current liabilities
Cash		10,000	Decrease in Cash

The net effect of the declaration and payment of a cash dividend is to reduce retained earnings (and, thus, total stockholders' equity) and Cash (and, thus, total assets). (Solution = d.)

QUESTION

13.   (L.O. 7) Barney's Corporation has an investment in 1,000 shares of Phil Jones Corporation common stock with a cost of $29,000. These shares are used in a property dividend to stockholders of Barney's. The property dividend is declared on March 23 and scheduled to be distributed on April 30 to stockholders of record on April 15. The market value per share of Phil Jones stock is $42 on March 23, $44 on April 15, and $45 on April 30. The net effect of this property dividend on retained earnings is a reduction of:
a. $29,000.
b. $42,000.
c. $44,000.
d. $45,000.

Approach and Explanation: Write down the journal entries involved in accounting for this dividend. Examine each account in the entries for its effect on retained earnings. Summarize the results. The entries and their effects on retained earnings (RE) would be as follows:

				Effect on RE	
3/23	Investments in Securities..	13,000		-0-	
	Gain on Appreciation of Securities		13,000	↑	$13,000
	[($42 x 1,000) - $29,000 = $13,000]				
	Retained Earnings..	42,000		↓	42,000
	Property Dividends Payable		42,000	-0-	
4/30	Property Dividends Payable	42,000		-0-	
	Investments in Securities..		42,000	-0-	
	Net effect on retained earnings =			↓	$29,000

(Solution = a.)

TIP: Although a property dividend gets recorded at the **fair value** of the asset to be distributed, retained earnings is decreased by the **carrying value** of the asset due to the recognition of the increase or decrease in the fair value of the asset (this increase or decrease goes through net income, which is closed into retained earnings).

QUESTION
14.   (L.O. 7) The net effect of the declaration and payment of a liquidating dividend is a decrease in:
a.   retained earnings and a decrease in total assets.
b.   total paid-in capital and a decrease in total assets.
c.   total paid-in capital and an increase in retained earnings.
d.   total stockholders' equity and an increase in liabilities.

Explanation: A dividend based on paid-in capital (rather than retained earnings) is termed a **liquidating dividend**, because the amount originally paid in by stockholders is being reduced or "liquidated." (Solution = b.)

QUESTION
15.   (L.O. 8) What effect does the declaration and distribution of a 30% stock split-up effected in the form of a dividend have on the following?

	Retained Earnings	Total Paid-in Capital	Total Stockholders' Equity
a.	Decrease	Increase	No Effect
b.	Decrease	No Effect	No Effect
c.	Decrease	No Effect	Decrease
d.	No Effect	No Effect	No Effect

Approach and Explanation: Write down the journal entries for the declaration and distribution of a large stock dividend. Analyze the accounts in each entry separately to determine the impact on the three items requested.

The journal entry to record the declaration will reduce retained earnings and increase stock dividend distributable (a component of total capital stock and, therefore, a component of total paid-in capital) by the par value multiplied by the number of shares to be distributed in the dividend. That entry will **decrease retained earnings** and **increase total paid-in capital** by identical amounts, and thus have **no effect on total stockholders' equity**. The entry to record the distribution will reduce the dividend distributable balance (one capital stock account) and increase the common stock account (another capital stock account). Thus, the distribution entry will have **no effect** on any total within the major classifications of stockholders' equity. (Solution = a.)

QUESTION
16.   (L.O. 3, 8) A 300% stock dividend will have the same impact on the number of shares outstanding as a:
a.   2-for-1 stock split.
b.   3-for-1 stock split.
c.   4-for-1 stock split.
d.   5-for-1 stock split.

Approach and Explanation: Set up an example with numbers. For instance, assume we begin with 10,000 shares outstanding. A 300% stock dividend (or stock split-up effected in the form of a dividend) will mean 30,000 new shares will be distributed and there will then be 40,000 total shares outstanding. A 2-for-1 split will cause 10,000 shares to be replaced by 20,000. A 3-for-1 split will result in 30,000 total shares. A 4-for-1 split will cause the 10,000 shares to be replaced by 40,000 shares. The example proves that a 300% stock dividend (shares are increased **by** 300%) has the same effect on the number of shares outstanding as does a 4-for-1 split (each share is replaced with four shares). (Solution = c.)

QUESTION
17. (L.O. 8) Pat Trim Corporation declared a stock dividend of 10,000 shares when the par value was $1 per share, the market value was $5 per share, and the number of shares outstanding was 200,000. How does the entry to record this transaction affect retained earnings?
a.   No effect
b. $10,000 decrease
c. $40,000 decrease
d. $50,000 decrease

Approach and Explanation: Analyze the data to determine the size of the stock dividend. Prepare the journal entry to record the declaration of the stock dividend and analyze the entry's effect on retained earnings. Comparing the 10,000 dividend shares to the 200,000 outstanding shares prior to the dividend yields a 5% relationship; thus, the stock dividend is an ordinary (small) stock dividend. An ordinary stock dividend is recorded by transferring retained earnings equal to the market value of the dividend shares to paid-in capital. Therefore, 10,000 shares multiplied by $5 means retained earnings is to be charged for $50,000. (Solution = d.)

QUESTION
18. (L.O. 8) A 4-for-1 stock split will cause a decrease in:
     a.   total assets.
     b.   total stockholders' equity.
     c.   retained earnings.
     d.   the par value per share.

Explanation: A stock split involves the issuance of additional shares of stock to existing stockholders according to the number of shares presently owned. A stock split does **not** result in the capitalization of any retained earnings; rather, the par value per share is reduced in proportion to the increase in shares. Thus, in a 2-for-1 split, the number of shares are doubled and the par value per share is cut in half. Whereas with a 4-for-1 stock split, the number of total shares is four times what the number was before the split and the par value per share after the split is 1/4 of the par value per share before the split. Assets are not affected. (Solution = d.)

QUESTION
19. (L.O. 2, 9) The balance of the Retained Earnings account represents:
a.   cash set aside for specific purposes.
b.   the earnings for the most recent accounting period.
c.   the balance of unrestricted cash on hand.
d.   the total of all amounts reported as net income since the inception of the corporation minus the sum of any amounts reported as net loss and dividends declared since the inception of the corporation.

Approach and Explanation: Define retained earnings and select the answer that most closely matches that definition. Retained earnings is net income retained in a corporation. Retained earnings is often referred to as earnings retained for use in the business. Thus, net income (earnings for a period) increases the balance of retained earnings. Distributions of earnings to stockholders (owners) are called dividends; they reduce the balance of retained earnings. (Solution = d.)

QUESTION
20. (L.O. 9) Assume common stock is the only class of stock outstanding in the B-Bar-B Corporation. Total stockholders' equity divided by the number of common stock shares outstanding is called:
a.   book value per share.
b.   par value per share.
c.   stated value per share.
d.   market value per share.

Approach and Explanation: Briefly define each of the answer selections. **Book value** per common stock share represents the equity a common stockholder has in the net assets of the corporation. When only one class of stock is outstanding, book value per share is determined by dividing total stockholders' equity by the number of shares outstanding. **Par value** is an arbitrary value which does not have much significance except in establishing legal capital and in determining the amount to appear in the Common Stock account for each share issued. **Stated value** refers to an arbitrary value that may be placed on a stock by the board of directors. Stated value has about the same significance as par value. **Market value** refers to the price for which a stock is currently being bought and sold in the open market. (Solution = a.)

QUESTION
21. (L.O. 9) A corporation has two classes of stock outstanding. The return on common stock equity is computed by dividing net income:
a. minus preferred dividends by the number of common stock shares outstanding at the balance sheet date.
b. plus interest expense by the average amount of total assets.
c. by the number of common stock shares outstanding at the balance sheet date.
d. minus preferred dividends by the average amount of common stockholders' equity during the period.

Explanation: The return on common stock equity is computed by dividing the amount of earnings applicable to the common stockholders' interest in the company by the average amount of common stockholders' equity during the period. The amount of earnings applicable to the common stockholders is the amount of net income for the period less the dividends declared on preferred stock during the period. (Solution = d.)

CHAPTER 16

DILUTIVE SECURITIES AND EARNINGS PER SHARE

OVERVIEW

During the past four to five decades, many corporations have engaged in heavy merger activity. These business combinations have utilized an increasing amount of dilutive securities such as convertible bonds, convertible preferred stocks, and stock warrants. The accounting procedures for each of these are discussed in this chapter.

Executives of corporations are usually given some type of stock-based compensation. The type of plan used can materially affect the corporation's financial statements. Accounting procedures for employee stock options and other stock-based compensation plans such as restricted-stock plans are discussed in this chapter.

Earnings per share (EPS) is typically the most widely quoted financial ratio. The computation of earnings per share is complicated by situations where dilutive securities, as well as common stock, are outstanding. EPS computations are also discussed in this chapter.

SUMMARY OF LEARNING OBJECTIVES

1.   **Describe the accounting for the issuance, conversion, and retirement of convertible debt securities.** The method for recording convertible bonds at the date of issuance follows that used to record straight (nonconvertible) debt issues. Companies amortize any discount or premium that results from the issuance of convertible bonds, assuming the bonds will be outstanding to maturity. If bonds are converted into other securities, the principal accounting problem is to determine the amount at which to record the securities exchanged for the bonds. The book value method is used in practice and is considered GAAP. The retirement of convertible debt is considered a debt retirement, and the difference between the carrying amount of the retired convertible debt and the cash paid should result in a gain or loss.

2.   **Explain the accounting for convertible preferred stock.** When convertible preferred stock is converted, a company uses the book value method. It debits Preferred Stock and any related Paid-in Capital in Excess of Par, and credits Common Stock and Paid-in Capital in Excess of Par (if any excess exists).

3.   **Contrast the accounting for stock rights issued to existing shareholders and stock warrants issued with other securities.** *Stock warrants:* Companies should allocate the proceeds from the sale of debt securities with detachable stock warrants between the two securities. Warrants that are detachable can be traded separately from the debt, and, therefore companies can determine their market value. Two methods of allocation are available: the proportional method and the incremental method. Nondetachable warrants do not require an allocation of the proceeds between the debt securities and the warrants; companies record the entire proceeds as debt. *Stock rights:* No entry is required when a company issues rights (warrants) to existing stockholders. The company needs only to make a memorandum entry to

indicate the number of rights issued to existing stockholders and to ensure that the company has additional unissued stock registered for issuance in case the stockholders exercise the rights.

4. **Describe the accounting for stock compensation plans under generally accepted accounting principles.** Companies must use the fair-value approach to account for stock-based compensation. Under this approach, a company computes total compensation expense based on the fair value of the options (that are expected to vest) on the grant date. Companies recognize compensation expense in the periods in which the employee performs the services. Restricted-stock plans follow the same general accounting principles as those for stock options. Companies estimate total compensation cost at the grant date based on the fair value of the restricted stock; they expense that cost over the service period. If vesting does not occur, companies reverse the compensation expense.

5. **Discuss the controversy involving stock compensation plans.** When first proposed, there was considerable opposition to the recognition provisions contained in the fair-value approach, because that approach could result in substantial compensation expense that was not previously recognized. Corporate America, particularly the high technology sector, vocally opposed the proposed standard. They believed that the standard would place them at a competitive disadvantage with larger companies that can withstand higher compensation charges. Offsetting such opposition is the need for greater transparency in financial reporting, on which our capital markets depend.

6. **Compute earnings per share in a simple capital structure.** When a company has both common and preferred stock outstanding, it subtracts the current year preferred stock dividend from net income to arrive at income available to common stockholders. The formula for computing earnings per share is net income less preferred stock dividends, divided by the weighted average of shares of common stock outstanding.

7. **Compute earnings per share in a complex capital structure.** A complex capital structure requires a dual presentation of earnings per share, each with equal prominence on the face of the income statement. These two presentations are referred to as basic earnings per share and diluted earnings per share. Basic earnings per share relies on the number of weighted average common shares outstanding (i.e., equivalent to EPS for a simple capital structure). Diluted earnings per share indicates the dilution of earnings per share that would have occurred if all potential issuances of common stock that would have reduced earnings per share had taken place. Companies with complex capital structures should exclude antidilutive securities when computing earnings per share.

*8. **Explain the accounting for stock-appreciation rights.** The accounting for stock-appreciation rights depend on whether the rights are classified as equity- or liability-based. If equity-based, the accounting is similar to that used for stock options. If liability-based, companies re-measure compensation expense each period and allocate it over the service period using the percentage approach.
     *This material is covered in Appendix 16A in the text.

9. **Compute earnings per share in a complex situation. For diluted EPS, make the following computations: (1) For each potentially dilutive security, determine the per share effect assuming exercise/conversion. (2) Rank the results from most dilutive to least dilutive. (3) Recalculate EPS starting with the most dilutive, and continue adding securities until EPS does not change or increases (from an antidilutive security). The antidilutive security is then omitted from the EPS calculation.
     **This material is covered in Appendix 16B in the text.

TIPS ON CHAPTER TOPICS

TIP: When accounting for convertible bonds and bonds issued with detachable warrants, follow the basic recording rules for bonds discussed in **Chapter 14** (see your *Problem Solving Survival Guide*). These include:

1. Record the par (face) amount of the bonds issued in the Bonds Payable account.

2. Record an excess of issuance price over par for the bonds in the Premium on Bonds Payable account; record an excess of par over issuance price in the Discount on Bonds Payable account.

3. Record debt issuance costs in an asset account to be amortized over the life of the bonds.

4. Remove all related amounts from the accounts when the debt is extinguished. The net carrying amount of the debt is eliminated from the accounts when the debt is settled.

TIP: An options market exists that works similarly to the stock market. For example, an investor may purchase a share of Apple stock for $100 per share or he may purchase an option to buy Apple stock. Assume the option allows the holder to buy Apple stock for $110 anytime within the next six months. This type of option is created by the marketplace, not by Apple Corporation. Therefore, the Apple Corporation is not involved with accounting for this type of security. In this chapter, the only type of options addressed are employee stock options which are granted by the related corporation.

TIP: A **dilutive security** is a security which would reduce earnings per share (EPS) if it became common stock. An **antidilutive security** is one which would result in an increase in the amount reported as EPS or a decrease in the amount reported as a net loss per share.

TIP: In computing diluted EPS, any antidilutive security is to be excluded. This means that a convertible bond will be assumed to be converted to common stock for the purposes of computing diluted EPS **if** the effect of that assumption is dilutive. The convertible bond will **not** be assumed to be converted in computing EPS **if** the effect of that assumption is antidilutive.

TIP: Assume a corporation has no discontinued operations, no extraordinary item, and no cumulative effect of a change in accounting principle. If the corporation has a **loss per share** result from the basic EPS formula, any and **all assumptions will be antidilutive**; therefore, a single EPS presentation will be made. A loss per share can result in the basic formula for the following conditions:

1. Corporation has a net loss on its income statement for the period.

2. Corporation has net income for the period but the amount of preferred dividends for the period exceeds the amount of net income.

3. Corporation has a net loss and preferred stock dividends (this situation results in a large negative numerator for the EPS ratio).

EXERCISE 16-1

Purpose: (L.O. 1) This exercise will illustrate how to record the issuance of convertible debt and its subsequent conversion to common stock.

Oviedo Oatmeal Corporation has 300,000 shares of its $10 par value common stock outstanding with a market price of $52 per share on January 1, 2010 when it issues convertible bonds. The debt issue is comprised of 1,000 bonds at $1,000 par with a 20-year term and a 10% stated interest rate. Each bond is sold at 101 and is convertible into 20 shares of common stock. Oviedo Oatmeal incurs costs of $80,000 related to the issue. The straight-line method is to be used to amortize any related premium or discount. An underwriter advises the issuer that the bonds would likely have sold for 99 without the conversion feature.

Instructions
(a) Record the issuance of the convertible bonds on January 1, 2010.
(b) Explain why a portion of the issuance proceeds is or is not allocated to the conversion feature.
(c) Record the conversion of 50% of the bonds on January 1, 2012, using the book value method.
(d) Record the additional entry required on January 1, 2012 if 500 additional shares of common stock are issued by Oviedo Oatmeal as an inducement for conversion in either part (c) or part (d) above.
(e) Record the additional entry required on January 1, 2012 if costs of $21,000 are incurred in administering (but not inducing) the conversion that takes place in part (c) above.

Solution to Exercise 16-1

(a)	Cash...	930,000	
	Unamortized Bond Issue Costs	80,000	
	Bonds Payable...		1,000,000
	Premium on Bonds Payable....................................		10,000

        ($1,000 x 1,000 = $1,000,000 par)
        ($1,000,000 x 101% = $1,010,000 issuance price)
        ($1,010,000 - $80,000 = $930,000 net proceeds)
        ($1,010,000 - $1,000,000 = $10,000 premium)

> **TIP:** No portion of the proceeds from the issuance of convertible debt should be allocated to the conversion feature; therefore, **none** of the proceeds should be recorded as paid-in capital. Thus, convertible bonds do not affect paid-in capital until they are converted to stock.

> **TIP:** Bonds issued with nondetachable stock warrants are similar to convertible bonds and are accounted for in the same manner; all of the proceeds are recorded in liability accounts.

(b) No portion of the proceeds from the issuance of convertible debt is allocated to the conversion feature for accounting purposes because the FASB indicates that the conversion option is inseparable from the debt security.

(c)

Bonds Payable (50% x $1,000,000)	500,000	
Premium on Bonds Payable (50% x $10,000 x 18/20)	4,500	
Unamortized Bond Issue Costs		36,000
(50% x $80,000 x 18/20)		
Common Stock		100,000
(50% x 1,000 bonds x 20 shares x $10 par)		
Paid-in Capital in Excess of Par (Difference)		368,500*

*Par value of bonds converted (50% x 1,000 x $1,000)	$ 500,000
Related unamortized premium (50% x $10,000 x 18/20)	4,500
Book value of bonds converted	504,500
Unamortized bond issue costs (50% x $80,000 x 18/20)	(36,000)
Net book value of bonds converted	468,500
Par value of stock issued (50% x 1,000 bonds x	
20 shares x $10 par)	(100,000)
Additional paid-in capital recorded	$ 368,500

Explanation: The net book value of bonds payable is removed from the accounts and that net amount is recorded in appropriate stockholder equity accounts. No gain or loss is recorded.

> **TIP:** The **book value method** of recording the conversion of bonds payable to common stock simply removes the net book value of the bonds from debt accounts and records that amount in appropriate stockholder equity accounts. **No gain or loss is recorded** when the book value method is used.
>
> **TIP:** Recall from **Chapter 14** that **book value** is synonymous with **carrying value** and **carrying amount**.

(d)

Debt Conversion Expense (500 x $52)	26,000	
Common Stock (500 x $10)		5,000
Paid-in Capital in Excess of Par [500 x ($52 - $10)]		21,000

Explanation: When an additional payment is needed to make bondholders convert, the payment is for a service (bondholders converting at a given time) and should be reported as an expense. The additional payment is called a **sweetener** to induce conversion; it should be recognized as an expense of the current period at an amount equal to the fair value of the additional securities or other consideration given.

(e)

Paid-in Capital in Excess of Par	21,000	
Cash		21,000

Explanation: If the administrative costs of conversion are viewed to be costs of issuing the stock, treatment similar to any other stock issuance costs is used, which will mean a charge to additional paid-in capital in this case. When a corporation is in the process of initial formation, stock issuance costs are charged to additional paid-in capital (as is shown in this solution). If the costs are viewed as connected with an inducement to convert, they should be expensed in the current period.

EXERCISE 16-2

Purpose: (L.O. 2) This exercise will illustrate how to account for convertible preferred stock.

Roy Rogers Corporation has 1,000 shares of $50 par 6% convertible preferred stock outstanding at December 31, 2010. Each share was issued in a prior year at $54. The preferred stock is convertible into $10 par common stock.

Instructions
(a)   Record the conversion of 100 shares of preferred stock if one share of preferred is convertible into four shares of common.
(b)   Record the conversion of 100 shares of preferred if the conversion ratio is 6:1.

Solution to Exercise 16-2

(a)	Convertible Preferred Stock (100 x $50)...................................	5,000	
	Paid-in Capital in Excess of Par—Preferred (100 x $4)........................	400	
	Common Stock (100 x 4 x $10)...		4,000
	Paid-in Capital in Excess of Par—Common.............................		1,400
	[100 x ($54 - $40)]		

(b)	Convertible Preferred Stock (100 x $50)...................................	5,000	
	Paid-in Capital in Excess of Par—Preferred (100 x $4)........................	400	
	Retained Earnings [100 x 6 x $10 - (100 x $54)]	600	
	Common Stock (100 x 6 x $10)..		6,000

Approach: Use the following guidelines to record the conversion of preferred stock to common stock:
1.   No gain or loss is recorded. This is a capital transaction. A corporation cannot record an accounting gain or loss when dealing with its stockholders in their capacity of being owners of the business.
2.   The amount originally recorded (at issuance) in the Convertible Preferred Stock account and a related additional paid-in capital account is removed from those accounts and recorded in the Common Stock account and a related additional paid-in capital account. As usual, the par amount goes in the Common Stock account and any excess goes in an additional paid-in capital account.
3.   If the par value of the common stock exceeds the recorded value of the preferred, the difference is charged to retained earnings (or some states allow for a charge to additional paid-in capital from other sources).

EXERCISE 16-3

Purpose: (L.O. 3) This exercise will review the accounting procedures for the issuance of debt securities with detachable warrants.

A new issue of 1,000 bonds was sold at 102.5 on January 1, 2010. Each bond had a face amount of $1,000 and one detachable warrant attached. One warrant allowed the holder to purchase 10 shares of $10 par common stock at $43 per share. The market value of the common stock at January 1, 2010 was $46. Shortly after issuance of the bonds and warrants, quotes were 98.5 for a bond ex-warrant and $48 for a common stock warrant. A few months later, 800 warrants were exercised. Two years later, the remaining 200 warrants expired.

Instructions
(a)   Record the issuance of the 1,000 bonds with detachable warrants.
(b)   Record the exercise of 800 warrants.
(c)   Record the expiration of 200 warrants.
(d)   Indicate the effect of each of the entries [(a), (b), and (c)] above on (1) assets, (2) total paid-in capital, and (3) number of common stock shares outstanding. State the direction and amount of each effect.
(e)   Explain how the journal entry for part (a) would differ if the market value of a bond ex-warrant was unknown.

Solution to Exercise 16-3

(a)   Cash (1,000 x $1,000 x 102.5%)..................................... 1,025,000
Discount on Bonds Payable... 22,628[b]
    Bonds Payable (1,000 x $1,000)....................................... 1,000,000
    Paid-in Capital—Stock Warrants....................................... 47,628[a]

$$^a \frac{\$48,000}{\$48,000 \; + \; \$985,000} \; \times \; \$1,025,000 = \$47,628 \text{ amount to allocate to warrants}$$

[b]$1,025,000 total proceeds - $47,628 allocated to the warrants
    = $977,372 allocated to the bonds.
  $1,000,000 face amount of bonds - $977,372 carrying value of bonds
    = $22,628 to record for discount on bonds payable.

Explanation: The proportional method is used; thus, the proceeds are allocated to the two securities based on their relative market values. The amount to be allocated to the warrants is determined by the formula:

$$\frac{\text{MV Warrants}}{\text{MV Warrants} \; + \; \text{MV Bonds Ex - Warrants}} \; \times \; \frac{\text{Total}}{\text{Proceeds}} \; = \; \frac{\text{Paid - in Capital}}{\text{To Record}}$$

The formula above computes the amount of proceeds to be allocated to the warrant. The remaining proceeds are recorded in bond accounts (the par value of the bonds always goes in the Bonds Payable account). The $22,628 excess of the bonds' par value over the proceeds allocated to the bonds [$1,000,000 - ($1,025,000 - $47,628) = $22,628] represents a discount on the bonds.

TIP: The amount of proceeds to be allocated to the bonds can be independently verified by using the formula above and substituting the "Market Value of the Bonds Ex-Warrants" in the numerator of the fraction. The result will then be the amount of "Debt to Record."

TIP: By use of the formula above, the proceeds from the issuance of **bonds with detachable stock warrants** are allocated between the bonds and the stock warrants based on the relative market values of the two securities. This is referred to as the **proportional method** and is the preferred method. If the market value of the bonds ex-warrants is not known or not determinable, the warrants are recorded at their market value and the remaining proceeds are allocated to the debt. This latter approach is called the **incremental method**.

TIP: Recall from your study of bonds payable that a bond's price is quoted in terms of a percentage of its par value. Carefully compute the bond's price before proceeding with the formula in this exercise. A very common error would be to use $98.50 for the price of one bond in this situation rather than the **correct** price of $985.00 (98.5% of $1,000 par = $985.00).

TIP: Warrant prices are quoted like stock prices—in terms of dollars. The price of a bond ex-warrants refers to the price of a bond without warrants.

TIP: When using the proportional method, the amount determined for allocation to the warrants should be close (but usually **not** equal) to the market value of the warrants. In part (a) of this problem, $47,628 is close to $48,000 (1,000 x $48); therefore, the amount determined by the formula is reasonable.

(b)   Cash (800 x 10 x $43)... 344,000
Paid-in Capital—Stock Warrants (800/1,000 x $47,628) 38,102
       Common Stock (800 x 10 x $10)... 80,000
       Paid-in Capital in Excess of Par.. 302,102*

*Cash proceeds from exercise (800 warrants x 10 shares each x $43 exercise price)	$ 344,000
Amount recorded on the books for the warrants exercised (800 warrants exercised out of 1,000 outstanding = 80%; 80% x $47,628)	38,102
Total consideration received for stock issued	382,102
Par value of stock issued (800 x 10 x $10)	(80,000)
Excess of consideration received over par for stock issued upon exercise of warrants	$ 302,102

TIP: The number of shares of stock obtainable upon the exercise of one warrant does **not** effect the computations and recording in part (a) [issuance date of bonds plus warrants] but it **does** effect the computations in part (b) [exercise date of the warrants].

(c)   Paid-in Capital—Stock Warrants ($47,628 - $38,102) 9,526

Paid-in Capital from Expired Stock Warrants............................   9,526

(d)   Effect on:

	(1)	(2) Total	(3) Number of Common
	Assets	Paid-in Capital	Shares Outstanding
(a)	Increase $1,025,000	Increase $47,628	No effect
(b)	Increase $344,000	Increase $344,000	Increase 8,000
(c)	No effect	No effect	No effect

(e)   The incremental method would be used. Thus, the market value of the warrants would be used to record the warrants and the remaining proceeds would be recorded in debt accounts. The entry would be as follows:

Cash (1,000 x $1,000 x 102.5%)   1,025,000
Discount on Bonds Payable..   23,000
    Bonds Payable (1,000 x $1,000)..   1,000,000
    Paid-in Capital—Stock Warrants (1,000 x $48)......................   48,000

EXERCISE 16-4

Purpose: (L.O. 3) This exercise reviews the accounting rules for the issuance of stock rights to existing stockholders.

Hot Videos Corporation wished to raise additional capital. One right was distributed for each of the 100,000 shares of stock outstanding. Four rights and $30 cash were required to purchase one new share of $10 par value common stock. Ninety percent (90%) of the rights were exercised and the rest expired three weeks after their issuance. The market value of the stock was $32 per share at the date the rights were distributed and $35 per share at the date the rights were exercised.

Instructions
(a)   Explain the most likely reason for the distribution of the stock rights to existing stockholders. Why are these rights good for a very limited time period?
(b)   Record the issuance of the rights.
(c)   Record the exercise of the rights.
(d)   Record the expiration of the rights.

Solution to Exercise 16-4

(a)   The existing stockholders likely have the preemptive right (privilege to purchase newly issued shares in proportion to their holdings before the new issuance); thus, they must have the first opportunity to acquire new shares. The distribution of the rights (warrants) is a way to administer that opportunity. The rights have a short life because the corporation is anxious to sell the new shares to somebody; if the existing stockholders do not wish to buy them, they are offered to the general public.

(b)   Only make a memorandum entry at the grant (issuance) date. The corporation has received no consideration; no exchange has taken place; there are no proceeds to allocate.

(c)
Cash	675,000*	
Common Stock (22,500 x $10)		225,000
Paid-in Capital in Excess of Par		450,000
($675,000 - $225,000)		

*100,000 x 90% = 90,000 rights exercised
 90,000 rights ÷ 4 = 22,500 common stock shares issued
 22,500 shares x $30 = $675,000 proceeds

> **TIP:** When the rights are exercised, the issuance of the stock is recorded as any other stock issuance. At this date, assets and owners' equity are increased by the amount of the proceeds received.

(d)   Only make a memorandum entry at the expiration date.

ILLUSTRATION 16-1
ACCOUNTING FOR STOCK COMPENSATION PLANS (L.O. 4)

The following guidelines pertain to accounting for a stock option, purchase, or award plan:

1. The consideration that a corporation receives for stock issued through a stock option, purchase, or award plan consists of cash or other assets, if any, plus services received from the employee.

2. Compensation for services should be measured by the **fair-value method.** Companies compute **total compensation expense** based on the fair value of the options on the date the employer grants the options (i.e. grant date) to employees. Only options that are expected to eventually vest are considered. Public companies estimate fair value by using an appropriate option pricing model. After this expense is computed, it is **not** adjusted up or down for changes in the stock price that occur subsequent to the grant date.

3. Compensation cost should be recognized as an expense of one or more periods in which an employee performs services (often called **the service period**) by a debit to Compensation Expense and a credit to Paid-in Capital—Stock Options. The grant or award may specify the periods, or the periods may be inferred from the terms or from the past pattern of grants or awards. Unless otherwise specified, the service period is the vesting period—the time between the grant date and the vesting date. The vesting date is the date the employee's right to receive or retain shares of stock or cash under the award is no longer contingent upon the employee remaining in the service of the employer.

4. If **employees fail to exercise** the stock options before their expiration date, the company does not adjust the compensation expense. An unexercised stock option does not nullify the need to record the costs of services received from executives and attributable to the stock option plan.

5. If an **employee forfeits a stock option** because the employee fails to satisfy a service requirement (e.g., leaves employment), the company should adjust the estimate of compensation expense recorded in the current period (as a change in estimate). A company records this change in estimate by debiting Paid-in Capital—Stock Options and crediting Compensation Expense for the amount of cumulative compensation expense recorded to date for the departing employee's forfeited options. This entry thus decreases compensation expense in the period of forfeiture.

6. The exercise of stock options is recorded by a debit to Cash for the amount of the exercise price, a debit to Paid-in Capital—Stock Options for the amount of compensation expense related to the options being exercised, a credit to Common Stock for the par value of the stock being given to the employee upon exercise of the options and a credit to Paid-in Capital in Excess of Par for the excess of the fair value of these options at the grant date (which is equal to the sum of the exercise price [amount of cash] and the compensation expense related to these options) over the par value of the stock given to the employee upon exercise of the options.

EXERCISE 16-5

Purpose: (L.O. 4) This exercise will illustrate the application of the fair-value method in accounting for a compensatory stock option plan.

Worldwise Corporation granted options for 10,000 shares of its $10 par value common stock to certain executives on January 1, 2010, when the stock was selling for $44 per share. The options stipulate a price of $44 per share for the stock and must be exercised between January 1, 2012 and December 31, 2014, at which time they expire. The options state that the service period is January 1, 2010 through December 31, 2011. An option pricing model determined that, at the date of grant, the estimated fair value of these options was $500,000.

Instructions

(a)   Prepare the journal entries for the following (items 3 and 4 are independent assumptions):
(1)   To record the issuance of the options (grant of options) on January 1, 2010.
(2)   To record compensation expense. Date the entry(s). Assume all employees remain employed by the corporation.
(3)   To record the exercise of the options, assuming all of the options were exercised on the earliest possible date, January 1, 2012.
(4)   To record the expiration of the options, assuming all of the options were **not** exercised because the market price fell below the exercise price before January 1, 2012 and stayed below that level for the balance of the option period.
(b)   Describe the intrinsic value method of accounting for stock options that was used prior to a FASB Standard that now requires the fair-value method to be used.

Solution to Exercise 16-5

(a)
(1)   **January 1, 2010**
          No entry

(2)   **December 31, 2010**
          Compensation Expense 250,000
                    Paid-in Capital—Stock Options   250,000

                             December 31, 2011
          Compensation Expense 250,000
                    Paid-in Capital—Stock Options   250,000

(3)   **January 1, 2012**
          Cash   440,000
          Paid-in Capital—Stock Options 500,000
                    Common Stock   100,000
                    Paid-in Capital in Excess of Par   840,000

                             December 31, 2014
(4)   Paid-in Capital—Stock Options 500,000
                    Paid-in Capital from Expired Stock Options   500,000

TIP:	Refer to **Illustration 16-1** for an explanation of the accounting procedures for stock option plans.
TIP:	The **option price** is often called the **exercise price**.

(b)   Prior to the issuance of SFAS 123(R) many companies used the intrinsic method. The intrinsic method computed compensation expense as the excess of the market price at the date of grant over the option price. (In the situation at hand, that amount would be zero.) The intrinsic method used the same time period of recognizing expense (service period) as does the fair-value method.

EXERCISE 16-6

Purpose: (L.O. 4) This exercise will illustrate the proper accounting for a restricted-stock compensation plan.

On January 1, 2010, Comustat Company issues 2,000 shares of restricted stock to its CFO. The stock has a fair value of $30 per share on January 1, 2010. The stock is for a service period of the next four years. Vesting occurs at the end of that four year period. The par value of the stock is $1 per share.

Instructions
(a)   Prepare the journal entry to record the issuance of the restricted stock on January 1, 2010.
(b)   Explain the nature of the Unearned Compensation account and where its balance is to be reported on a balance sheet.
(c)   Prepare the journal entry at December 31, 2010 to record the related expense for 2010.
(d)   Assume the CFO leaves the company on July 3, 2012 (before any expense has been recorded for 2012). Company policy calls for the employee to forfeit his/her rights to the stock when the employee leaves the company before vesting occurs. Prepare the journal entry on July 3, 2012 to record the forfeiture.

SOLUTION 16-6

(a)
Unearned Compensation (2,000 X $30)	60,000	
Common Stock (2,000 X $1)		2,000
Paid-in Capital in Excess of Par (2,000 X $29)		58,000

Explanation: The debit to Unearned Compensation (often called Deferred Compensation Expense) is for the total compensation expense to be recognized over the next four years (service period).

(b)   Unearned Compensation represents the cost of employee services yet to be performed. The balance of this account, is to be reported in the stockholders' equity section of the balance sheet. It is a contra-equity item, similar to treasury stock.

(c)
Compensation Expense	15,000	
Unearned Compensation		15,000

(d)	Common Stock	2,000	
	Paid-in Capital in Excess of Par	58,000	
	Compensation Expense		30,000
	Unearned Compensation		30,000

ILLUSTRATION 16-2
STEPS IN COMPUTING EARNINGS PER SHARE (EPS) (L.O. 6, 7, *9)

Step 1:   Compute the weighted average number of common stock shares outstanding.

A.   When common shares are issued for assets during the period, weight them according to the length of time in the period the stock is outstanding in relation to the total time in the period.

B.   When common shares are issued in connection with a stock split or stock dividend declared during the period, give retroactive treatment to these shares. Retroactive treatment here means to restate the shares outstanding before the split or stock dividend. Give retroactive treatment even if the stock dividend or split is declared after the end of the period (but before the financial statements are published). Also, restate EPS in financial statements for prior periods presented.

> **TIP:**   See **Illustration 16-3** for a short-cut method of computing the weighted-average number of common stock shares outstanding.

Step 2:   Compute basic EPS (EPS before any assumptions or adjustments).

$$\text{Basic Formula:}\quad \frac{\text{Net Income} - \text{Preferred Dividends}}{\text{Weighted-Average Number of Common Shares Outstanding}}$$

The numerator should be the income available to common stockholders which is net income minus preferred stock dividend requirements. Thus, in the numerator, deduct the preferred dividends actually declared. If the preferred stock is cumulative, deduct the preferred's current year preference as to dividends, even if no dividends were declared. Dividends in arrears for prior years have no effect on the current year's basic EPS calculation, they were used for EPS calculations in prior years.

> **TIP:**   Dividends declared and/or paid during the year on common stock have no effect on this computation.
>
> **TIP:**   If there is a net loss rather than a net income, the amount of the loss is increased by the preferred dividends.

ILLUSTRATION 16-2 (Continued)

Step 3: Compute diluted earnings per share.

A.   The basic formula is adjusted as follows:

$$\frac{\text{Net Income - Preferred Dividends} \pm \text{Adjustments}}{\substack{\text{Weighted Average Number of Common Shares Outstanding } + \\ \text{Weighted Average Number of Potential Common Shares}}}$$

B.   Treatment of convertibles: Use the **if converted** method.

1.   Assume the convertible is converted to common stock, if the effect of that assumption is dilutive.

> **TIP:**   **Dilution (dilutive)** is a reduction in earnings per share. **Antidilution (antidilutive)** is an increase in earnings per share amounts or a decrease in loss per share amounts.
>
> **TIP:**   A quick test to determine if a convertible debt instrument is antidilutive is as follows: if the amount of interest net of taxes per common share obtainable upon conversion exceeds basic EPS, the effect is antidilutive.
>
> **TIP:**   A quick test to determine if a convertible preferred stock is antidilutive is as follows: if the amount of preferred dividends per common share obtainable on conversion exceeds basic EPS, the effect is antidilutive.

2.   For a convertible preferred, add back the preferred dividends (that had been deducted in the basic formula) in the numerator and add an appropriate weighted average number of potential common shares (assumed to be outstanding) in the denominator of the diluted EPS formula.

3.   For convertible debt, add back interest and deduct tax savings due to interest in the numerator and add an appropriate weighted average number of potential common shares in the denominator.

> **TIP:**   In using the "if converted" method for a convertible bond, interest expense is added back in the numerator of the EPS formula and the related tax effect is deducted. In using the "if converted" method for a convertible preferred stock, preferred dividends are added back in the numerator (because they were deducted in the numerator of the basic formula); however, there is **no** related tax effect because preferred dividends are not a tax deductible item.

ILLUSTRATION 16-2 (Continued)

4. Assume the conversion takes place at the beginning of the period for which EPS is being calculated or at the date of the issuance of the convertible, whichever is later (more recent).

5. If there is a scale of conversion rates, use the rate that is the most advantageous from the standpoint of the security holder.

C. Treatment of options and warrants:

1. Assume the options and warrants are exercised **if** the effect of that assumption is dilutive.

> **TIP:** An option or warrant is dilutive if the average market price of the common stock during the period is greater than the exercise price of the option or warrant.

2. Use the **treasury stock method**. Assume that the proceeds (from the exercise of the options or warrants) are used to purchase treasury stock at the **average market price** for the period. Thus, shares will be added to the EPS denominator because of the assumed exercise, and then a smaller number of shares will be deducted from the denominator because of the assumed purchase of treasury stock. Weight the resulting **net** number of common equivalent shares according to the time they are assumed to be outstanding.

3. Assume the exercise occurs at the beginning of the period or at the date of the issuance of the options or warrants, whichever is the later.

D. Treatment of contingent issuance agreements.

1. Common stock contingently issuable with the only condition being the mere passage of time should be assumed to be outstanding for computing diluted EPS.

2. Common stock contingently issuable upon condition of the attainment or maintenance of a level of earnings should be considered outstanding in computing diluted EPS **if** that level is currently being attained.

3. Common stock contingently issuable upon condition of the attainment of a market price level should be considered outstanding shares **if** that level is met at the end of the current year.

ILLUSTRATION 16-2 (Continued)

TIP: An entity with a **simple capital structure,** that is, one with only common stock outstanding, must report **basic-per-share** amounts for income from continuing operations and for net income on the face of the income statement. An entity with a **complex capital structure** (i.e., a structure with one or more potentially dilutive securities outstanding) must report **basic and diluted per share** amounts for income from continuing operations and for net income on the face of the income statement with equal prominence.

TIP: Securities such as options, warrants, convertible bonds, convertible preferred stock, or contingent stock agreements are referred to as "potential common stock" or "potentially dilutive securities."

TIP: The computation of diluted EPS should not assume conversion, exercise, or **contingent issuance** of securities that would have an **antidilutive** effect on earnings per share. Shares issued on actual conversion, exercise, or satisfaction of certain conditions for which the underlying potential common shares were antidilutive shall be included in the computation as outstanding common shares from the date of conversion, exercise, or satisfaction of those conditions, respectively. In determining whether potential common shares are dilutive or antidilutive, each issue or series of issues of potential common shares should be considered separately rather than in the aggregate.

TIP: When a company has a complex capital structure and a dual presentation of earnings per share, it must disclose a reconciliation of the numerators and denominators of the basic and diluted per share computations, including individual income and share amount effects of all securities that affect EPS.

TIP: Including potential common shares in the denominator of a diluted per-share computation for continuing operations always will result in an antidilutive per-share amount when an entity has a *loss* from continuing operations or a *loss* from continuing operations available to common stockholders (that is, after any preferred dividend reductions). Although including those potential common shares in the other diluted per-share computations may be dilutive to their comparable basic per-share amounts, no potential common shares should be included in the computation of any diluted per-share amount when a loss from continuing operations exists, even if the entity reports net income.

ILLUSTRATION 16-2 (Continued)

TIP: Convertible securities may be dilutive on their own but antidilutive when included with other potential common shares in computing diluted EPS. To reflect maximum potential dilution, each issue or series of issues of potential common shares shall be considered in sequence from the most dilutive to the least dilutive. That is, dilutive potential common shares with the lowest "earnings per incremental share" shall be included in diluted EPS before those with a higher earnings per incremental share. (Options and warrants generally will be included first because use of the treasury stock method does not impact the numerator of the computation.)

TIP: An entity that reports a discontinued operation, an extraordinary item, or the cumulative effect of an accounting change in a period should use income from continuing operations (adjusted for preferred dividends) as the "control number" in determining whether those potential common shares are dilutive or antidilutive. That is, the same number of potential common shares used in computing the diluted per-share amount for income from continuing operations should be used in computing all other reported diluted per-share amounts even if those amounts will be antidilutive to their respective basic per-share amounts.

For example, assume that Corporation A has income from continuing operations of $2,400, a loss from discontinued operations of $(3,600), a net loss of $(1,200), and 1,000 common shares and 200 potential common shares outstanding. Corporation A's basic per-share amounts would be $2.40 for continuing operations, $(3.60) for the discontinued operations, and $(1.20) for the net loss. Corporation A would include the 200 potential common shares in the denominator of its diluted per-share computation for continuing operations because the resulting $2.00 per share is dilutive. (For illustrative purposes, assume no numerator impact of those 200 potential common shares.) Because income from continuing operations is the control number, Corporation A also must include those 200 potential common shares in the denominator for the other per-share amounts, even though the resulting per-share amounts [$(3.00) per share for the loss from discontinued operations and $(1.00) per share for the net loss] are antidilutive to their comparable basic per-share amounts; that is, the loss per-share amounts are less.

This material is covered in **Appendix 16B in the text.

ILLUSTRATION 16-3
SHORT-CUT METHOD FOR COMPUTING WEIGHTED AVERAGE
NUMBER OF COMMON STOCK SHARES OUTSTANDING* (L.O. 6)

Step 1: Begin with the number of common shares outstanding at the beginning of the period. Assume they were outstanding the entire year; multiply the number by 12/12 to get an equivalent amount. Enter the equivalent amount in the Weighted Average column.

Step 2: Take the first transaction that occurred during the year that changed the number of shares outstanding and properly adjust the balance in the Weighted Average column.

a.   **If shares were issued for assets, weight the new shares** by multiplying them by a fraction. The numerator of the fraction is the number of months in the period the shares were outstanding; the denominator is the number of months in the year. Add this equivalent amount in the Weighted Average column; arrive at a new balance.

b.   **If shares were issued in a stock dividend or a stock split, retroactively adjust for these shares** by taking an appropriate multiple of the existing balance in the Weighted Average column. Ignore the date of the stock dividend or split; the multiple is determined by the size of the stock dividend or split. Arrive at a new balance.

c.   **If shares were acquired as treasury stock or retired by the corporation, weight** the shares for the time they were **not** outstanding and deduct this equivalent amount from the existing balance. Arrive at a new balance.

Step 3: Take each of the other transactions that occurred during the year that changed the number of common shares outstanding and properly adjust the balance in the Weighted Average column as shown in Step 2 above. Handle each transaction in order of date.

EXAMPLE:

Data:

January 1, 2010	100,000 shares were outstanding.	
April 1, 2010	Issued 40,000 shares for cash.	
June 1, 2010	Declared a 40% stock dividend.	
October 1, 2010	Declared a 2-for-1 split.	
December 1, 2010	Issued 60,000 shares for cash.	

*The reporting period is assumed to be one year.

ILLUSTRATION 16-3 (Continued)

Computation:

Date		Weighted Average	
1/1/10	100,000 x 12/12 =		100,000
4/1/10	40,000 x 9/12 =		30,000
	New balance		130,000
6/1/10	40% stock dividend	x 140%**	
	New balance		182,000
10/1/10	2-for-1 split	x 2***	
	New balance		364,000
12/1/10	60,000 x 1/12		5,000
	New balance		369,000

**The appropriate multiple for a stock dividend is 100% plus the percentage used in the dividend. Thus, 100% + 40% dividend = 140% as the multiplier.

***The appropriate multiple for a stock split is the size of the split. Thus, for a 2-for-1 split, multiply by 2.

> **TIP:** Notice how the computation for the weighted-average number of common stock shares outstanding for the period differs from the computation for the actual number of common stock shares outstanding at the end of the period. The number of common stock shares actually outstanding at December 31, 2010 can be computed as follows:
>
> | Date | | Actual Shares |
> |------|---|---|
> | 1/1/10 | Balance | 100,000 |
> | 4/110 | Issued for assets | 40,000 |
> | | New balance | 140,000 |
> | 6/1/10 | 40% stock dividend | 56,000 |
> | | New balance | 196,000 |
> | 10/1/10 | 2:1 split | 196,000 |
> | | New balance | 392,000 |
> | 12/1/10 | Issued for assets | 60,000 |
> | | New balance | 452,000 |
>
> **TIP:** Assume that in addition to the transactions listed above, a 10% stock dividend was declared on January 7, 2011, before the financial statements for 2010 were issued. The weighted average number of common stock shares outstanding for purposes of computing EPS for 2010 would be 405,900 (369,000 x 110% = 405,900) and the actual number of common stock shares outstanding to be reported on the balance sheet at December 31, 2010 would be 452,000.

EXERCISE 16-7

Purpose: (L.O. 6) This exercise will apply the guidelines for computing the weighted average number of common stock shares outstanding.

When the number of common stock shares varies during the year, the weighted average number of common stock shares outstanding must be calculated before the EPS can be computed.

Listed below are the details regarding common stock shares outstanding for four different companies:

1.   Michael Jackson Corporation had 100,000 shares of common stock outstanding on January 1, 2010. On March 1, 2010, 6,000 shares of common stock were issued for cash.

2.   Jimmy Buffet Corporation had 100,000 shares of common stock outstanding on January 1, 2010. On March 1, 6,000 shares of common stock were issued for cash. On July 1, a 4-for-1 split was declared.

3.   Emmy Lou Harris Corporation had 100,000 shares of common stock outstanding on January 1, 2010. On March 1, 2010, 6,000 shares of common stock were reacquired by the corporation.

4.   Elton John Corporation had 100,000 shares of common stock outstanding on January 1, 2010. On March 1, 2010, 6,000 shares of common stock were issued for cash. On June 1, 2010, a 10% stock dividend was declared. On December 1, 2010, 12,000 shares of common stock were issued for cash.

Instructions
(a)   Compute the weighted average number of common stock shares outstanding for 2010 (to be used to compute EPS) for **each** of the **independent** situations above.
(b)   Compute the number of common stock shares outstanding to be reported on the balance sheet at December 31, 2010 for Elton John Corporation (situation 4).

Solution to Exercise 16-7

(a)   **Approach and Explanation:** Use the short-cut method explained in **Illustration 16-3**.

Date		Weighted Average
1. 1/1/10	100,000 x 12/12 =	100,000
3/1/10	6,000 x 10/12 =	5,000
	New balance	105,000

TIP:	The weighted average calculation for common stock shares uses the same concept that is applied in computing equivalent units of production for a manufacturing firm. In the situation above, the computation indicates that having 6,000 shares outstanding for ten months of the year is equivalent to having 5,000 shares outstanding for twelve months. The weighted average number of shares outstanding is sometimes referred to as equivalent shares.

	Date		Weighted Average
2.	1/1/10	100,000 x 12/12 =	100,000
	3/1/10	6,000 x 10/12 =	5,000
		New balance	105,000
	7/1/10	4-for-1 split	x 4
		New balance	420,000
3.	1/1/10	100,000 x 12/12 =	100,000
	3/1/10	(6,000) x 10/12 =	(5,000)
		New balance	95,000
4.	1/1/10	100,000 x 12/12 =	100,000
	3/1/10	6,000 x 10/12 =	5,000
		New balance	105,000
	6/1/10	10% stock dividend	x 110%
		New balance	115,500
	12/1/10	12,000 x 1/12 =	1,000
		New balance	116,500

TIP:	If you want, you can prove the answer of 116,500 by a more complex procedure as follows:

Dates Outstanding	Actual Shares[a]	Restatement	Fraction	Weighted Shares
1/1/10 to 2/28/10	100,000	1.1	2/12	18,333
3/1/10 to 5/31/10	106,000	1.1	3/12	29,150
6/1/10 to 11/30/10	116,600		6/12	58,300
12/1/10 to 12/31/10	128,600		1/12	10,717
				116,500

[a]See solution to part (b) for computations.

A stock dividend or a stock split requires retroactive restatement of shares for the computation of EPS. A 10% stock dividend causes a 10% increase in the number of shares outstanding. Therefore, to restate the number of shares outstanding at a certain date in the past as to give retroactive effect to a subsequently declared 10% stock dividend, the old number of shares is multiplied by 110% (which is 1.1 in decimal form).

> **TIP:** When shares are issued for **assets**, they are weighted for the number of months they are outstanding in relation to the number of months in the period for which EPS is being computed. When shares are issued in a stock dividend or a stock split, they are **not** weighted; rather, retroactive adjustment is made for these additional shares in the weighted average shares calculation. The reason for the difference in treatment is that when assets are received, the entity has more resources and, therefore, an opportunity to increase the net income figure by earning a rate of return on those new assets for the months the new resources are available. When shares are issued in connection with a stock dividend or stock split, there are no new resources and, therefore, no changes in net income. In order for EPS figures for successive periods for a company to be meaningful, they must all be based on the rearranged capital structure; therefore, stock dividends and stock splits must be handled retroactively. This **retroactive treatment** causes adjustment to the weighted average shares computation for EPS **for all periods presented**. Therefore, when the financial statements for a prior period are republished in comparative statements, the EPS amounts for the prior period are to be restated for all stock dividends and stock splits occurring subsequent to the prior period. Thus, a stock dividend declared in 2010 calls for retroactive restatement of the 2009 EPS figure when the 2009 income statement is republished in 2010 for comparative purposes.

(b)

Date		Actual Shares
1/1/10	Balance	100,000
3/1/10	Issued for assets	6,000
	New balance	106,000
6/1/10	10% stock dividend	10,600
	New balance	116,600
12/1/10	Issued for assets	12,000
	New balance	128,600

EXERCISE 16-8

Purpose: (L.O. 7) This exercise will illustrate the application of the treasury stock method.

Jeremy Sherr Corporation had 200,000 shares of common stock outstanding during 2010. On January 1, 2010 40,000 stock options were granted. Each option entitles the holder to purchase one share of common stock at $40. The options become exercisable in 2012. Net income for 2010 was $400,000. The average market price of stock during 2010 was $50; the closing market price was $54.

Instructions
(a)   Compute the amount(s) that Jeremy Sherr Corporation should report for earnings per share for 2010.
(b)   Explain how your answer(s) to Part (a) would change if the options were issued on April 1, 2010 rather than January 1, 2010.

Solution to Exercise 16-8

(a)   **Explanation and Approach:** Follow the steps for computing EPS as outlined in Illustration 16-2.

Step 1:   **Compute the weighted average number of common stock shares outstanding.**
There were no changes in the 200,000 shares of common stock outstanding during 2010. Therefore, the weighted average is <u>200,000</u> shares.

Step 2:   **Compute basic EPS before any assumptions** (basic formula without adjustment).

$$\frac{\$400,000 \ - \ \$0}{200,000} = \underline{\$2.00}$$

Step 3:   **Compute diluted earnings per share.**
- Use the treasury stock method for the options.
- Use the quick test to determine if these options are dilutive. Compare the option price and the current market price. The option price ($40) is less than the average market price ($50), so the options will have a dilutive effect on EPS.
- Adjust the basic formula:

$$\frac{\$400,000 \ - \ \$0}{200,000 \ + \ 40,000^{a} \ - \ 32,000^{b}} = \underline{\$1.92}$$

^{a}Number of shares to be issued upon exercise of options.
^{b}Number of shares that could be purchased for the treasury at $50 (average market price for the period) per share from the proceeds of the exercise of the options:
    40,000 x $40 = $1,600,000 proceeds
    $1,600,000 ÷ $50 = 32,000 assumed treasury shares

> **TIP:**   Notice the incremental number of shares calculated by use of the treasury stock method is 8,000 in this example (40,000 - 32,000). If the average market price was less than the option price, the number of assumed treasury shares would exceed the number of shares assumed issued upon exercise of the options, and the result would be to decrease the denominator from the figure used in the basic formula. That decrease in the denominator would have an antidilutive effect on EPS; therefore, the exercise of the options would **not** be assumed in that circumstance. **Never make assumptions in computing diluted EPS that are antidilutive.**
>
> **TIP:**   Notice why the treasury stock method is so named; the proceeds from the assumed exercise of stock options are assumed to be used for the purchase of treasury stock.

Jeremy Sherr Corporation should report a dual presentation for 2010 as follows:

$2.00 basic earnings per share, and
$1.92 diluted earnings per share

(b)   The exercise of the options would be assumed to have taken place on April 1 rather than at the beginning of the year. Therefore, the assumed shares in the denominator would have to be weighted as follows:

$$9/12 \ (40,000 - 32,000) = 6,000$$

Therefore, the computation for diluted EPS would then be:

$$\frac{\$400,000}{200,000 \ + \ 6,000} = \underline{\$1.94} \text{ diluted EPS.}$$

*EXERCISE 16-9

Purpose: (L.O. 7, 9) This exercise will illustrate the proper treatment of convertible securities in the EPS computations. It will also demonstrate how to test for dilution when more than one potentially dilutive security exists.

The following data pertain to the Star Trek Corporation at December 31, 2010:

Net income for the year	$1,600,000
6% convertible bonds issued at par in a prior year, convertible into 200,000 shares of common stock	$3,000,000
8% convertible, cumulative, preferred stock, $100 par, issued in a prior year (each share is convertible into 6 shares of common)	$2,000,000
Common stock, $10 par, issued in prior years	$6,000,000
Additional paid-in capital	$3,400,000
Retained earnings	$5,200,000
Tax rate for 2010	40%

There were no changes during 2010 in the number of common stock shares, preferred stock shares, or convertible bonds outstanding. There is no treasury stock held.

Instructions
(a)   Compute the basic earnings per share for 2010.
(b)   Compute the diluted earnings per share for 2010.
(c)   Explain whether a dual presentation should be presented for EPS for 2010.

Solution to Exercise 16-9

(a) $2.40 (See Step 2 below.)

(b) $1.86 (See Step 3 below.)

(c)   Yes, a dual presentation must be reported in 2010 because the corporation has some dilutive securities outstanding.

> **TIP:** Whenever a situation involves the EPS computation(s), follow the steps (in order) listed in **Illustration 16-2**. By using this organized approach to these situations, you are less likely to overlook guidelines that may affect your solution.

Approach and Explanation:

Step 1:   **Compute the weighted average number of common stock shares outstanding.**
There were no changes in the number of common shares outstanding during 2010. There are no treasury shares; thus, the number of shares outstanding is equal to the number of shares issued. The number of common shares issued can be computed by:

$$\$6,000,000 \div \$10 \text{ par} = 600,000 \text{ shares}$$

Step 2:   **Compute basic EPS (before any assumptions).**

$$\frac{\$1,600,000 - \$160,000^{a}}{600,000} = \underline{\$2.40}$$

[a]8% x $2,000,000 par = $160,000 preferred dividends.

> **TIP:** Recall that with cumulative preferred stock, the preferred's current year preference as to dividends is deducted in the basic EPS formula, whether or not the dividends were declared.

Step 3:   **Compute diluted earnings per share.**

$$\frac{\$1,600,000 - \$160,000 + \$180,000^{a} - \$72,000^{b} + \$160,000}{600,000 + 200,000 + 6(20,000)^{c}} = \underline{\$1.86}$$

[a]6% x $3,000,000 par = $180,000 interest expense.
[b]$180,000 interest x 40% tax rate = $72,000 tax effect of interest.
[c]$2,000,000 par ÷ $100 per share = 20,000 shares of preferred issued.

> **TIP:** Notice why the "if converted method" is so named; the earnings per share computation assumes conversion of the convertible securities.

When there is more than one potentially dilutive security outstanding, the steps for computing diluted earnings per share are as follows:

1. Determine, for each dilutive security, the per share effect assuming exercise/conversion.
2. Rank the results from Step 1 from smallest to largest earnings effect per share; that is, rank the results from most dilutive to least dilutive.
3. Beginning with the earnings per share based upon the weighted average of common shares outstanding ($2.40 in this problem), recalculate earnings per share by adding the smallest per share effects from Step 2. If the results from this recalculation are less than $2.40, proceed to the next smallest per share effect and recalculate earnings per share. This process is continued so long as each recalculated earnings per share is smaller than the previous amount. The process will end either because there are no more securities to test or a particular security maintains or increases earnings per share (is antidilutive).

> **TIP:** This means that dilutive potential common stock with the lowest "earnings per incremental share" will be included in diluted EPS before those with a higher "earnings per incremental share."

The 3 steps are now applied to the Star Trek Corporation. The Star Trek Corporation has two securities (6% and 8% convertible bonds) that could reduce EPS.

The first step in the computation of diluted earnings per share is to determine a per share effect for each potentially dilutive security.

Step 1: Determine the per share effect of each dilutive security.
Convertible bonds:

Interest expense for year (6% x $3,000,000)	$180,000
Income tax reduction due to interest (40% x $180,000)	72,000
Interest expense avoided (net of tax)	$108,000

Number of additional common shares issued assuming conversion of bonds	200,000

Per share effect:

Incremental Numerator Effect: $\dfrac{\$108,000}{200,000 \text{ shares}} = \$.54$
Incremental Denominator Effect:

Convertible preferred stock:

Dividend requirement on cumulative preferred (20,000 shares X 8% X $100)	$160,000
Income tax effect (dividends are not a tax deduction)	none
Dividend requirement avoided	$160,000

Number of additional common shares issued assuming conversion of preferred (6 x 20,000 shares)	120,000

Per share effect:

Incremental Numerator Effect:	$160,000	=	$1.33
Incremental Denominator Effect:	120,000 shares		

Step 2: Rank the results from Step 1.

The ranking of the two potentially dilutive securities is as follows (lowest earnings per incremental share to the largest):

	Effect Per Share
1. 6% convertible bonds	$.54
2. 8% convertible preferred	1.33

Step 3: Determine diluted earnings per share.

The next step is to determine earnings per share giving effect to the ranking above. Starting with the earnings per share of $2.40 computed previously, add the incremental effects of the options to the original calculation, as follows:

6% Convertible Bonds

Numerator from previous calculation	$1,440,000
Add: Interest expense avoided (net of tax)	108,000
Total	$1,548,000
Denominator from previous calculation (shares)	600,000
Add: Number of common shares assumed issued upon assumed conversion of bonds	200,000
Total	800,000
Recomputed earnings per share ($1,548,000 ÷ 800,000 shares)	$1.94

Since the recomputed earnings per share is reduced (from $2.40 to $1.94), the effect of the 6% bonds is dilutive.

Next, earnings per share is recomputed assuming the conversion of the 8% preferred stock. This is shown below:

8% Convertible Preferred

Numerator from previous calculation	$1,548,000
Add: Dividend requirement avoided	160,000
Total	$1,708,000
Denominator from previous calculation (shares)	800,000
Add: Number of common shares assumed issued upon conversion of preferred stock	120,000
Total	920,000
Recomputed earnings per share ($1,708,000 ÷ 920,000 shares)	$1.86

Since the recomputed earnings per share is reduced, the effect of the 8% convertible preferred is dilutive. Diluted earnings per share is $1.86.

ILLUSTRATION 16-4
ACCOUNTING FOR STOCK- APPRECIATION RIGHTS (L.O. 8)

The use of stock-appreciation rights is a stock-based compensation plan whereby the company gives an executive the right to receive compensation equal to share appreciation. Share appreciation is the excess of the market price of the stock at the date of exercise over a pre-established price. The company may pay the share appreciation in cash, shares, or a combination of both. The company simply awards the executive cash or stock having a market value equivalent to the appreciation over a period of time. The accounting for stock appreciation rights depends on whether the company classifies the rights as equity or as a liability.

   a. **SARs-Share-Based Equity-Awards.**

      In an equity SAR, the holder receives (upon exercise) the shares with a market value in an amount equal to the share price appreciation (the difference between the market price and the pre-established price). At the date of grant, the company determines a fair value for the SAR and then allocates this amount to compensation expense over the service period of the employees, similar to the accounting for stock options granted.

   b. **SARS-Share- Based Liability Awards.**

      In a liability SAR, the holder receives a cash payment (rather than shares) equal to the amount of share price appreciation. The company's compensation expense therefore changes as the value of the liability changes.

The following procedures are followed:

1. Measure the fair value of the award at the grant date and accrue compensation over the service period. Debit Compensation Expense and credit Liability Under Stock Appreciation Plan.
2. Remeasure the fair value each reporting period, until the award is settled, and adjust the compensation cost each period for changes in fair value pro-rated for the portion of the service period completed. (In a period that the value of the stock declines, a negative expense may be recorded as a debit to Liability Under Stock Appreciation Plan and a credit to Compensation Expense.)
3. Once the service period is completed, determine compensation expense each subsequent period by reporting the full change in market price as an adjustment to compensation expense.
4. The payout to the employee removes the liability and an entry is made to debit Liability Under Stock Appreciation Plan and to credit Cash.

ANALYSIS OF MULTIPLE-CHOICE TYPE QUESTIONS

QUESTION
1. (L.O. 1) For the purpose of inducing conversion, a corporation with convertible bonds increases the number of common shares into which this debt may be converted. Upon conversion, the fair value of the additional shares given should be reported as:
  a.   an expense of the current period.
  b.   an extraordinary item.
  c.   a direct reduction of owners' equity.
  d.   a deferred expense.

Explanation: When an issuer offers some form of additional consideration (cash, other assets, or common stock), called "sweetener," to induce conversion of convertible debt, *SFAS No. 84* requires that the sweetener be recognized as an expense equal to the fair value of the additional securities or other consideration given. (Solution = a.)

QUESTION

2. (L.O. 1) The Goodings Corporation issued 1,000 8% convertible bonds with a face value of $1,000 each at a price of 102. An underwriter advised the corporation that without the conversion feature, the bonds could not have been issued at a price above 99. At the date of issuance, the amount to be recorded as paid-in capital attributable to the conversion feature is:
   a. $0.
   b. $10,000.
   c. $20,000.
   d. $30,000.

Approach and Explanation: State the rule related to accounting for the issuance of convertible bonds. All proceeds received from the issuance of convertible debt are to be recorded in liability accounts; none of the proceeds is to be allocated to the conversion feature under current generally accepted accounting principles. The journal entry to record the issuance of these bonds is no different than the recording of bonds without the conversion feature. That entry would be as follows for the bonds in question:

Cash	1,020,000	
Bonds Payable		1,000,000
Premium on Bonds Payable		20,000

(Solution = a.)

QUESTION

3. (L.O. 1) A corporation issued convertible bonds with a face value of $800,000 at a discount. At a date when the unamortized discount was $50,000, the bonds were converted to stock having a par value of $200,000 and a market value of $870,000. Using the book value method, the amount of gain/loss to record on the conversion is:
   a. $0.
   b. $70,000.
   c. $120,000.
   d. $670,000.

Approach and Explanation: Reconstruct the journal entry to record the conversion. The book value of bonds is removed from the accounts and that book value amount is recorded in appropriate stockholders' equity accounts. There is **never** a gain or loss recognized when the book value method is used to record the conversion of bonds to stock. The journal entry is as follows:

Bonds Payable	800,000	
Discount on Bonds Payable		50,000
Common Stock		200,000
Paid-in Capital in Excess of Par		550,000

Support for the book value method is based on the argument that an agreement was established at the date of the issuance either to pay a stated amount of cash at maturity or to issue a stated number of shares of equity securities. Therefore, when the debt is converted to equity in accordance with the preexisting contract terms, no gain or loss should be recognized upon conversion.

(Solution = a.)

QUESTION

4. (L.O. 3) A corporation issues bonds with detachable warrants. The amount to be recorded as paid-in capital is preferably:
   a. zero.
   b. calculated by the excess of the proceeds over the face amount of the bonds.
   c. equal to the market value of the warrants.

d.   based on the relative market values of the two securities involved.

Explanation: When both the market value of a warrant and the market value of a bond ex-warrant are known, the proportional method is to be employed; hence, the proceeds are allocated to the warrant (paid-in capital) and the debt instrument (liabilities), based on the relative market values of the warrants and bonds. The incremental method (answer section "c") would be appropriate in this case if the market value of the bonds ex-warrants is not known. Answer section "a" (zero) is appropriate only if the warrants are nondetachable (another type of convertible debt instrument). (Solution = d.)

QUESTION
5.   (L.O. 3) The distribution of stock rights to existing common stockholders will increase paid-in capital at the:

	Date of Issuance of the Rights	Date of Exercise of the Rights
a.	Yes	Yes
b.	Yes	No
c.	No	Yes
d.	No	No

Approach and Explanation: Quickly reconstruct and review the journal entries involved in accounting for stock rights. Analyze the effect of each entry on paid-in capital. At the date of issuance of the rights, there is no debit and credit entry; thus, no effect on paid-in capital. At the date of exercise, assets and paid-in capital increase by the exercise price multiplied by the number of related shares. (Solution = c.)

TIP: A **stock right** is defined as a privilege extended by a corporation to acquire additional shares of its capital stock. A **stock warrant** is defined as the physical evidence of stock rights. The warrant specifies the number of rights conveyed, the number of shares to which the rightholder is entitled, the exercise price, and the exercise period. Although the terms "stock right" and "stock warrant" have distinct meanings, they are often used interchangeably; thus, "to record the issuance of stock rights" means the same thing as "to record the issuance of stock warrants."

QUESTION
6.   (L.O. 4) Stock options allowing selected executives to acquire 10,000 shares of $1 par common stock are granted on January 1, 2010. The market price at January 1, 2010 is $22. The option price is $10. The options are for services to be performed over four years from the date of grant. The options become exercisable on January 1, 2012 and expire on December 31, 2014. An option pricing model estimates the fair value of each option to be $30. The amount of compensation cost related to these options to be charged to expense for 2010 (using the fair value method) is:
a. $60,000.
b. $75,000.
c. $120,000.
d. $150,000.
e. $0.

Explanation: The fair value of the options = $30 X 10,000 = $300,000. The fair value of the options is the measure of compensation cost to be recognized as expense over the service period (which is stated to be four years). $300,000 ÷ 4 years = $75,000 per year. (Solution = b.)

QUESTION

7.   (L.O. 4) Stock options allowing selected executives to acquire 10,000 shares of $1 par common stock are granted on January 1, 2010. The market price at January 1, 2010 is $22. The option price is $10. The options become exercisable on January 1, 2012 and expire on December 31, 2014. The option pricing model estimates the fair value of each option to be $30. The amount of compensation cost related to these options to be charged to expense for 2010 if the intrinsic value method is used is:

a. $0.
b. $24,000.
c. $30,000.
d. $60,000.
e. $120,000.

Approach and Explanation: (1) Compute the total compensation cost. It is the excess of the market price over the option price at the grant date. Therefore, ($22 - $10) X 10,000 shares = $120,000 total compensation cost. (2) Determine the service period—span of time over which the employees are to provide services in exchange for the options. Unless otherwise specified, the service period is the vesting period—the time between the grant date and the vesting date. In this case, that is years 2010 and 2011. (3) Divide total compensation cost ($120,000) by the service period (2 years) to arrive at $60,000 per year. Note: The intrinsic value method is **no** longer acceptable to be used for reporting purposes. (Solution = d.)

QUESTION

8.   (L.O. 4) On January 1, 2010 Stuart Chandler, Inc. granted stock options to officers and key employees for the purchase of 100,000 shares of the company's $1 par common stock at $20 per share as additional compensation for services to be rendered over the next two years. The options are exercisable during a four-year period beginning January 1, 2012 by grantees still employed by Stuart Chandler. The market price of Stuart Chandler's common stock was $26 per share at the date of grant. An option pricing model estimates the fair value of each option to be $32. Assuming the fair-value method is used, the journal entry to record the compensation expense related to these options for 2010 would include a credit to the Paid-in Capital—Stock Options account for:

a. $50,000.
b. $300,000.
c. $600,000.
d. $1,600,000.
e. $3,200,000.

Approach and Explanation: Reconstruct the journal entry to record the compensation expense for 2010. It would be as follows:

Compensation Expense   1,600,000
    Paid-in Capital—Stock Options   1,600,000

The total compensation cost is determined by the fair value of an option ($32) multiplied by the number of options granted (100,000 options). The total compensation cost is allocated to the periods included in the service period (two years). $3,200,000 ÷ 2 = $1,600,000. (Solution = d.)

QUESTION

9.   (L.O. 6) Peter Wong Corporation had net income reported for 2010 of $880,000. During 2010 dividends of $120,000 were declared on preferred stock and $200,000 were declared on common stock. There were no changes in the 200,000 shares of common stock or the 40,000 shares of preferred stock outstanding during 2010. There were no potentially dilutive securities outstanding. The earnings per share to be reported for 2010 is:

a. $4.40.
b. $3.80.
c. $3.67.

d. $2.80.
e.   none of the above.

Approach and Explanation: Write down the basic EPS formula. Solve using the data in this question.

$$\frac{\text{Net Income} \ - \ \text{Preferred Stock Dividends}}{\text{Weighted Average Number of Common Shares Outstanding}}$$

$$\frac{\$880,000 \ - \ \$120,000}{200,000} = \underline{\$3.80}$$

(Solution = b.)

QUESTION
10.(L.O. 6) The following data pertain to the Colby Corporation:

January 1, 2010	Shares outstanding	500,000
April 1, 2010	Shares issued	80,000
July 1, 2010	Treasury shares purchased	30,000
October 1, 2010	Shares issued in a 100% stock dividend	550,000

The number of shares to be used in computing earnings per common share for 2010 is:
a.   682,500.
b.   1,090,000.
c.   1,095,000.
d.   1,100,000.
e.   1,130,000.

Approach and Explanation: Follow the steps listed in **Illustration 16-3** to compute the weighted average number of common stock shares outstanding for 2010.

Date		**Weighted Average**
1/1/10	500,000 X 12/12 =	500,000
4/1/10	80,000 X 9/12 =	60,000
	New balance	560,000
7/1/10	30,000 X 6/12 =	(15,000)
	New balance	545,000
10/1/10	100% stock dividend	X 200%*
	New balance	1,090,000

*The appropriate multiple for a stock dividend is 100% plus the percentage used in the dividend. Thus, 100% + 100% dividend = 200% as the multiplier. (Solution = b.)

QUESTION
11.   (L.O. 6) Refer to **Question 10** above. The number of shares actually outstanding at the end of 2010 is:
a.   550,000.
b.   1,100,000.
c.   1,130,000.
d.   1,160,000.

Explanation:

Date		**Weighted Average**
1/1/10	Balance	500,000
4/1/10	Issued for assets	80,000
	New balance	580,000
7/1/10	Acquired for treasury	(30,000)
	New balance	550,000
10/1/10	100% stock dividend	550,000

New balance   1,100,000
                                                          (Solution = b.)

QUESTION

12. (L.O. 6) At December 31, 2009 Opal Company had 200,000 shares of common stock and 5,000 shares of 8%, $100 par value cumulative preferred stock outstanding. No dividends were declared on either the preferred or common stock in 2009 or 2010 On February 10, 2011, prior to the issuance of its financial statements for the year ended December 31, 2010, Opal declared a 100% stock split on its common stock. Net income for 2010 was $480,000. In its 2010 financial statements, Opal's 2010 earnings per common share should be:

a. $2.40.
b. $2.20.
c. $2.00.
d. $1.20.
e. $1.10.
f. $1.00.

Explanation: $\dfrac{\$480,000 - 5,000(8\% \times \$100)}{200,000 \times 2} = \underline{\$1.10}$

Dividends on **cumulative** preferred stock are deducted in the numerator, whether declared or not. However, only the current year's preference is used; dividends in arrears for prior years do not affect the EPS computation. Stock dividends and stock splits are given retroactive treatment for all periods presented, even if they occur after the end of the current year, but before the financial statements are issued. (Solution = e.)

QUESTION

13. (L.O. 6, 7) Tempo, Inc. had 200,000 shares of common stock issued and outstanding at December 31, 2009. On July 1, 2010 an additional 200,000 shares were issued for cash. Tempo also had stock options outstanding at the beginning and end of 2010 which allow the holders to purchase 60,000 shares of common stock at $20 per share. The average market price of Tempo's common stock was $15 during 2010. The market price of Tempo's common stock was $25 at December 31, 2010. What is the number of shares that should be used in computing diluted earnings per share for the year ended December 31, 2010?

a. 400,000
b. 300,000
c. 360,000
d. 415,000
e. 320,000
f. 280,000

Approach and Explanation: Use the treasury stock method to compute the number of shares to be used in determining diluted EPS. **However**, only make assumptions about the exercise of stock options when those assumptions are **not** antidilutive. A quick test to determine whether these options are dilutive or antidilutive is to compare the average market price ($15) with the option price ($20). The market price is **not** higher; therefore, the assumed exercise of stock options in applying the treasury stock method when computing EPS will have an antidilutive effect. Therefore, no assumptions should be made. Only the weighted average actual outstanding shares should be used in computing EPS in this situation.

Jan. 1	Shares outstanding: 200,000 x 12/12	=	200,000
July 1	Issued for assets: 200,000 x 6/12	=	100,000
	Weighted average shares outstanding	=	300,000 (Solution = b.)

> **TIP:** You could calculate EPS using the basic formula and calculate diluted EPS assuming the exercise of the options and application of the treasury stock method. Because this would entail an assumption of $1,200,000 proceeds being used to buy back stock at $15 (average market price) per share, this would result in making adjustments to the denominator as follows:

> - Add 60,000 shares because of assumed exercise of options.
> - Deduct 80,000 shares because of assumed purchase of treasury stock with $1,200,000 proceeds from assumed exercise of options.
>
> The net result of these assumptions is a **decrease** in the number of shares used to calculate diluted EPS, which indicates an antidilutive effect on EPS. Thus, these assumptions should **not** be made in the scenario described in this question.

QUESTION

14.   (L.O. 6, 7) Refer to the facts of **Question 13** above. If the average market price of Tempo's common stock was $25 rather than $15 during 2010, what is the number of shares that should be used in computing diluted earnings per share for the year ended December 31, 2010?

a.   330,000
b.   448,000
c.   412,000
d.   320,000
e.   348,000
f.   312,000

Approach and Explanation: Use the treasury stock method to compute the number of shares to be used in determining diluted EPS. The weighted average number of shares actually outstanding is 300,000 (see Explanation to **Question 13** above for this computation). The average market price of the common stock ($25) should be used in determining the number of assumed treasury stock shares in computing diluted EPS. The average market price ($25) of Tempo's common stock exceeds the option price ($20); thus the effect of assuming the exercise of the options and purchase of treasury stock with the assumed proceeds is dilutive. Thus, the computation of the number of shares used in computing diluted EPS is as follows:

Weighted average actual shares outstanding	300,000
Shares assumed issued upon exercise of options	60,000
Assumed shares purchased for the treasury ($1,200,000 ÷ $25)	(48,000)
Shares used for denominator of diluted EPS	312,000

(Solution = f.)

> **TIP:**   A comparison of 312,000 shares (determined by use of the treasury stock method) with the weighted average number of common stock shares actually outstanding (300,000) indicates a dilutive effect on EPS.

QUESTION

15.   (L.O. 7) A convertible bond issue should be included in the diluted earnings per share computation as if the bonds had been converted into common stock, if the effect of its inclusion is:

	Dilutive	Antidilutive
a.	Yes	Yes
b.	Yes	No
c.	No	Yes
d.	No	No

Explanation: A convertible security is a potentially dilutive security. All potentially dilutive securities should be included in the diluted EPS computation, if the effect of inclusion is dilutive. **No** antidilutive assumptions are to be made in computing diluted EPS. (Solution = b.)